C000183326

Sue,

With many thanks [for]
all your help.
We hope you enjoy
reading it!

Alan & Pat

Was It Something I Said?

Was It Something I Said?

by

Alan Lettin

The Memoir Club

First published in 2005 by
The Memoir Club
Stanhope Old Hall
Stanhope
Weardale
County Durham

British Library Cataloguing in
Publication Data.
A catalogue record for this book
is available from the
British Library

ISBN: 1-84104-101-7

Typeset by TW Typesetting, Plymouth, Devon
Printed by CPI Bath

Contents

List of Illustrations

Foreword

When asked for directions, an Irishman replied, 'Well, for sure and I wouldn't be starting from here.'

No one fifty years ago, aspiring to lead a profession and destined to become President of his specialty association, Consultant Surgeon to St Bartholomew's Hospital and the Royal National Orthopaedic Hospital, Master of a City Company and Senior Vice-President of the Royal College of Surgeons, would have chosen to be born to so-called working-class parents, however proud and industrious, in London's pre-war East End. Such were the author's childhood surroundings until he qualified in medicine, with innumerable distinctions along the way, in 1956.

His account chronicles his early years amongst the back streets of Leytonstone and wartime evacuation, and reveals how, by dint of intelligence, application and hard work, and no doubt also a touch of cockney sagacity, he climbed to the peak of British Surgery, on the way earning immense gratitude from so many who had benefited from his surgical skill.

The phrase *Was it something I said?* crops up repeatedly throughout the book as he describes various disappointments which he attributes to his verbal gaffes. Clearly he has insight, but those of us who know him well often wonder why, having conquered so much adversity, tact, second nature to most of us, often eludes him.

There is much more to this account than simply the progress of one who, overcoming hurdle after hurdle, each of them an obstacle that few of his peers would have encountered in their childhood, achieves his goal. One clue to his success may lie in his mother's, often repeated, aphorism 'God helps those who help themselves'.

Having read the draft, I telephoned to ask if I could make an offer for the film rights! Tongue in cheek, perhaps, but among the numerous records of life in that part of London at the time, I doubt whether many are written with such human interest. I can just imagine the inevitably exaggerated and no doubt distorted film script based on it all. Could this perhaps therefore turn out to be 'the book of the film'?

As I read, I wondered who else would, like me, find it interesting: family, friends, surgical and other colleagues. The field, though, I judge to be very much wider than this. I have already mentioned that it is more than simply an account of success triumphing over early adversity. It is the very readable story, through the author's eyes, of the contemporary scene in which he grew up and trained to become a surgeon, and of the subsequent changes in surgical training and healthcare in which he played a significant part. The field of interest, therefore, is wide, not least perhaps in years to come, as an insight, in personal terms, into late twentieth century London and the medical scene.

Perhaps it is too much to hope that some young people in similar circumstances today might also read it and be encouraged to contemplate the possibility of a future seemingly, to them, quite beyond their reach. Those of us who had an easier ride may be left wondering whether we could have done the same!

Sir Rodney Sweetnam KCVO, CBE, FRCS

Preface

Late one evening during the winter of 1990/1991, I was lying in bed listening to the radio. Bernard Levin, a rather acerbic and controversial journalist and broadcaster, and an American journalist were discussing the problems which Britain faced at that time. They came to the conclusion that the class system, a burden from which the United States was free, was at least in part responsible. Surely not. In the last decade of the twentieth century Britain was a land of equal opportunity, regardless of social background; at least, from my own experience, it seemed to be so.

My bed was in the Master's Lodge of Barber Surgeon's Hall in the heart of the City of London, with a wonderful view of the floodlit dome of St Paul's Cathedral through one of the windows. I, born and brought up in the East End of London, almost but not quite within the sound of Bow Bells, was Master of the Worshipful Company of Barbers – one of the oldest and most prestigious Livery companies in the City of London, of which I was a Freeman.

St Bartholomew's Hospital, an even more prestigious institution where I had been appointed to the consultant staff in 1967, and where I was now surgeon in charge of the Orthopaedic Department, was but a stone's throw away. Furthermore I was also a member of the consultant staff of the Royal National Orthopaedic Hospital, a renowned postgraduate teaching hospital specialising in disorders of the musculoskeletal system. I had been elected to the Council of the Royal College of Surgeons of England in 1984 and had served on its Court of Examiners, as well as examining for the Universities of London, Cambridge and Liverpool. I had been called upon to serve on many local, regional and national committees where my background appeared to be no handicap. At that time it was not possible to predict what the future had in store for me but, whatever it might be, I was confident that social class would play no part.

Whether the story of my life suggests that my confidence may have been misplaced is for the reader to decide. Whilst coming to that judgement, I hope that my recollections of my childhood in 'the corner shop' before the Second World War, and my experience of evacuation during that war, will prove of general interest. My perceptions of the National Health Service, undergraduate and postgraduate education and training and their associated themes may interest the social historian as well as my grandchildren for whom this book is intended in the hope that they may find it an interesting and perhaps even an inspiring part of their heritage. Above all I hope that it encourages others from a disadvantaged background to achieve their hopes and ambitions, no matter how unrealistic they may at first appear.

Acknowledgements

To the junior staff and colleagues who have encouraged and supported my endeavours over the years

Chapter 1

Family background

Lettin is an unusual name but it can be found scattered around the United Kingdom and in the old Commonwealth and the United States. Its origins are a matter for speculation, particularly if the variations Letten and Letton are taken into account. It is possibly derived from the village of Letton in Herefordshire or a village of similar name near Shippam in Norfolk. There are certainly written references to the name Letton in Norfolk and Suffolk in the thirteenth, fourteenth and fifteenth centuries.

The name Josiah Lettin appears in 1686 in the archives of New Jersey in a dispute over a purchase of land. Josiah was the son of Richard Lettin who was born in Salford, Bedfordshire in 1609, emigrating to America in 1638. Josiah acquired other land from the Indians in 1681and in the original deeds his name is misspelt Latting. Part of the present day Lattingtown on Long Island is situated on this land. Josiah's descendants subsequently used the name Latting and, with customary American zeal, the present-day members of that family have traced the earliest known ancestors of the Lettin-Latting family to Pierre Lettin who, in 1494, lived in Malines in the Spanish Netherlands, where a family coat of arms is recorded in the old City records.

John (Jahan) Lettin, a wool comber, left Flanders in 1567 with his wife, a young son and one servant, and settled in Norwich where, by letters patent two years earlier, Elizabeth I allowed thirty Dutchmen to trade. By the end of the sixteenth and the beginning of the seventeenth centuries, the name is recorded in the parish records of a cluster of villages in Lincolnshire and Bedfordshire. Over the next two to three hundred years it occurs sporadically elsewhere but not in London until the mid seventeenth century.

My great-grandfather, Thomas Lettin, a woodcarver, was born in Birmingham in 1830 according to the 1871 census but so far it has been impossible to establish a link to the descendants of the wool comber from Flanders or indeed to his forefathers. Thomas married Catherine Jones from Cardiff and they had two daughters and two sons, one of whom, my grandfather Thomas Henry Lettin, also a woodcarver, was born in 1860 in Shoreditch, East London. In 1883 he married Ellen Le Croisette, whose Huguenot ancestors in England can be traced back at least to 1742 when John Le Croisette was baptised in St Martin-in-the-Fields.

My grandfather, Thomas, died in 1905 at the early age of forty-three years, having fathered fifteen children (including a set of twins) of whom

My father (extreme left) with nine of his ten surviving brothers and sisters with their mother in 1918

eleven survived into adult life. Frederick Lettin, my father, was born on 7 October 1893 in Bethnal Green and, at the time of his father's death, there would have been four younger children. I presume his mother and the young children would have been supported by the older children who would have been working by this time, as was the custom in the days before Social Security. They seemed to move house at frequent intervals, perhaps doing what was called a 'moonlight flit' to avoid paying the rent. By all accounts he was devoted to his mother, for he in his turn supported her in her final years when she suffered from severe asthma, a condition which has affected some of her great-grandchildren. Surviving photographs show that she and her Le Croisette sisters were very good-looking women in their youth.

After her death in 1919, he felt free to marry Louisa Marion Tabberer, my mother, who was known as Marion. Her first love – her cousin Leonard Tabberer – had been killed in the last few days of the First World War. She was born at 7 Norah Street, Bethnal Green in 1894, the eldest surviving daughter of thirteen children, with one older brother and seven surviving younger brothers and sisters, and so assumed much of the responsibility for their upbringing at No. 12 Hereford Street, Bethnal Green. This small terraced house must have been full to overflowing, with an elderly silk weaver, a reminder of the industry introduced into the East End of London by the Huguenot refugees in the eighteenth century, occupying an upstairs room, and her mother's widowed mother also living there, although, of course, the children, one born every two years or so until 1914, would not all have lived there at the same time.

Her father, Henry Tabberer, another Huguenot name, was a French polisher who worked for Waring & Gillow's for most of his life. He was born in Shoreditch in 1869, one of five children who were orphaned when the eldest, Great-Uncle Fred, was just fifteen years old. He arranged an apprenticeship for my grandfather, a job in service for one sister and admission to an orphanage for the youngest brother and sister, before joining the Royal Marines. No counselling or Social Security, just common sense, initiative and a sense of responsibility which would be hard to find in a young teenager today. After leaving the Marines, he married and became foreman in the Naval Dockyard at Chatham, and would travel up to London in his retirement on the early morning train to visit his 'little brothers and sisters', as he called them, well into his seventies. His back was ramrod straight and his boots brightly polished, a credit to the Royal Marines. When he died he left me the gold pocket watch which was presented to him when he retired but sadly this was stolen from me in a burglary many years later. In spite of their early hardships, all five brothers and sisters led useful and productive lives well into their seventies and eighties.

My maternal grandmother, Emma Ellen Brown, was born in 1873, also in Bethnal Green. Her mother, also Emma Ellen Brown, married Charles Brown at St James the Great, Bethnal Green on the 9 September 1867. Not only did the bride and groom have the same surname but their respective fathers had the same Christian name, Charles, as well. I have their original marriage certificate on linen paper and it is clear that neither the bride, the groom nor their fathers could sign their own names. The signatures were entered by the minister, each followed by a small cross, this in spite of the fact that the men were skilled tradesmen employed in the furniture-manufacturing industry which flourished in the East End of London before the introduction of mass-produced, machine-made furniture.

John Hollingshead in *Ragged London in 1861* wrote:

> That vast district of eastern London familiar to the public under the broad title of Bethnal Green would exhaust a twelvemonth in a house-to-house visitation. It is flat, it is ancient, dirty, and degraded; its courts and alleys are almost countless, and overrunning with men, women, boys, cats, pigeons, and birds. Its children are ragged, sharp, weasel-like; brought up from the cradle – which is often an old box or an egg-chest – to hard living and habits of bodily activity. Its men are mainly poor dock labourers, poor costermongers, poorer silk-weavers clinging hopelessly to a withering handicraft, the lowest kind of thieves, the most ill-disguised class of swell-mobsmen, with a sprinkling of box and toy makers, shoe makers and cheap cabinet-makers. Its women are mainly hawkers, sempstresses, the coarsest order of prostitutes, and aged stall-keepers, who often sit at the street corners in old sedan-chairs, and sometimes die, like sentinels, at their posts. Its broadest highways are chiefly lined with the most humble shops. There are steaming eating-houses, half filled with puddings as large as sofa squabs, and legs of beef, to boil down into a cheap and popular soup; birdcage vendors; mouldy, musty dens full of second-hand garments, or gay 'emporiums' in the ready-made clothing line; pawnbrokers, with narrow, yellow side entrances, whose walls are well marked with the traces of traffic; faded grocers; small print shops, selling periodicals, sweetstuff, and stale fruit; squeezed-up barbers, long factories and breweries, with the black arches of the Eastern Counties Railway running through the midst. Every street of any pretension is generally guarded at its entrances by public-houses smelling of tobacco, stale beer, and sawdust; and the corners of every leading thoroughfare cutting into the heart of the district are watched over by glittering genii in the shape of gin-palaces.

This was the environment into which my grandparents were born.

In spite of my grandfather's regular employment it was necessary for my grandmother to take in washing to make ends meet, which my mother and the older children collected and delivered, besides helping with the ironing. My mother also earned a few pennies scrubbing floors and often remembered how she knocked the skin off her knuckles on the fixings for the silk-weavers' looms which remained on the floors long after the looms had been consigned to history.

Clothes and toys were almost always second-hand 'hand-me-downs'. A Mrs Charles, a well-to-do lady from Tunbridge Wells, would arrive from time to time with bundles of clothes. She never failed to notice that the children were always clean and tidy and the house spick and span, with the front step whitened and the kitchen grate blackleaded and polished. The harshness of my mother's childhood had a profound effect on her throughout her life. Nothing was ever wasted, neither material things nor time. Nothing was bought unless absolutely necessary. 'Waste not, want not' and 'Look after the pennies and the pounds will look after themselves' were her watchwords. She was determined that she would never find herself in such impoverished circumstances again.

My father and mother met at the Bedford Institute in Wheeler Street, Spitalfields, which was run and largely financed by Mr Theodore Godlee, a London solicitor, and his sister, Miss Mary Jane Godlee, members of a well-known Quaker family. Sir Rickman Godlee, a surgeon at University College Hospital and President of the Royal College of Surgeons, was a brother, and Lord Lister, of antiseptic fame, was their uncle. There is a portrait of Sir Rickman Godlee hanging at the top of the main staircase of the College in Lincoln's Inn Fields, which bears a striking resemblance to my memory of Theodore Godlee whom I met, in my early childhood, at the Bedford Institute.

Curiously, UCH and the College of Surgeons played a large part in my own life but the Bedford Institute played a far greater part in the lives of my parents, their brothers and sisters and innumerable other children and young adults from London's East End at the turn of the nineteenth century and the first half of the twentieth century. Mr Godlee, the boss, looked after the boys' activities – football, cricket, gymnastics and swimming. There was an annual athletic sports day at Mr Godlee's field at Whipps Cross, Walthamstow, with transport provided, and an annual camp at Whitley, which many of the boys continued to attend in their adult years. For the girls, Miss Godlee ran sewing classes and household management and, of course, religious instruction but I think very little physical activity. Both she and her brother were remembered with affection and gratitude throughout my parents' lives.

In spite of this strong Quaker influence, my parents were married in St Matthew's Church, Bethnal Green, on the 21 June 1919. My father is described as an 'instrument maker'; I'm not sure what this implies but I know that his work was such that he was exempt from military service in the First World War in which two of his brothers were seriously wounded. My mother worked for W.D. & H.O. Wills, the cigarette and tobacco

My mother seated to the left of her mother and father with her eight surviving brothers and sisters in the garden of 57 Aden Grove at her sister Win's wedding in 1932

manufacturers. She made the very large cigars of the sort smoked by Winston Churchill. This was piecework. Each worker was provided with a quantity of tobacco leaf from which a minimum number of cigars were rolled by hand. The quicker and the more cigars produced, the bigger the wages at the end of the week. My mother was proud of the fact that Mr Wills himself often complimented her on her work on his tours of the factory.

At this time they were living in a flat at 56 Dynevor Road, Stoke Newington, other parts of the house being occupied by members of my father's family. Their only recreations were the Bedford Institute, of course, and attending political meetings addressed by the pioneers of the Labour Movement. They were particularly inspired by George Lansbury, a Christian Socialist, described as 'a man of energy with love of his fellows and an idealistic leader'. He was at one time editor of the *Daily Herald*, a newspaper they took until its demise. I do not think they were ever members of the Labour Party, although my father was a member of the Amalgamated Engineering Union, and there is no doubt where their sympathies lay.

My father became unemployed in the worldwide industrial depression which began in the early 1920s but, by virtue of my mother's thrift and skill as a cigar maker, they had saved enough money to buy, in 1924, the freehold and goodwill, and stock, such as it was, of a small shop in one of the pleasanter parts of East London – 42 Cobbold Road, Leytonstone E11, for £600 – advised inevitably by Theodore Godlee. Perhaps even more remarkably, my mother was able to buy 57 Aden Grove, Stoke Newington within a year or two for her parents and still unmarried brothers and sisters to rent, putting Bethnal Green, and the fear that they might end their lives in the Workhouse and be buried in paupers' graves, behind them.

Chapter 2

The shop

Forty-two Cobbold Road was much the same as any of the numerous corner shops built in the urban sprawl in the towns and cities of late Victorian England. It was on the corner of Cobbold and Courteney Road – the end of a terrace of three similar houses, with the shop itself occupying the equivalent of the bay-windowed front room, front door and passage of the adjoining houses. Behind the shop was the shop parlour with a window looking into the shop, intended to be a sitting room but rarely used as such, becoming a storeroom in the later years. The back section, narrower than the front, an almost universal design in working-class housing of the period, was separated from the boundary wall by a narrow alley, a door in the wall opening onto Courteney Road. A small lobby, with stairs to the upper floor, separated the shop parlour from the living room, possibly eight feet by ten feet, one wall of which was almost completely occupied by a 'Triplex' grate, my mother's pride and joy, installed soon after I was born. The open fire, with a small back boiler, provided hot water; a side oven, and a small oven above, were used for cooking, much like a present-day Aga.

A small table fitted into the bay window and was pulled out on the rare occasions when visitors came to tea. Four straight back chairs and a 'Singer' treadle sewing machine in one corner and a 'Marconi' wireless set on top were the only other pieces of furniture. A built-in dresser in the alcove beside the Triplex grate housed the crockery above, with kitchen utensils and food below. It was a basic, warm room but hardly comfortable and remained unchanged for the whole of the time I lived there. A door led to the scullery, even smaller, with a gas cooker, sink and a mangle (clothes wringer) and a built-in copper heated by a fire underneath for the weekly wash.

My father built a small glazed lean-to outside the back door of the scullery (leaving off a door to keep the rates down!) to provide some protection from inclement weather when visiting the outside lavatory. The yard was about fifteen feet square, paved, apart from a strip of soil about a yard wide along one side which was almost completely taken up by the chicken run. On the opposite side, the yard opened onto Courteney Road through two large wooden gates (made by my father) in the boundary wall. The flank wall of the first house in Courteney Road was the fourth side of

The author aged 6 in front of the shop, November 1937

the yard and built onto it was what had originally been a stable but was now used as a garage for the 'Singer Eight' EV 561 – one of the very few cars in the neighbourhood.

Upstairs, the quite large front bedroom over the shop was occupied by my parents and in which I was born on Tuesday 6 January 1931. Behind it a smaller room with a window overlooking the alley was mine. The landing led to a small bathroom (another pride and joy) – very unusual in a working-class home where a tin bath was brought into the kitchen once a week from the yard and filled with hot water from the copper, each member of the family taking his or her turn with a hot water top-up in between. Beyond the bathroom there was another bedroom above the living-room which, in the years before the war, was occupied by various lodgers.

In these early years trade was poor. The previous owners, a Mr Funnel and his two daughters, had let the business run down and it did not provide much of an income but it did provide a roof at least. My father looked after the shop and my mother continued working until shortly before I was born, walking a mile or so to Maryland Point Station and then catching a train to Liverpool Street, which was close to the Wills factory in Ropemaker Street. Although there were thousands unemployed, the demand for expensive hand-made cigars was undiminished! It was imperative to support Mother's income in any way possible. Before the purchase of the car, the stable (now the shed) was used as a changing room by a local football club who played on nearby Wanstead Flats. The whitewashed walls and rows of clothes pegs remained the only evidence of the place where they changed and stored their goal posts and drank their tea – made by my mother – after their games, for they too were eventually unable to afford the small cost and left, owing several weeks' rent!

The back room upstairs was occupied for a time by my father's youngest sister, Elsie, before she left in 1929 to join another sister and a brother in California, never to return. She was followed by Bert Hasler, with whom my parents established a local milk round. The bottles were sterilised and filled in premises behind another shop at the end of Cobbold Road, but the three-wheeled milk cart remained in the back yard long after Bert left and provided something to play on in my early years. I often think how hard he and the other delivery men worked, pushing their milk carts and their bakers' barrows around the streets in the early morning, whatever the weather. No wonder life expectancy was short in those days. The milk was often sold from a churn and I still have the pint measure with which it was transferred to the customer's enamelled container. This proved to be an ill-fated enterprise and Bert left, again owing money, which my mother never ceased trying to recover.

Perhaps most surprising of all, he was followed by Bill Stratton, a dentist who, I suppose, qualified before dental registration was introduced in the 1920s. Can you imagine a dental surgery in a back room above a shop in the East End of London? I presume he slept in the same room as he treated the patients. I cannot remember a bed but I do remember a treadle-powered drilling machine and a spittoon and a wall-mounted tray on which he placed his instruments. Two cheap dining-room chairs stood on the landing outside the door for patients to use whilst they waited to be seen. He was his own dental mechanic, making false teeth in the shed at the end of the yard. I often watched him using the wax impressions he had taken of the patients' gums to make a plaster of Paris mould on which the dentures were made. I still have one or two of his old instruments in my workshop.

Unfortunately Bill Stratton was too fond of the drink and we were a teetotal house, my mother having signed the pledge, whatever that may have been, although my father always denied having done so and took the occasional drink at Christmas. One night Bill Stratton came home drunk and my mother would not let him in but I suppose he must have returned at some time for his equipment, no doubt owing my mother money. He was, however, very well-regarded by his patients, for they would return years after he had left if they needed further treatment or repairs to their broken dentures, asking in the shop where he could be found.

The last of the lodgers was Tommy Sibley, whom my mother had met at a whist drive – her favourite pastime. He was an elderly widower who, at one time, had been the landlord of the Hare & Hounds pub in Lea Bridge Road, Leyton, but, in spite of that, he must have been to all intents and purposes a non-drinker when he arrived in 1938 or early 1939. I was very fond of Tommy. He took me to see the various sights in London and I was fascinated when he talked about Paris, which he had once visited. I know nothing more of his past but his daughter, a nurse at St Pancras Hospital, came to visit him once, wearing, I remember, her outdoor nurse's uniform. Tommy left London in 1940, my mother having found him a lodging with an elderly spinster, Miss Inglis, in the village of the Mereside in Huntingdonshire, close to where I was evacuated. He subsequently died there and was buried in the local cemetery at Ramsay.

The LMS suburban railway line crossed in turn Cobbold and Courteney Roads at an angle, about a hundred yards from the shop, which was therefore at the apex of a triangle – the sides formed by the two roads and the railway line. This ran above ground on brick arches except where it crossed the roads, when the arches became iron bridges with high sides, obscuring the wheels of the trains. I remember as a little boy thinking that the trains slid along the rails! The arches marked the horizon of my small childhood world, centred on the shop and inhabited by its customers and calling commercial travellers. Tom Hood School occupied the opposite corner and most of the far side of Courteney Road, followed by a few houses with long front gardens and then the railway arches. Tom Hood, the author of 'The Song of The Shirt' was presumably a local resident long before the school was built around the turn of the nineteenth century. I imagine that the most famous pupil was Bobby Moore, the idolised Captain of England's World Cup winning team of 1966, but that, of course, was many years later. The pupils would come into the shop to buy sweets and the staff cigarettes and tobacco.

Courteney Road met Cobbold Road at a T-junction and the school extended along a part of Cobbold Road outside the triangle towards St Margaret's Church. On the opposite side of the road there were two old cottages approached by long gardens, relics of the market gardens of a previous era. Mrs Warne, an elderly lady with a dusky complexion, always dressed in black with skirts reaching her ankles, lived in one with her husband and four grown-up children, two boys and two girls. Two long greenhouses either side of a drive occupied the land in front of the cottage. Behind, there were one or two sheds used by her sons. 'Coo', the eldest, with an obviously repaired hare-lip, ran a car repair business and John, the other, was a self-employed builder and both of them came into the shop to buy cigarettes but had little to say. Kit, the elder daughter, helped to run the house and Thora, the younger, worked as an usherette at the Rex Cinema. Mr Warne was occasionally seen riding an old bicycle but was generally kept out of view. In retrospect I think he may have been suspected, or even convicted, of interfering with small boys. Sometimes I was invited to visit the greenhouses and to see his fish, and I was always closely questioned by my parents afterwards. He was not much interested in horticulture and I imagine that the property was inherited by Mrs Warne. He had been a bricklayer and I learned more from him about English and Flemish bond than about plants! I remember being invited to the house, probably on my eighth birthday, to see one of the earliest TV broadcasts, *The Circus*, on a tiny screen. Mrs Warne was a frequent customer and she could remember when the Red Coats held their annual camps in bell tents pitched on Wanstead Flats. She was something of a soothsayer and I can remember that she predicted that my frequent childhood ailments would be over by the time I was seven years of age. I think she was right.

The cottage next door was derelict and the garden overgrown. Next to that there was a factory producing waterproof garments but not much custom for the shop. A row of terraced houses extended to St Margaret's Church where I was baptised. An elderly widower, Mr Bull, lived in one of them and his two sons, one of whom worked for the electricity board, the other for London Transport, lived nearby. Their children were a little older than me and Doreen Bull would sometimes baby-sit on the rare occasions when both my parents went out together. I still see her brother Freddy, now in his eighties, from time to time. He was conscripted into the Royal Marines early in the war and took part in every major landing, including D-Day. He, like most of his generation, is reluctant to talk about his experiences but D-Day was the worst because of the rough sea and he and many of the marines were seasick before they went ashore to establish the beachhead in preparation for the main assault. Once secure, this group of experienced and battle-hardened men were withdrawn in preparation for further landings, the last of which was the capture of the island of Walcheren in the Schelde Estuary, to open up the Port of Antwerp for allied shipping. He was one of only three of his original commando unit to survive the war. All the Bull family were talented artists and Freddy may be found on Sunday mornings with his paintings hanging on the railings of Green Park in London.

Old Mr Bull was a frequent visitor to the shop, and would spend a great deal of time discussing politics with my father after buying an ounce of tobacco or so. At Christmas he would make some of his watercolours into calendars, which we would sell for him. During the war my father sent a calendar to each of his relatives in California in return for the food parcels they had sent to us. Old Mr Bull specialised in sunsets and seascapes, one of which I brought back from America on a visit in 1987, and it hangs on the wall behind me in my study.

The Warnes' neighbours on the other side were the Pegleys with a similar plot of land, but this time with a semi-detached house to one side and at the front, adjacent to the road. Behind the house was a nice flower garden but other than that the land was occupied by lock-up garages. Those fortunate enough to own cars in those days did not park them in the road but usually rented a garage often some distance from their homes. Mr Pegley was a self-employed ropemaker and I remember that, in some old sheds beyond the garages, there was a large brick trough filled with tar in which the ropes were soaked after the fibres had been twisted together. The tar permeated his clothes and even his skin, which had a sallow dusky look, and the smell lingered in the shop, to which he was a frequent customer, buying and smoking Wills Gold Flake cigarettes. He had the contract to make the official hangman's ropes for the Home Office but benefited considerably during the war from making the scrambling nets and ships' fenders for the services. The Pegleys were probably the most affluent of the local residents.

The house next to Pegleys' was occupied by a rather secretive family, the head of which appeared from time to time, between spells in prison, it was rumoured. Next came 'Poona Villa', technically detached and probably one of the earliest houses to be built in the road, occupied by Mrs Medcalf, a rather haughty lady who shopped at Sainsbury's and was rarely seen without her cigarette in a very long cigarette-holder. She had little to do with her neighbours and her husband, a master mariner, was not often at home. Her son, Gordon, was two years older than me but was never allowed to play in the street with the riff-raff and was regarded as rather odd but later became one of my greatest friends for the rest of his life. He married another of my childhood schoolfriends, Jean Croft, with whom I am still in touch.

A variety of terraced houses occupied the interval between 'Poona Villa' and the railway arch, most of the occupants coming into the shop from time to time. I remember particularly Mrs White, whose husband worked in the building trade and after the war became self-employed. 'Now we will have to vote Conservative, not Labour,' she announced one day in the shop.

On the opposite side of the road the house next door to the shop was divided into upstairs and downstairs flats. Mr and Mrs Badger were downstairs, both rather short and heavily built. Bill Badger, an amateur weightlifter with bulging biceps, worked in the docks and spent the war as a sub-mariner. Upstairs there lived a postman, nicknamed 'Sambo', and his family. (I have no idea how he acquired the nickname, for he was not black. In fact, it was most unusual to see a coloured person in those days.) They moved out and the Laceys moved in. She was a small, bird-like woman with a very large husband, a bus driver who was seen only intermittently and was rumoured to have another wife elsewhere. Of their three children, Frankie and Roy were nearest to me in age and were frequent playmates in the street but not special friends.

The third house in this little terrace was occupied by Mrs Clark who had been left a widow with seven children when her husband, Syd, died in the early 1930s. He was a pepper grinder with the Co-op but rather fancied himself as a painter and decorator, specialising in grain and varnishing, a technique aimed at imitating natural wood, much in demand in those days. My mother thought it was rather special and Syd Clark had applied his limited expertise to most of the downstairs woodwork in our house. I think my father rather had his doubts! Syd had probably been reasonably well-insured and the family was not on the breadline but then, of course, the older children would have been working.

They were in many ways a tragic family. The youngest, Georgie, with whom I played as a very young child, died in 1935 at the age of six (my mother kept the memorial card – something she always did). This was my first encounter with death and I remember the event vividly. On the day of a funeral all the neighbours would draw their curtains and people, often strangers, would stop and stand in the street as the cortege slowly passed, the men raising their hats. Frankie was a couple of years older than me and I had a lot to do with him at one time but as soon as he left school he ran away with the travelling funfair which visited Wanstead Flats on bank holidays. He was quite fearless and thought nothing of climbing out onto the flat roof of Tom Hood School to retrieve a lost ball. May was a pretty, but flighty, girl and Phoebe, I now realise, had cerebral palsy but she was strongly supported by the church. Freddie was a little simple but managed menial jobs. The older boys all served in the war. Percy, the eldest, was blinded in the Western Desert, Reggie was lost at sea, but Stanley survived and married a girl from the next road. Mrs Clark was a frequent customer and was known as 'Mrs Humming Top' because she never stopped talking. She usually ended her sentences with 'D'yer blame me?' In later years she had a stroke, which left her with a completely paralysed left arm and, as a consequence, she often came into the shop with the back of her dress tucked into her knickers!

Next came a row of simple houses owned by the LMS railway and occupied in the main by their employees. Mr Mapley was a plate-layer and an infrequent customer, but this was amply compensated for by his large blonde wife, who smoked Players Weights and had a loud raucous laugh. She always took a great interest in me from the time I was a baby until I went to university. She was a frequent visitor to the Lord Rookwood pub at the other end of Cobbold Road and there was, I think, some doubt as to her morals. I liked her, for she was a genuine good-hearted cockney! In fact, most of the customers spoke with that characteristic accent, which is instantly recognisable, even when modified. My father had a particularly strong accent, my mother less so, and so it was inevitable that I would have one too, to my later embarrassment. Worse was the poor grammar – an even greater embarrassment – but both were corrected with time. Nowadays such accents are cultivated. I also acquired a wide vocabulary of cockney rhyming slang, much of which is unknowingly incorporated in abbreviated form into everyday speech, such as 'blowing a raspberry' (raspberry tart – fart) and 'use your loaf' (loaf of bread – head). Bad language, apart from the odd 'bloody', was not a feature of everyday speech as it is today, where almost every sentence includes the F-word, even among the higher echelons of the Civil Service. My mother, I think, would never have tolerated it in the shop, preferring to lose custom – no doubt the Quaker influence.

A railway guard, Mr Gibbs, and his wife lived next to Mapleys'. They were not regular customers but he would be seen turning the corner on his way to work with his rolled-up red and green flags sticking out of the top of his regulation bag. I think perhaps the Gibbs had something to hide, for their granddaughter, Ella, lived with them and they kept themselves to themselves. She disappeared for some time and when she returned she was a most attractive teenager. Children often disappeared quite suddenly, I later discovered, to long-stay hospitals, with tuberculosis or polio, to return later, sometimes still in plaster, sometimes in callipers. Infantile paralysis and TB were never mentioned and seemed to be regarded as a social disgrace, supposedly due to lack of parental care.

At the end of this terrace there were a couple of houses on either side of the railway arch owned by Nevilles Bakery, whose premises occupied some of the adjoining land in addition to the arches. The first was occupied by the Whitworths. She was a rather dignified lady, who, perhaps, had come down in the world, he a rather dapper self-employed tailor, inevitably well-dressed. They had a daughter, May, and a son, Derek, a little older than me, whose tailor-made suits I wore when he had grown out of them; I eventually outgrew him but by then I was wearing a school blazer.

Mrs Taylor, her husband, and children Sylvia, Doris and John, lived in the next house. I remember Doris reading a Mickey Mouse book to me. I was quite often invited into their house to play with John. Mr Taylor worked at night as a stoker in the bakery and Mrs Taylor had come from a rather better-off family and was a bad household manager. She was frightened to tell her husband that they were usually in debt and they survived 'on tick'. Goods were commonly bought but paid for at the end of the week when the breadwinner received his wages. Mrs Taylor and others sometimes maintained their cash flow by taking their goods to Coomb's, the pawnshop in the High Road. Not just jewellery but also bed linen and clothes. Sometimes they could not raise the money to redeem them and my mother bought the pawn tickets and then redeemed the goods herself. I had a nice pair of solid gold cuff links acquired in this way, which were unfortunately stolen at the same time as my gold watch.

Careful scrutiny of the photograph of the shop taken in November 1937 reveals a notice in the lower window of the door to the left of my head. 'Relief Tickets taken'. 'Relief' was the equivalent of Social Security and tickets, which could be exchanged for food, were issued to means-tested recipients. Then, as now, whenever money was being given away there was dishonesty, resentment and ill-feeling. Politicians never seem to benefit from the experience of a previous age. Needless to say the recipients often wanted cigarettes and tobacco, rather than food, in exchange for their relief tickets and my parents complied for fear of losing custom which they could ill afford to do. The tickets, which were worth five shillings each, were taken to an office in Dawlish Road, Leyton, by my father where they were redeemed for cash. One or two families went hop-picking every summer to supplement their incomes but it was unlikely that they mentioned it when applying for relief!

Most of the houses were rented and so the occupants changed from time to time and my recollections relate only to the families, particularly those with children, whom I came to know in my early childhood. The first house in Courteney Road was occupied by Mrs Graves, a very stout lady, her husband, and children, June, and Arthur, who was my best friend in those pre-war years. They moved in 1939 and I often wonder what happened to him. The next house was occupied by the Braids. Mr Braid and his son, Georgie, were self-employed builders, who pulled their materials and equipment from job to job in a two-wheeled cart. The wheels, like those on the bakers' carts, were of large diameter. I suppose it must have made it easier to pull.

Mr Hemmings and his wife and son, Peter, lived next door. He worked at Beckton Gas Works. Then came the Ralphs and children, Renée and Billy. The next three houses were occupied by members of the Tompkins family, rag and bone men, like Steptoe and Son! The end house was adjacent to their yard and they kept two ramshackle four-wheeled carts and their two cart-horses under the railway arches. It was reputed that old man Tompkins slept with a loaded pistol beside his bed to protect a chest of drawers filled with golden sovereigns! His two sons would travel with their horse-drawn carts to more prosperous neighbourhoods collecting scrap which was subsequently sorted by their wives, who separated the rags from the more valuable items which would often be sold on – no doubt adding more sovereigns to the chest! I often played with Alfie and 'Arfer' (Arthur), the next generation, sometimes clambering over the carts in the evening at the end of the day's work. To my great surprise I saw Alfie one day, a number of years later, plodding through Woodford Bridge on the same old cart collecting scrap. I now wish I had stopped the car to talk to him, but twenty years had passed and our lives had taken different paths.

The railway arches on the opposite side of Courteney Road were occupied by the Beechcroft Breezeblock Company. Breezeblocks were made by mixing cement, ash and clinker together and the wet mix was then shovelled into hand presses to make rectangular blocks, probably twelve inches by eighteen inches in size, equivalent to six standard bricks. They were used as a cheap substitute for bricks, particularly in the construction of internal partition walls. It was hard physical work. The men, often stripped to the waist in summer, were usually covered with a dusting of cement. It was piece-work and the men were reluctant to leave the presses, even for food and drink. With the agreement of the management, my father would visit the yard each morning to take orders from the men.

Pint milk bottles would be warmed in hot water (not too hot or the bottles would break) in the scullery behind the shop and filled with tea. Small loaves were cut in half and each half provided three slices of bread, including the crust, which were spread with margarine, and sometimes jam or fish paste, but that, of course, increased the basic price. Later, at the appropriate times, Father would return with the orders, and also cigarettes and tobacco, and distribute them to the men as they worked. As I got older I would help him. All the sales were 'on tick', of course, and on Friday evenings the men would come to the shop to pay after they had collected their week's wages. Sometimes when they didn't, my father had to catch them at work and it was not unknown for them to move to other jobs without paying their bills – money we could hardly afford to lose. During the war, when most of the workmen were in the Services, the work was done by Italian POWs who were transported daily from a nearby camp on a bombsite. Productivity fell alarmingly.

The inside of the shop was divided by an L-shaped counter, the long arm of the 'L' facing the door and lined with sweets. The short arm was the provision counter, with a small machine for slicing the bacon. At the junction of the two stood a glass-sided cabinet, which held the patent medicines. The walls behind the counters were lined with shelves. To this day I can remember exactly where the bags of flour, packets of tea, jars of jam and so on were to be found. Cigarettes, tobacco and chocolate were displayed behind the main counter, just out of reach of the 'light-fingered' customers.

The author's mother and father in the shop circa 1950

We sold everything that would yield a profit, however small, even paraffin oil, which was stored in a tank in the lean-to behind the house. This was collected at the side door, to avoid carrying it through the shop. I still have the measures with Queen Victoria's excise marks stamped on them. Groceries, provisions, soap, bread, milk, even small items of clothing such as socks and stockings (bigger items to order) were sold. It really was a general store.

The goods more often than not were supplied in bulk. Sugar came in hundredweight sacks, but Tate & Lyle's supplied the blue paper bags into which it was weighed. On the other hand, for soda and soap flakes, for example, my father had to make the bags, shaped like funnels, from brown paper. Tea could be bought loose. Dried fruit was supplied compressed into wooden boxes and weighed and sold as required. The empty boxes would be chopped and bundled up and sold for kindling for a penny a bundle. I don't remember my parents making any attempt to teach me to count or read before I started school and I suppose I must have learned something by helping with the weighing and measuring and stacking the shelves. As I got older I was allowed to count the takings in the till at the end of the day.

Goods were often wrapped in newspaper which customers brought into the shop but no one seemed to be any the worse for what would now be considered a very unhygienic practice. Trade was never very brisk in those days and my father would read the papers between customers when he was not making toys out of odds and ends and the remnants of packing cases. I learned very early on in life how to use tools, most of which I still possess and use frequently, never without thinking of my father, who used them before me, and how he would gently chide me if anything I made was not quite 'true' (accurate). He could turn his hand to almost any task – woodwork, metalwork, plumbing, bricklaying and, of course, home decorating. For him this was preferable to shopkeeping!

'Frenlite Flour' was supplied by French's Flour Mills from Ware, Hertfordshire, and every year they gave prizes for a window display featuring their products. Mother always entered but never won more than a small consolation prize – cutlery, aluminium saucepans and, once, a couple of large preserving pans. These were used to make jam in the summer and marmalade in the winter for sale in the shop. My father cut the orange peel by hand whilst listening to the wireless in the evenings. He always listened to Raymond Gram Swing, an American commentator whose broadcasts preceded Alistair Cooke's *Letter From America.* We kept chickens in the run in the yard, hens for the eggs, cockerels for sale and for our own use at Christmas. They were bought as day-old chicks in 'Club Row', a Sunday street market almost entirely devoted to livestock in the East End close to where my mother's family had lived. It was a wonderful place to visit as a child and almost any small live animal, fish or bird could be bought or sold. On one visit I remember a beautiful replica of a costermonger's cart pulled by two goats, which I did so want. My Uncle Will promised to buy it for me but, of course, he never did.

There was no room for more than about four or five people between the counter and the shop door, a space that was partly occupied by a small refrigerator in later years and a fruit machine (one-armed bandit) standing on crates of soft drinks. It was, I believe, illegal to use coinage and so those wishing to try their luck bought brass tokens to feed the machine and were rewarded with similar tokens, which were then converted back to real money if they were lucky enough to win.

In another money-making enterprise, my father went into partnership with Jack Roth, whom we named the 'Sausage King'. They rented premises in Odessa Road, Forest Gate, and bought the appropriate equipment but, although the sausages were absolutely delicious and sold well, they were uneconomical; the business was unprofitable and went bankrupt. Fortunately, the house and shop had been bought in my mother's name, otherwise we might have been homeless as well as jobless. A salutary lesson, which I have not forgotten.

Commercial travellers visited the shop regularly, hoping for orders and were usually known by the name of their product. 'Mr Galloway' sold patent medicines, notably 'Galloway's Cough Syrup'. He was always immaculately dressed – bowler hat, black overcoat, a rolled umbrella and a waxed moustache – and he invariably gave me a silver threepenny piece. Could this have been an inducement for a good order? 'Mr Peak Freen', a tall man with a stoop, a very sallow complexion and a somewhat obsequious manner, sold biscuits which were delivered in square tins and sold loose. Their broken biscuits, a mix of all varieties, were the most popular – no doubt because they were the cheapest. 'Kempy', on the other hand (Kemp's Biscuits), was a hail-fellow-well-met type with a red face, flat cap and a raucous laugh.

Some travellers did their rounds on foot, just taking orders, but others who delivered the goods at the time obviously needed transport. 'Mr Brooke Bond', selling his tea, had a little red van, and Mr Edwards, bowler-hatted with a greasy brown shop coat, supplied provisions from the back of a rather battered old van from his address in Old Hill Place, Stamford Hill. I mention the address particularly for, years later, the company making 'Simplex Cement', used to anchor artificial joints to bone, was situated there and gave me a small research grant.

Wholesalers providing a wide variety of products were responsible for most of the deliveries. Goodridges delivered the hardware with a horse and cart, the driver sitting up front in all weathers, with no more than his flat cap and a leather cape covering his shoulders and his knees to protect him. His moustache was beer stained and his face weather-beaten but he was a firm favourite with me because he always gave me some chaff, from the nosebag he was obliged to carry to feed the horse during the working day, to feed my rabbits. On one occasion I can remember a cart, rather like an American covered wagon drawn by two oxen, standing in the road outside the shop delivering Atora beef suet (obviously a publicity stunt), which is sold to this day.

Another vivid memory is of Lizzie Tompkins, one of the rag and bone family, running to the shop with her small son, who had set fire to himself, wrapped in a blanket. 'Mr Clarnico', in the shop hoping for an order for Clarnico sweets, immediately dashed out and took Lizzie and the child in the back of his little Austin 7 to Queen Mary's Hospital in Stratford. He was no doubt rewarded with orders for many months to come.

Living in a shop selling sweets and chocolates might seem like paradise to a child but I was never allowed unlimited access to the stock. On one occasion I coveted a large Clarnico Easter Egg decorated with little blue flowers, which remained unsold after Easter, no doubt too expensive for our usual customers. I was allowed to have it only because an aunt paid for it.

One of the more colourful commercial travellers was 'Greeny', who sold haberdashery, stationery, greeting cards and the like, with a pork-pie hat perched on the back of his head, a long raincoat always unfastened, and a ready line of cockney patter. It was not surprising that during the war he took to buying damaged property and later became a very successful property developer. He worked for Dennis Brothers, whose empty semi-derelict premises still stand in Shoreditch High Street opposite the junction with the Bethnal Green Road.

Further along Shoreditch High Street, perhaps even in Bishopsgate, was Anlaby House – Jeremiah Rotherham's large wholesale warehouse where my mother bought the small items of clothing (mainly socks and stockings) to sell in the shop. Bigger items such as bed linen and other household goods would be bought to order. The warehouse was destroyed in the Blitz but continued to trade from temporary buildings in the car park behind.

The shop was open every day of the year, from 8 a.m. to 7 p.m., apart from Sundays, bank holidays, and Christmas Day when it would be closed for the afternoon and, of course, on early closing day (by law) on Thursdays. On Thursday afternoon we would drive up to 'Jerry's' (Jeremiah Rotherham's) in our small Singer 8 blue saloon car, EV 561, which my mother had bought for £100 soon after I was born with possibly the last of her savings from cigar making. She would never consider hire purchase or the 'never-never' as she called it. If you wanted something you had to save for it, a principle which I have always followed.

Anlaby House had a revolving door and just inside was a commissionaire of the kind employed in most large buildings, I suppose as a security officer. They were invariably ex-servicemen and wore a very smart distinctive uniform with their medal ribbons boldly displayed and their stripes on their arms. (They were almost invariably sergeants.) The commissionaire always gave me a boiled sweet of the more expensive kind, wrapped in paper, unlike the sweets we sold in the shop. Sometimes, instead of accompanying my mother, my father and I would walk to Liverpool Street Station and then look at the magnificent locomotives hissing steam, the drivers polishing the brass fittings, the air filled with that distinctive smell instantly recognisable. Through the windows of the Pullman coaches, the subdued lighting of the table lamps on the white tablecloths set for dinner were part of another world. To this day I enjoy being part of that other world, using the dining-car whenever the opportunity arises on a train journey.

On the way to Liverpool Street Station we passed what I suppose would have been a naval outfitters with mannequins in the windows dressed in naval officers' uniforms. I identified particularly with what I thought was a small boy dressed in a sailor suit, but I suppose it must have been a midshipman's uniform. I begged my father to buy it for me but he told me I would have to join the Navy if I wanted to wear a suit like that, whereupon I decided to be a sailor when I grew up!

When my mother completed the afternoon's business, we drove the short distance to my grandparents' house in Stoke Newington, which was shared with a married aunt, her husband and baby daughter, and an unmarried aunt and uncle. There we would have what was called 'tea' – usually smoked haddock or grilled bloater or herring, bought from an impressive fishmonger's in Ridley Road, Dalston, with bread and butter. I was encouraged to eat the soft roes because my mother believed that they were good for the brain. It is interesting that so many old wives' tales have been found to have some scientific basis!

I can remember one such Thursday evening – it must have been in 1934 or 5 – when my grandfather returned home from work with his Gladstone bag and the attaché case, in which he carried his French-polishing materials, looking particularly gloomy. It was his last working day, but not as one might think an occasion for celebration. From now his only source of income would be his old-age pension of ten shillings and sixpence a week. The son and daughter still at home were the only other means of support. Grandfather did manage to get some part-time work later on, renovating furniture for a second-hand dealer called Kaminsky, who used to put the clock back by ten or fifteen minutes in the afternoons so that granddad worked a little longer than he was paid for, a trick he soon rumbled. We have a rather nice Victorian sofa table he re-polished and bought from Kaminsky for £4. 10s. – so perhaps those extra minutes he worked have been repaid over the years!

The journey home across Hackney Marshes or along Lea Bridge Road in the dark winter was often through thick fogs – 'peasoupers' which enveloped London until the 1950s. My father always tried to drive behind a bus because buses had powerful foglights focussed on the kerb, but of course we had to stop whenever the bus stopped to pick up or set down passengers. Those Thursday afternoon jaunts must have come to an end when I left Cannhall Road School in 1942.

CHAPTER 3

Early schooldays

I SUFFERED FROM ALL OF THE CHILDHOOD AILMENTS, which invariably meant being confined to bed for a week or so on the advice of Dr O'Brien or Dr Harcourt, local general practitioners with a surgery on the corner of Lansdown Road and the High Road, Leytonstone. Unlike many families, we were usually able to afford the 2*s.* 6*d.* fee for a home visit. Being confined to bed had some compensations, especially in the wintertime when a fire would be lit in the bedroom and before falling asleep one could watch the embers glow red as the fire died down in the evening. There was no electricity upstairs, but a night light in a saucer of water provided a flickering light, casting curious shadows on the walls. The wireless would be brought upstairs and it would be quite a problem connecting up the outside aerial and the power from downstairs. I vividly remember listening to the medical bulletins broadcast during the last hours of the life of King George V in 1936 as I lay in bed with the measles. My father would come upstairs from time to time to hear the latest bulletin and no doubt relay the news to the customers in the shop below. No one would have thought it possible that the little boy in bed upstairs would meet many of the King's descendants in the years to come.

Rheumatic fever, seldom encountered in Britain today, was the most serious illness from which I suffered. I remember all too clearly the severe pain I experienced in my knees and ankles. Dr O'Brien insisted that I stay in bed for three months because of the danger of permanent damage to the heart valves. I was not allowed to undertake any strenuous exercise for several years after that and as a result I did not learn to swim, for example, until adolescence. The pain in my knees occurred intermittently in bed at night for many years, and my mother would rub Wintergreen Ointment into the painful joints for what were called 'growing pains' unrelated to the rheumatic fever. The pains were, of course, not related particularly to the process of growing, and there are those who doubt their existence but I have no doubts whatsoever that 'growing pains' do occur and subside with the approach of adolescence.

As a result of these ailments I had passed my sixth birthday before I started school. I was put into a class of children my own age at Trumpington Road School, a local authority building built, no doubt, to the standards laid down by the School Boards following the Education Acts at the end of the nineteenth century. I was absolutely lost. I had no friends and no effort had been made at home to teach me the three Rs. I remember being asked if I knew the alphabet. I did not know what the alphabet was! I was desperately unhappy and was picked on by two boys in particular, Roy Amore and Philip Wakefield, the first as fair-headed as the other was dark. My mother, of course, complained to the staff but the headmistress, Miss Mack, who drove a little Austin 7 motorcar with GB plates on the back (showing off because she had been abroad, my parents said) was unsympathetic. One afternoon I left school at playtime and walked home and, in doing so, crossed a very busy main road. This was the last straw and I was subsequently taken to the Education Office in Kirkdale Road, Leytonstone, and it was agreed that I could be transferred to Cannhall Road School, which was further from home but did not involve crossing a main road. This relieved my mother of the duty of taking me and fetching me from school each day, four journeys in all, for school hours were nine until twelve and then two until four, and invariably pupils returned home for a mid-day meal. There were no 'school dinners' in those days but we did have free school milk in the morning break. I was befriended on the first day by a pretty little girl with auburn curls and a pink dress whose name was Jean Croft. Almost seventy years have passed and we still keep in touch. The classroom was rather austere, with an open coal fire in winter, protected by a heavy-duty fireguard, removed from time to time by the school caretaker when he added more coal.

Miss Farrow, our teacher, was a pear-shaped lady, in her fifties, I suppose, with short bobbed hair turning grey, and she wore long skirts, woollen jumpers, woolly stockings and flat sensible shoes, typical of schoolteachers of the day. We sat in double desks and concentrated on the three Rs. I distinctly remember learning to spell phonetically, C-A-T, D-O-G and similar words, and thinking what an impossible task we faced having to learn to spell every single word in this laborious fashion! At the end of each summer term we would move up a class but Miss Farrow stayed with us and the curriculum gradually expanded to include drawing and painting. For nature study we grew hyacinth bulbs in glass vases of water and twigs of hazel, pussy willow and horse chestnut in containers on the windowsill and watched the catkins develop and the sticky buds unfold. It was wonderfully exciting for children without gardens or access to the countryside. Miss Farrow would bring frog spawn in a jamjar and we would watch the tadpoles develop, but I think they all died before turning into frogs!

There was little physical activity, which I suppose was a good thing in view of the restrictions placed upon me, but we did have teams and played rounders or star relay once a week in the playground. I was always very competitive, wanting my team to win! We made paper chains at Christmas time to decorate the classroom and sent Christmas Cards to each other posted in an imitation pillar box; to be chosen as 'postman' was a great privilege. I was quite good at handicrafts and made a pair of moccasins, weaving with green and fawn wool on a cardboard loom. They were awarded a Certificate of Merit at an exhibition of schoolwork at the Town Hall, but strangely my parents, perhaps unaware that my work was on show, did not go.

Every Tuesday afternoon Miss Cooper, the headmistress, another stout lady, with a large mole on her left cheek, would sit at the teacher's desk and those of us with more affluent parents would line up to one side to buy 6*d.* National Savings Stamps. These were pale blue in colour and depicted the head of a Roman Centurion in crested helmet. The stamps were stuck into a little book which, when full, could be exchanged for a 15*s.* 0*d.* National Savings Certificate, which in turn would be worth a pound five years later, I think. My mother gave me the money to buy a stamp each week and I distinctly remember an occasion, I suppose it must have been in the summer of 1939, when the boy in front of me in the queue asked Miss Cooper why we bought savings stamps. Without being asked, I immediately replied, 'We are saving up for the war,' which incurred Miss Cooper's rebuke. 'Don't be silly,' she said. 'There isn't going to be a war.' This was the first time I can remember speaking out of turn but it was not the last. Clearly talk of war must have been in the air.

Discipline was firm but I do not remember children misbehaving unduly. The teachers were respected by pupils and parents alike and their actions were never questioned. Truancy was not a problem. My parents warned me that if I did not go to school, the School Board Man would catch me as he rode around the streets on his bicycle, and I would be sent to a Reform School. That was enough. I wonder whatever happened to the School Board Man and Reform Schools?

There was no homework and so after school we played in the street, often until it was dark – cricket with a tennis ball with the lamppost as a wicket, football under the Courteney Road railway arch, with the goals permanently chalked on the walls on either side. Graffiti had yet to be invented. Other street games were hopscotch, five stones, and marbles played in the gutter. A special treat in winter was to sit around a night watchman's coke fire when the roads were being re-surfaced. His hut was constructed of tarpaulins tied over a metal frame. The strip of road under repair in a nearby street was cordoned off and at night marked with red hurricane lamps which the watchman re-filled with paraffin, besides keeping an eye on the equipment.

I had a small white ridge tent, second-hand no doubt, probably acquired in exchange for a packet or two of 'fags', and in the summer we would sometimes spend the day camping on nearby Wanstead Flats. We would take a cooking pan and a few potatoes, cut them up into chips with our much prized sheath knives and fry them over an open fire made from collected twigs. They were never allowed to cook properly because we couldn't wait to eat them and as a consequence they were virtually raw, perhaps a little brown on the outside. My father would arrive on his bicycle from time to time to make sure we were all right. I think our parents warned us all never to talk to strangers but we were never told why, and probably would not have understood anyway. The danger we believed was kidnapping but we never understood what the consequences might be. Whether 'Boblar' was a man or a myth, I never knew, but he was to be avoided at all costs, according to the older children, because we assumed he would kidnap us. Those of us with bicycles would sometimes cycle to the Woolwich Free Ferry and spend a half-day or so travelling back and forth across the Thames, pretending we were on a ship at sea. The older, more adventurous boys would sometimes cycle the thirty miles or so to Southend along the newly built Southend Arterial Road, which had cycle tracks along the greater part of its length, but I was never allowed to do this.

One or two families would perhaps have a week's holiday at Southend, or even Clacton, and pay my father to take and collect them in the car. If there was room, I sometimes went too for the ride but we never had a family holiday as such ourselves because one or other of my parents had to stay to look after the shop. The Society of Friends had a Convalescent Home on Canvey Island and Miss Stewart, one of my mother's friends from the Bedford Institute, was, I think, a trustee and arranged for us to stay for a week at modest cost. Canvey Island had yet to be developed. The Convalescent Home consisted of a series of wooden huts with connecting walkways and a larger building with a dining room and a sitting room, in what, at the time, seemed to be extensive grounds with a lawn and fruit trees but in reality I imagine was probably no more than an acre. My mother and I seemed to spend most of the time clambering on the sloping sea walls, built centuries before by the Dutch, picking 'sea spinach' which we took home in two large canvas bags to sell in the shop.

If my father had taken us by car he would have had to close for the day and so we went by train from Wood Grange Park Station. Although Leytonstone Station was nearer, the fare from Wood Grange Park was less. I can remember struggling to carry one of the large bags of spinach from the station and wishing we had gone to Leytonstone! On every station there was a 'penny in the slot' weighing machine and, whilst waiting for the train at the beginning of a holiday, it was usual to weigh oneself and then repeat the process on the way home. A gain in weight was a measure of the success of the holiday for, unlike today, working-class men, women and children were generally undernourished. One year I went to Canvey with my father. This was much more like a holiday and I remember we visited the fairground on several occasions and won a jam pot and a china egg-timer in the form of a paper seller who held the sand-filled hour-glass in one hand.

My mother was not pleased when we returned home because she considered our prizes were the consequence of unnecessary expenditure. Yet she was not really mean, just thrifty. My father would often tell her that if everyone was like her there would be no trade! She was in many ways quite generous, especially in her support of the Bedford Institute, where a bazaar was held every autumn at which I remember meeting Theodore Godlee. My mother collected discarded clothes from the more prosperous neighbours (the Pegleys) throughout the year for the jumble sale and she personally ran a sweet stall stocked mainly with sweets and chocolates, donated as a result of her efforts, by the major manufacturers, because, of course, the Rowntrees, the Frys and the Cadburys were all Quaker families and philanthropy was part of their culture, extending to their business enterprises.

Christmas was always spent at my grandparents' house in Stoke Newington with aunts and uncles and cousins, members of my mother's large family, some of whom we met at no other time during the year. I always thought of it as a large house, but in fact there were the same number of rooms at 42 Cobbold Road, if the shop itself is included. The rooms at my grandparents' house were rather larger, but the basic plan was the same – two large rooms at the front up and down and a narrower, back section downstairs with kitchen and scullery and an inside lavatory (something I was not used to) and a bathroom and another bedroom upstairs. Underneath was a large cellar which extended under the pavement outside so that the coal could be emptied straight down a hole after lifting off the decorative cast-iron grating.

At the time I thought that the house had a flat roof, but this was an illusion created by a parapet which extended along the whole length of the terrace of houses lying along each side of Aden Grove and no doubt built to the same plan by a speculative Victorian builder. The little rectangular garden was tended by my unmarried uncle, Will. A small lawn was flanked by narrow borders and, towards the end, a rustic pergola with climbing roses crossed from side to side. There was just enough space beyond to accommodate the Anderson Shelter in 1939 and, as in so many other gardens, the excavated soil covering the top was made into a rock garden. I remember particularly the snapdragons in the borders and how the flowers opened when pressed from side to side between the finger and thumb. The garden, the inside lavatory and the cellar made it seem a much better house than my own.

The house was always full and Christmas dinner followed the King's Christmas broadcast, which gave us the time to get to Stoke Newington after closing the shop at mid-day. We always had a couple of chickens from those that we kept in the backyard, as well as a big piece of bacon cooked in a large iron cooking-pot (which I still have), followed by my grandmother's Christmas Pudding. I looked eagerly for the occasional silver threepenny piece incorporated in the mix several weeks before.

The large double doors separating the two big rooms at the front of my grandparents' house were opened and fires were lit. The rooms were decorated with paper chains and holly, but there was no Christmas tree and the children had already emptied their Christmas stockings at home but brought some of the more special gifts with them. One year I had a small Hornby train set, which I had previously seen in the window of a second-hand shop, and then I realised for certain that Father Christmas did not exist. Apart from the obligatory fruit and sweets, I usually received a book. Rather surprisingly, at home the only book we possessed was the Bible my mother had received as a prize during her schooldays and so reading for pleasure has never been a feature of my life. I was, however, pleased to receive volume one and volume two in successive years of the *Wonder Encyclopaedia for Children*, published by Odhams Press, the publishers of the *Daily Herald*, which I have kept because they were so precious. I also remember two other books of short stories published by Odhams, which may have been birthday presents.

'Tea' comprised winkles and shrimps accompanied by bread and butter and perhaps celery, followed by tinned fruit and jelly and then Christmas cake with tea to drink. After tea we usually played party games and had a singsong. One Christmas I was given a book with cardboard scenery and cutout figures and a script for the pantomime *Cinderella*. This my cousin Joan and I presented to the family and over the last sixty years each succeeding generation has continued *Cinderella* with the same scenery and figures, sometimes reluctantly, but the pantomime can now be seen on home-made video! At the last performance in 2002, my teenage granddaughters surprised us all by surreptitiously rewriting the script in a contemporary idiom.

By the time the children went to bed, sharing the bedrooms with the ladies, the supplies of beer stacked in crates in the front passage were becoming seriously depleted. Uncle Will would call for a whip-round and a visit would be made to Albert at The Albion pub at the end of the road for replacements. On returning, the men would play cards, usually Knockout Whist, well into the early hours of Boxing Day, sleeping on the floors of the downstairs rooms.

Breakfast on Boxing Day morning was informal but my mother's brothers all began the day with a pint mug of cocoa made with hot water but without milk. It tasted really horrible. Their individual mugs remained on the dresser after they had left home and this was probably the only occasion on which they were used. Meantime, granddad, who sat up all night in a small armchair in the kitchen to 'keep the fire in', washed, stripped to the waist, at an outside tap with Lifebuoy soap, just as he'd done winter and summer every day since childhood, when the only water supply came from a communal tap in a yard in Shoreditch.

The children were taken for a walk to Clissold Park to see the wallabies and other small animals in their enclosures and my father would return home to open the shop for two or three hours on Boxing Day morning, before returning in time for a cold lunch made from the leftovers of the day before. My uncles were strong Tottenham Hotspur supporters and in the afternoon I would be included in the trip to Whitehart Lane if Spurs were playing at home, sometimes even travelling by taxi if the buses were full. After tea, once the expenses had been apportioned, uncles, aunts and cousins bade farewell until next year, and I longed for the day when I would be allowed to stay up and play cards and sleep on the floor with the men. That day arrived at Christmas 1941 and I remember I could hardly keep my eyes open. Sadly the opportunity never occurred again for that Christmas marked the end of those wonderful family Christmases of my childhood.

As my birthday on 6 January fell so soon after Christmas, I usually received combined Christmas and birthday presents, which, as those born close to Christmas know, is a great disappointment. I can remember having only one birthday party during my childhood, when I was five years old. The shop parlour was cleared and our customers' children of a similar age were invited to tea. My mother had brought home the discarded Christmas tree which had stood in the foyer of the Rialto Cinema and the children each received a present from the tree. The most popular was a small tinplate bird which, when wound up, rocked to and fro as if picking up food in its beak. I remember all the children shouting, 'I want a pecking bird' and being rather tearful because there were too few birds to satisfy everyone.

The shop parlour, as far as I can recall, was never again used for a social event!

Chapter 4

The War

THE SECOND WORLD WAR – 'THE WAR' – was, for my generation, a watershed in the lives of those who lived throughout it. They measured time by it. In conversation events occurred before, during, or after the war, although the duration of each period of time is so widely disparate.

The summer of 1939 was glorious, but preparations for the inevitable conflict were already underway. I recollect gangs of men digging in what my parents, with recollections of the First World War, called trenches on Wanstead Flats. They were, in fact, air-raid shelters dug on the cut-and-cover principle, lined and roofed with concrete and later fitted with primitive bunks in readiness for the civilian population to shelter from the anticipated air raids. The school summer holidays had already begun and curious children followed the work-in-progress, running errands for the men, buying cigarettes and soft drinks from the nearby shops, with a penny or two for reward. The work eventually reached what we called the Sand Hills on the far side of Wanstead Flats, on the boundary of Manor Park, about a mile from the shop.

Once, when I was running errands for the men, I suddenly realised it was early closing day and I hurried home, expecting to find my parents waiting for me to join them on the usual Thursday afternoon business trip to Shoreditch and subsequent tea with my grandparents. When I arrived at the shop it was, of course, closed. The side door was opened by Tommy Sibley, our lodger, telling me that my parents had already left. I immediately set off to try to catch them before Tommy, already in his seventies, had time to stop me. I knew they intended picking up my aunt and her two young children on the way, so I hurried to their house, only to find that they had already left, and so I set off to walk to Stoke Newington. I had, of course, made the journey by car so many times that the route presented no difficulty, but halfway along the Lea Bridge Road it started to rain and I was dressed in no more than a summer shirt and trousers. Finally, to everyone's consternation, a very bedraggled eight-year-old arrived at 57 Aden Grove, having completed the seven-mile journey in about three hours. I imagine that when we got home, poor Tommy was berated for not stopping a very self-confident and self-willed boy from making such a journey.

Later, anti-aircraft gun and searchlight enplacements were built near the Sand Hills and a barrage balloon unit appeared on the flats at the end of

Courteney Road. Barrage balloons were a wonderful idea; the large silver hydrogen-filled balloons were attached by a stout cable to a winch sometimes mounted on the back of a lorry, sometimes, for example, in the playground of Cannhall Road School, more permanently fixed to the ground. When the balloons were inflated and reeled out, any low-flying aircraft would obviously become entangled in the cables and so the dive bombing employed by the Luftwaffe so effectively in Warsaw was prevented. Sometimes enemy aircraft would shoot at them and the blazing balloons made a very spectacular sight in the sky.

Large metal water storage tanks for use by the Auxiliary Fire Service (AFS) if the mains supply failed were placed where there was sufficient space. Anderson Shelters made from heavy-duty galvanised corrugated iron were distributed to individual households for erection in their gardens. Those without a garden could have a Morrison Shelter, which was essentially a steel box designed to fit under a table – too big for our small kitchen. The supply of a shelter was subject to a means test and the Pegleys were not entitled to one, so they agreed to have our Anderson Shelter in their garden for us all to share. The shelters were dug half into the ground and half above ground and the excavated soil was placed over the top. Those who were able to install their own shelters often made nice rock gardens on the top. Later, gangs of workmen did the heavy work for those unable to do it themselves. The shelters often filled with water and later the teams of men returned to 'tank' them with concrete up to the outside ground level. I doubt that these preparations had been completed by the time war was declared.

On 3 September 1939 I can remember my father listening intently to Prime Minister Neville Chamberlain's broadcast announcing that we were at war with Germany. Almost immediately we set off in the car, following what must have been a pre-arranged plan, to collect my Aunt Beat and her two daughters, Joan aged four and Rita just two months old, to drive to farming friends in Huntingdonshire. My parents and other members of the family had become acquainted with the Beilbys, Ella and Frank, and their three children – some ten years earlier as a result of a friendship between my American relatives and Ella's brother in California, and had made brief visits to the farm from time to time over the intervening years. The following day my father brought his youngest brother's wife, Hilda, and their children, John and Joy, to join us. Aunt Beat and Joan and Rita stayed with Ella's widowed mother, Granny Robinson, in her bungalow nearby but my mother and Hilda and the remaining children were somehow accommodated in the farmhouse.

There seems to have been a general perception that London and other major cities were in imminent danger from the Luftwaffe and the

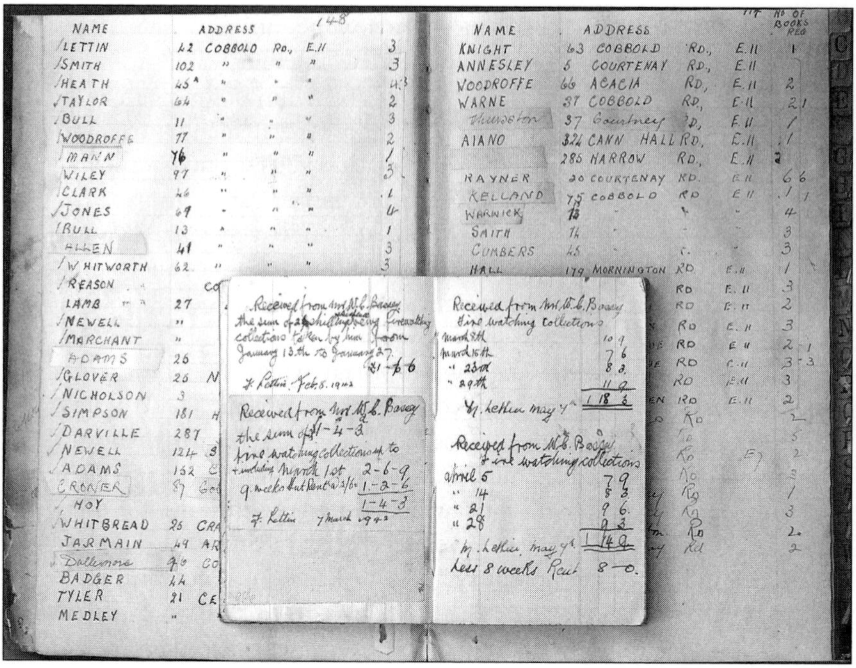

List of customers registered for staple foods, and fire-watching cash-book

evacuation of whole schools and hospital patients to the safety of the country was taking place according to plans formulated and tested as early as 1938. Ours was a private evacuation and had the advantage that our hosts were not strangers and we were not separated from our mothers, but of course our fathers stayed behind. In the event nothing much happened. There were a few insignificant air raids on London in what became known as the 'phoney war'. Over the next few weeks we and others like us drifted back home and we celebrated Christmas 1939 in the usual family fashion. By now there was a universal blackout. Windows were heavily curtained or covered with closely fitting blinds or shutters made of lightproof material, sometimes paper, sometimes cloth. There were no street lights and the upper half of the headlights of all road vehicles were covered with black paint. The interior lights on public transport were dimmed. Illuminated advertising signs were turned off. Air-raid wardens patrolled the streets and any chink of light brought a knock on the door and a reprimand.

Food rationing was introduced and everyone had a ration book, buff in colour for adults, green for children, which was renewed every six months. For the staple foods – butter, margarine, cooking fat, sugar, cheese, bacon and eggs, milk – each individual was obliged to register with a particular retailer who was provided with the appropriate rations for each customer each week on production of the ration book. I recorded the names of the customers registered with us in a ledger, a photograph of which is shown on page 32. I can't remember if I was asked to do it or if I was just trying to be helpful! The pages in the front part of the ration books were divided into dated squares and the appropriate square was cancelled when the rations were supplied. The pages in the back of the book were divided into vertical strips, each of which was worth a number of 'points' which could be exchanged for a variety of foods when available at any shop. Biscuits, sweets, tinned food, for example, would be on 'points'. The Ministry of Food would decide from time to time how many points should be cut from the ration book for such items. At the end of each week I would help my father to tie the points into bundles of 100, which were then taken in a special envelope to the Food Office. We often wondered if they bothered to count them themselves! Curiously meat was rationed by price. One shilling and ten pennyworth of meat was the ration and so the more expensive the cut the smaller the portion. A separate system of coupons was used for clothes. Because we supplied food and drink to the workers at the Beachcroft Breezeblock Company, it was necessary to record how much food and how many 'beverages' (I had never come across the word before) were supplied each day in order to claim the appropriate amount of rations from the wholesalers.

Rationing worked quite well on the whole and, though I have no doubt that extra food could be obtained on the black market for those who could afford it, I think there was very little abuse. It was very beneficial for the small shopkeeper because the registered customers were obliged to purchase their rations at the same shop each week and so a regular and consistent income was assured. Furthermore, the price of every commodity was controlled and so there was obviously no advantage to be gained from registering with the big cut-price shops (supermarkets of the day) in the High Street where before the war my mother could often buy sugar, for example, cheaper than from the usual wholesaler!

Apart from these necessary inconveniences, the war seemed a long way off and I have little recollection of the disastrous Norwegian campaign or the torpedoing of the *Royal Oak* in the supposed safety of Scapa Flow. Perhaps unconsciously I suppressed the bad news, but I do clearly remember the liberation of the British merchant seamen from the prison ship *Altmark* in a Norwegian fjord by HMS *Cossack* with the cry, 'It's all right, chaps, the Navy's here.' I remember the Battle of the River Plate when the cruisers, *Exeter*, *Ajax* and *Achilles* forced the German pocket battleship *Admiral Graf Spey* to scuttle itself outside Montevideo Harbour. I cut the photographs from the newspaper and stuck them into a scrapbook!

'Why are we fighting this was against the Germans?' I remember asking my father around this time.

'To keep our independence and the right to govern ourselves and make our own laws,' he replied.

I wonder if he and the thousands who died fighting for that ideal would think it all worthwhile now that nearly all our laws are made in Brussels.

There must have been sporadic air raids in the spring of 1940. I also remember seeing a German aircraft caught in the searchlight beams as we made our way to the air-raid shelter in the Pegleys' garden. It was intended for four people but eight squeezed in, sitting on benches on either side, around a paraffin stove and an oil lamp. At this stage the raids were short-lived and people were not sleeping in their domestic shelters. When the all-clear sounded we returned to bed and, the next day on the way to school, we found pieces of shrapnel, remnants of the anti-aircraft barrage from the guns which had boomed during the raid the night before.

We sometimes saw 'dog fights' during the day. We were close to the fighter stations at North Weald and Hornchurch where Spitfires and Hurricanes were based. On one occasion an enemy plane crashed into Mayville Road School, less than half a mile away from the shop. It must have been during the school holidays or on a weekend for I have no recollection of children being killed. After the raid, adults and children made their way to Mayville Road, which the police had cordoned off, looking for souvenirs. I went home triumphantly with what I thought was a piece of the German bomber, only to be deflated when my father told me that it was a sash pulley from one of the school windows!

Whether this was one of the sporadic air raids during the phoney war, which ended on 10 May 1940 when the German Army moved into Holland and Belgium, or whether it happened later, I do not know but around this time the Government was making vigorous efforts to evacuate the children remaining in London. On this occasion I was part of an official group of evacuees sent to Devon. There are numerous published photographs of the multitude of children at London mainline stations, each with a small knapsack, a gas mask in a cardboard box hanging by a string from the neck, and a luggage label with name and address, tied to a coat lapel. I, now nine years old, was one of them.

We left our tearful mothers behind in the early morning and I have no idea how we got to Paddington Station, where we boarded the train to Exeter. The journey seemed to be interminable with frequent stops and it was early evening by the time we arrived. We were distributed to the surrounding villages by bus and I found myself with a group of children, none of whom I knew, in the Village Hall in the little village of Hele. The WVS were in charge of arrangements and the local ladies who had agreed to take evacuees were waiting. What followed was rather like an auction. The ladies all claimed to have ordered 'girls', perhaps with the thought that they might help with the housework, but soon there were only boys left.

'You will have to take boys,' said the WVS lady in charge. 'There are no girls left' and I found myself with one other little boy, Ivor Ingram, left until last. The lady who took us was clearly not pleased but we soon arrived at her small semi-detached cottage opposite Whiteways Cider Factory, which her husband managed, at Hele. By this time it was getting dark and, shortly afterwards, I found myself sharing a bed with a boy I had never seen before.

I cannot remember now the name of the woman or her husband. Perhaps it was subconsciously obliterated from my memory for this proved to be a very unhappy interlude in my life. They had no children of their own and from the start she seemed to take a dislike to me and Ivor was clearly her favourite. However, I got on well with her husband, who took me to the factory where I saw how the cider was made and how the coopers made the barrels. He had a ferret and I would go with him in the evenings to the orchards to catch and shoot rabbits. I don't remember much about school but I do remember having an argument with a boy of similar age who lived in the adjoining cottage. I suppose I had learned from the chickens we kept in our back yard that a cock and a hen were necessary for eggs to produce chicks and, surprisingly for a country boy, he insisted that this was not so. The woman heard the argument and scolded me because, she said, 'I knew too much.' This seemed a ridiculous proposition to me. Clearly *something I had said* landed me in trouble once more.

This must have been around the time of the evacuation of the British Expeditionary Force from Dunkirk. That epic event has been recounted so frequently that it is difficult to disentangle personal recollections from the knowledge acquired from historical accounts, but I have no clear memory at all of the events of the last week in May 1940. We all know the part played by the little ships but few are aware of the 125,000 French troops evacuated (taking valuable places from British soldiers), 100,000 of whom elected to be re-patriated to so-called neutral Vichy France. After assembling on the South Coast they were given safe passage back to France, leaving only 7,000 subsequently joining De Gaulle's Free French Army. Small wonder that Churchill ordered the Royal Navy to sink the French Fleet at Oran.

The main railway line was easily seen from the cottage and how I wished to be on the train back to London. Soon my letters were answered and my mother arrived, unannounced, and took me home. There were so few teachers left in London that we had half-day schooling, attending in the morning or the afternoon on alternate weeks. I remember school dinners (lunches) were now provided for the first time, which seems illogical in retrospect since we were at school in either the morning or the afternoon and could well have eaten at home. On the whole I disliked them but I think they were meant to be nutritious and often included salads, which we never had at home!

The air raids meantime had intensified. We began sleeping in our Anderson Shelter, which we now had to ourselves every night, the Pegleys having built an air-raid shelter for themselves in one of their lock-up garages. When Britain failed to surrender after Dunkirk, the bombing of London began in earnest when, on the afternoon of Sunday 10 July, 400 bombers attacked and so the Battle of Britain had begun, escalating by September to become 'The Blitz'.

I do not know precisely when I was evacuated for the third time, back to the Beilbys' farm near Ramsay, Huntingdonshire, my Aunt Beat and Joan and Rita returning to Granny Robinson's bungalow at the same time. It must have been late August or early September because the corn was being harvested, but the harvest was later then because the corn was sown in the spring rather than in the autumn as it is now. The 'stooks' of corn were collected and piled carefully into traditional stacks until the threshing machine, pulled and then driven by a coal-fired traction engine (now collectors' items), arrived some time later, travelling from farm to farm.

The Bielbys' small mixed farm possessed two two-wheeled carts (tumbrels), each pulled by one of their three horses, not as massive as thoroughbred shires, but similar in appearance. Jesse Cowling, the licensee of The Plough in Mereside, where he also farmed, brought along his four-wheeled wagon to help bring the stooks into the yard. Frank Bielby would, of course, later help out with his carts on Jesse's farm. Such co-operation was commonplace. As the corn left the threshing machine, each man carried a filled two-hundredweight sack on his back to the barn, where the sacks were stacked until subsequently sold. Carrying such heavy weights is now forbidden by the Healthy & Safety Regulations. The straw was built into a stack, covered with a tarpaulin, and eventually used for animal bedding.

The farmhouse was on the road leading from the small town of Ramsay, a couple of miles away, to the village of Mereside, a mile or so in the opposite direction, beside a bridge crossing a substantial river draining into the forty-foot drain, one of the main man-made channels draining the Fens. The soil was rich, the land flat and featureless and the vegetation sparse, with scarcely a tree to be seen. Stables for three working horses, Blossom, Smart and Prince, and the house cow, Bessie, and various other rough and ready pens for half a dozen or so bullocks and a similar number of pigs, surrounded the farmyard. A purpose-built henhouse stood in the yard with a similar one on the bank on the opposite side of the river, each housing about fifty hens. It soon became my task to let the hens out each morning to range freely and the ducks to swim in the river, and to shut them up after their evening feed of corn. The eggs were collected each day, washed and stored in crates, to be collected by a carrier once a week.

There were three rectangular fields side by side, parallel to the road, through which the crops of corn, potatoes and sugar beet were rotated each year. Pasture for grazing was rented from an adjacent farm. This relatively small parcel of land and the livestock were sufficient to support Frank and Ella, Gordon, the farmhand, and 16-year-old Keith, their son, who worked full-time on the farm, and Joy their 9-year-old daughter, and now me, for whom Ella was paid, I believe, about ten shillings a week for my keep. Joan, her 19-year-old daughter, worked as a full-time nanny in Birmingham, returning occasionally for weekends.

The potatoes were harvested after the corn, a horse-drawn machine throwing them onto the surface. Casual workers, mainly women from the village, then put them into special wicker baskets, with wire mesh bottoms and rigid wicker handles spanning the opening. I sat in a horse-drawn cart as it slowly made its way along the rows of baskets. Keith, with one hand on the cart, hooked up the baskets with the other hand, throwing them over the cart so that they were upside down by the time I caught them to empty their contents into the cart and then to throw them out the opposite side, ready for the next row.

Surprisingly, I was not sent to school, perhaps because this was a private evacuation and the authorities were unaware of my existence. I was paid 7/6*d.* a week for the job I was doing on the farm and the only concession to my age was an 8 o'clock rather than the usual 7 o'clock start each morning. The potatoes were stored in clamps covered with straw and then earth until they were sold. After the potatoes came the sugar beet, which was mechanically lifted and I now worked each day with others cutting the tops off with a sort of machete as they lay on the ground. Gerald, a local carrier, was employed to transport the sugar beet to the sugar factory at Peterborough in his small lorry and he also helped out with the loading. One day, when we were sheltering from the rain by the side of a ditch, he used his coat to protect me but also took the opportunity to put his hand up the inside of my trouser leg (boys wore short trousers in those days). I found the whole episode rather curious and, of course, I had no idea why he was doing it. I mentioned it to Keith later that day. 'Oh, Gerald up to his old tricks again' was his response. So obviously his activities were well known. Perhaps too much is made of such things nowadays, particularly if there is a chance of compensation! I subsequently accompanied Gerald to the sugar beet factory, when a small 'back-hander' ensured that the sample of beet taken for inspection was fairly free of soil, resulting in a better price.

Once all the crops had been harvested, the stables and pens were mucked out. The soiled bedding was thrown straight into the yard where it was left until the following spring, before being spread on the land. Whenever there are animals, there are rats but, as they scurried out from their hiding places, they were either shot or impaled on the tines of the pitchforks. I cut off their tails, receiving sixpence per tail when I took them to Farmer Ingles, the local NFU representative who farmed in Mereside. A pigeon's head was worth a penny and a small bird, such as a sparrow, one farthing. Clearly such payments were intended to reduce the losses of precious foodstuffs and I made a point of collecting such items in a cocoa tin until I had sufficient to exchange for payment.

Petrol was still obtainable so my parents arrived for Christmas 1940, and I awoke on Christmas morning to find several new Dinky toys including a Hurricane and a Spitfire, a Blenheim and a Wellington Bomber, for which my father had made three hangars of characteristic shape. He also managed to bring my junior bicycle, a tent, a fishing rod and half a dozen or so mousetraps which I used to catch sparrows which fed on the corn which I fed to the chickens each evening. I had been keeping rabbits since the beginning of the war and had three breeding does, the offspring of which were either sold as babies for five shillings or fattened up and killed for food. One doe also arrived together with its hutch!

Meantime the Blitz had reached its zenith and on the night of 30 December, after my parents had returned to London the whole of the Docks and a large part of the East End were on fire. The red glow in the sky was visible on the farm eighty miles away. The able-bodied residents in every neighbourhood took their turn in fire-watching and my father had been elected to take charge in Cobbold Road. Threepence a week was collected from each household and from this 2/6*d.* was used to rent a shed in which the fire-fighters' equipment – one stirrup pump and one bucket (which I still have), a tin hat and some sand – was stored. Two pages from the account book are reproduced on page 32. The money was also available to meet other incidental expenses, such as the replacement of damaged clothing, but none seems to have been claimed. Unfortunately, there was very little the fire-watchers could do when an incendiary bomb set light to the mackintosh factory almost opposite the shop in Cobbold Road. Fortunately, the Fire Brigade prevented the fire from spreading to neighbouring properties but the factory itself was completely destroyed leaving only the perimeter wall standing.

Very few houses, however, escaped some damage during the raids. At the very least windows were blown in, to be replaced by opaque wire-reinforced plastic sheets, and lathe and plaster ceilings which had collapsed were covered with sheets of plasterboard. The more severely damaged houses were evacuated. The occupants emerging from their air-raid shelters, glad still to be alive, were housed elsewhere and once the houses were made habitable again they or other families returned.

I do not know whether my parents knew that I had not been to school but, after the Christmas holidays, arrangements were made for me to attend the village school in Mereside. There were three classrooms leading off a small lobby, one for infants, one for juniors and one for seniors. I was in the juniors and Miss Palmer was our teacher. Mr Parr, the Headmaster, rather surprisingly for so small and insignificant a school, was a Cambridge MA. At least that was what was on the sign outside – MA (Cantab). He took the senior class and every morning he stood in the lobby with the classroom doors open and played the morning hymn on one of his many musical instruments while Miss Palmer accompanied him on the piano. Sometimes it was a trumpet or perhaps a saxophone and on another day the violin, and I remember even a mandolin. My cousin Joan now lived in the village, her mother having returned to London, and I called for her as I walked past her house on the way to school.

I learned to knit at Mereside School but I don't remember learning much else. I suppose we did sums and read aloud but it was the knitting I remember – iron holders and egg cosies in green and fawn wool, which I sent back to my parents in London. I did, however, make a firm friend – Peter Clark, the son of the village electrician – and we often camped out at the weekend in a nearby field. We were surprised to wake up one morning to find ourselves surrounded by men from the RAF Regiment from nearby Upwood RAF Station. Our white tent had been spotted from the air and, as it was thought that perhaps it was a parachute, they came to investigate. We were told quite firmly that white tents were forbidden and so our camping weekends came to an end.

The river running alongside the farm was teeming with fish and I spent many happy hours on the bank with my fishing rod, a bent pin with a piece of bread for bait catching roach, perch and bream without much difficulty. Several anglers kept their equipment at the farm and when they came to fish I could usually scrounge one or two proper hooks and some live maggots, but unfortunately hooks and bait were completely swallowed by eels and could rarely be retrieved. Granny Robinson, however, enjoyed the eels!

I suppose the endless supply of iron holders and egg cosies caused further anxiety at home and after the Easter holidays I was transferred to the elementary school in Ramsay (not I hasten to add Ramsay Abbey Public School). I went on my bicycle, but sometimes the wind across the Fens was so strong that I was blown over and forced to walk. Ella made arrangements for me to leave my bike at a house near the school, where I was also provided with a mid-day meal.

The teaching was much more rigorous, although very much learning by rote. Towards the end of the term there was an exam, something I had not previously experienced and to my surprise I came top of the class. It was the practice for the pupils to sit in order of merit, from the back left-hand corner of the room row-by-row to the front. We occupied double desks. A girl had come second in order of merit and it was thought an unjust reward for my achievement that I should be obliged to sit next to a girl and so I had a double desk to myself! My new-found celebrity was not to last, for at the end of term I returned to London for what was to be a holiday. The Blitz had ended in May and the danger had receded, but the results of the bombing were only too evident. I never returned to the farm.

Schools in the country broke up later and returned later so that the children could help with the harvest so, after a mere fortnight's break, I returned to Cannhall Road School. I joined Mr West's class and was reunited with many of my former classmates, including Jean Croft, the girl who had befriended me on my first day at Cannhall. Mr West was an excellent teacher with whom I got on well and, surprisingly, Jean can still recall the occasions when he asked me to tell the class about my experiences on the farm. I suspect he had been excused military service because of ill-health; he always looked pale and sallow, yet he arrived each day at school on his racing bicycle. I did quite well in the exams but never managed to come top of the class again, always being beaten by at least four girls, one of whom was always Jean.

Fire-watching duties continued until September 1942, according to the cash-book. My father was also working part-time at night, carrying out emergency repairs to the machinery at Neville's Bakery. Ken Mullock, the full-time engineer, lived in Croydon and it would take him some time to reach the bakery in an emergency. Dad would have a meal after closing the shop and then spend the next five or six hours at Neville's, by which time the bread for distribution in the early hours of the morning had been baked. All the fit enough young men were in the forces and Mr Brett, the local removal man, sometimes needed an extra pair of hands and Dad would help him out while Mum looked after the shop, all of which benefited the family finances.

There are certain days or occasions in one's life which prove to be of enormous significance. Friday 6 March 1942 was the day that determined my future, the day I took what was then called 'the Scholarship', later the eleven-plus exam. This was held at the Leyton County High School for Boys, in Essex Road, Leyton. I had never been there before and again, somewhat surprisingly by today's standards, neither of my parents accompanied me. I was told to catch the 661 trolleybus at the top of Beachcroft Road in the High Road, Leytonstone, and ask the conductor to put me off at Essex Road. I suppose my previous experiences had made me self-reliant and I can recall two or three occasions, in addition to the seven-mile walk as an 8-year-old to my grandparents' home just before the outbreak of war, when I had made journeys on my own which would be regarded as quite unthinkable for a child today. A visit to the school dentist at the school clinic, a distance of about a mile there and back from Cannhall Road School along the busy High Road of Leytonstone, and a trip to Scott's ship *Discovery*, which was at that time moored on the Thames Embankment, with Willie Wilson with whom I shared a double desk in Mr West's class, come to mind. When we arrived we found that unaccompanied children were not admitted and so we asked an airman and a WAAF at the entrance of the gangway to take us on board and, not only did they do so, but they took us to a café afterwards for a meal. Baked beans on toast, I think.

I had always wanted a dog and Ruby (a nickname – I think his name was Rubens), one of the men working at the Beachcroft Breezeblock Company, used to bring his little wire-haired terrier with him when he came to the shop on Friday evenings to settle his bill. I really coveted that dog and one day a similar little terrier followed me home from school. I was made to take it to Leytonstone police station where I was told that it would be sent to Battersea Dogs Home and if no one claimed it I would be allowed to keep it. In due course I made the journey to Battersea, having been told which buses to take in order to get there. I remember being very surprised when the dog had its rectal temperature taken before I was allowed to take it home, after I had paid the 7/6*d.* fee.

I was promised a new adult-size bicycle if I passed the scholarship and true to his word my father took me to Reeds Cycle Shop in the High Road on the afternoon the results were announced and I rode my brand new Elswick bicycle back home. It was two or three months before I started at the High School and during this time I became very friendly with Frankie Clark the youngest of Mrs Humming Top's children, who lived next door but one. We decided to build a tunnel under the Laceys' back garden to link our respective homes. We began in Frankie's garden and converted his mother's mangle (clothes wringer) into a crane by removing one of the rollers and adding a jib, and as he dug down I hauled up the buckets of soil. The materials salvaged from bomb-damaged houses had been taken by the demolition crews to a place near the bandstand on Wanstead Flats, where it was available to anyone who could make use of it. Most children had 'barrows' made from old pram wheels and, using my barrow, we collected floorboards and joists to shore up our tunnel. We completed the shaft and boarded the sides but Frankie decided to begin excavating the tunnel itself on his own. Late one summer evening an anxious Mrs Clark came knocking on the side door. The sides of the shaft had collapsed, with Frankie underneath. Dad had to hurry round to get him out and so another adventure came to an end.

Leyton County High School for Boys in the 1940s (photo Paul Estcourt)

The Leyton County High School (LCHS) for Boys had its origin in the Leyton Technical Institution which was founded in 1898, and under the impetus of the 1902 Education Act, several other educational institutions were subsequently amalgamated into a single school, administered by the Essex County Council. After occupying temporary accommodation at various sites a new purpose-built school in Essex Road, Leyton, was opened in 1929. It was a pleasant brick two-storey building on nine acres of land with formal gardens in front and playing fields behind, built around two quadrangles separated by the Assembly Hall, the full height of the building. Dr Couch, the third Headmaster, ran the school along the lines of an independent public school without the 'fagging' and he alone administered corporal punishment, other members of the staff and prefects being permitted only to keep the boys in detention after school or give lines.

The four Houses, although named, were always known by the colours Gold, Red, Blue, and White and served to foster academic and sporting competition between their members. The curriculum was broadly based, leading after five years to the General Certificate of Education, after which most of the 500 or so boys left to seek employment, with just a few staying on in the small Sixth Form to take the Higher School Certificate two years later. Staff and pupils had been evacuated at the outbreak of war and the school buildings became the Leyton Centre to accommodate the boys from Leyton and the surrounding Grammar Schools, particularly Walthamstow (Sir George Monoux School), Chingford and Ilford. In September 1942, I joined Form 1L, the Leyton Form, the year the parent school returned from evacuation. In 1943 most of the visitors returned to their own schools and the return to normality began, with the more orthodox re-naming of the forms A, B and C. I remained in the 'A' Form for the next four years but never managed to exceed fourth position in the order of merit. On the whole I managed to keep out of trouble but I remember being accused of some misdemeanour, to which I indignantly responded 'I never done it, Sir,' a phrase I would have used at home. Sadly, I did not understand why I was additionally being reprimanded for my grammar as well as the supposed misdemeanour. It was clearly *something I said*!

Many of the more senior members of the staff had joined the school in the 1920s and such continuity paid dividends, but the younger members had been called up into the forces and were replaced by women, among whom was our form mistress, Mrs Cattell-Jones, known affectionately as 'Katy Bones' or simply 'Kate', whose husband had been a master of the school before his early death. She was a charming Welsh lady who could think no ill of any of her pupils, with many of whom she remained in contact for the rest of her life, particularly any who followed a career in medicine. She remembered my children's birthdays and presented them with silver napkin rings in infancy and was always looking to the future and never to the past. It was only after the death of our eldest child, Jenny, at the age of thirteen that we knew that her only child, a son, had died in early adolescence and would have been about my age. By the time of her death at the age of eighty-two, after being mugged, she was the most senior graduate of Aberystwyth University, having graduated in 1912. My wife and I had frequently been her guests at the Old Aberystwythians Dinners held in London each year and had met many prominent graduates of that university.

The teaching was good, but I single out our History master, Victor Cohen, nicknamed 'the Bear' on account of his appearance rather than his manner. The memory of his eccentricities has remained with me, and some of his techniques I have imitated whilst teaching medical students. There is always someone who will ask a question, not in the thirst for knowledge but to show off or make an impression. 'Good question, boy' the Bear would usually reply. 'If I knew the answer to that, I wouldn't be a schoolmaster.' I would substitute 'If I knew the answer to that, I would be awarded the Nobel Prize' but I then relented and tried to give an answer of some sort. I still remember that Peel's Ministry was divided into three parts – 'Bobby Peel', 'Orange Peel' and 'Potato Peel' – but I'm not sure that it was necessarily in that order! On arriving in class for the last period of the afternoon the Bear would ask, 'Any boy here got a watch?' Murray Rennie would invariably raise his hand and the Bear would respond, 'Your father must be very rich. I can't afford a watch. Tell me when it's quarter to four. I've got a train to catch.' Any boy misbehaving was ordered 'Stand on the form, boy' and spent the rest of the lesson standing on the seat of his desk. I don't think he knew a single boy by name, but his pupils did well in the exams and I think he was the best teacher I ever had.

The winter game was football and, though I played in the Form and House Teams, I was not good enough to get into the school junior team so, with my friend Len Miller who was in a similar position, we decided to form our own team which we called Cobbold Athletic. Eton Manor, a well-known East End Sports Club, had playing fields near Hackney Wick and we approached them for the use of a football pitch and, surprisingly, no doubt impressed by our initiative, they allowed us to use a pitch on Saturday mornings. We recruited a team but sadly it was too late to arrange for fixtures and Cobbold Athletic failed to find any opposition.

Once at the High School, homework, school sports on Saturday mornings and different term times resulted in less contact with old friends but also in the making of new ones. Curiously, the most lasting of those new friends proved to be the boy with the rather haughty mother, Gordon Medcalf, who lived almost opposite the shop and had never been allowed to play in the street with the rest of us. It was not until after his death more than half a century later that I learned that her reclusiveness and apparent haughtiness may have been due to the fact that Gordon had been conceived out of wedlock, and such a thing would have been shameful at that time and something to be kept secret. I remember the unmarried daughter of a near neighbour who became pregnant. The family would not allow her out of the house but my mother persuaded them to let her take the pregnant girl out each evening after dark (there were no street lights during the war) for a walk and to arrange her confinement in a private nursing home and the adoption of the new-born baby. Sadly, with the passing of the years, 'shame' has been supplanted by 'shameless' at all levels of society.

Gordon had passed the scholarship a couple of years earlier and was at Wansted County High School. Perhaps his mother thought that now I might prove to be a suitable companion. I had not renounced my old friends completely and Gordon joined us that summer when we formed our own 'Army' – about ten strong. Gordon was the CO and I was his deputy, with Eddie Adams as sergeant. We made very good replica rifles for the troops from blitzed floorboards, and issued them with passes made from cardboard. We climbed over the walls of the burnt-out mackintosh factory, cleaned away the burnt remnants of groundsheets and capes and swept the whole area for use as a parade ground. We also had day camps on Wanstead Flats using my tent, but our cooking still left much to be desired. I had a toy cinematograph projector which was turned by hand.

Unfortunately I only had one very short Mickey Mouse film, which we showed repeatedly in Gordon's cellar, sitting on benches made from blitzed floorboards.

We returned to school in September, and at the end of that summer holiday I effectively left my childhood friends behind, not deliberately, but it must be remembered that the school leaving age was fourteen and by the next summer holiday many of them had left school for full-time employment. Gordon and I had similar interests – initially, our Hornby clockwork train sets, which, when combined, resulted in an appreciable layout in his conservatory or garden. Subsequently we made scale model aeroplanes from balsa wood, and I was particularly keen on model boats, sailing boats at first and then models powered by an electric motor or steam, which we sailed on the pond on Wansted Flats. I still have them, still unpacked from our last move. I wonder what will eventually become of them?

Gordon, meantime, became more interested in electricity and radio and there is a wonderful book (I still have a copy) called *The Boy Electrician*, first published in 1920 but revised and re-printed many times since. With the aid of this book we made ourselves telephones using second-hand bits and pieces which we acquired for a few shillings from Cape's Junk Shop in the High Road, Leytonstone. We strung a wire across Cobbold Road from our upstairs front windows and were able to communicate with each other. No one, with perhaps the exception of the Pegleys, had telephones in those days. We believed our private telephone line was probably illegal and sooner or later we would be in trouble with the Post Office. We made crystal wireless sets and then one-valve receivers but Gordon became more and more ambitious, constructing ever more sophisticated apparatus, including a radio transmitter with which we transmitted gramophone records of one Billy Penrose playing the piano, which interfered with normal radio reception for about a quarter of a mile around. This was more likely to get us into trouble, but we kept very quiet about it. Gordon eventually obtained a First Class Honours Degree in Electronics as an external student of London University, which takes some doing, and made this his career.

At every bank holiday, a traditional travelling fair visited Wanstead Flats with roundabouts, coconut shies and other so-called games of skill, all aimed at relieving the participants of their money. We discovered in a corner of the shop some bottles of what was described on the label as 'metal polish' and sure enough every metal to which it was applied took on the appearance of silver, at least for a short period of time. A farthing would be indistinguishable from a sixpenny piece at a glance, and a ha'penny from a shilling.

The 'Roll A Penny' stall was a popular amusement, in which a penny was placed on its edge in the groove of a triangular wooden slide and allowed to roll down on to a board marked out in squares. When the penny landed on a square without touching the surrounding lines, the attendant would pay out threepence or sixpence, or whatever sum was marked on the square. Furthermore, the attendants would willingly, and very speedily, at a flick of the wrist, change silver coins for more pennies to enable one to continue playing. We could not lose when we exchanged our silvered farthings or ha'pennies for more pennies and, after rolling down a further penny or two, we moved on, especially if we saw a policeman, always fearful that our scam might be discovered. The silver would, of course, wear off before the attendants eventually added up their takings but they might have been surprised by the number of farthings amongst them.

Sporadic air raids continued but then 1944 brought the V1s (the 'doodlebugs'), pilotless aircraft loaded with explosives. The engine cut out when the aircraft reached its target, then the machine crashed to the ground and exploded. The first on 13 June hit a railway bridge in the East End. They came at irregular intervals, day and night, 4,000 over the next three months, and at school a rota of prefects kept watch on the roof and, on the appearance of a doodlebug, rang the fire bells. We would all troop from classrooms to the sandbagged ground-floor cloakrooms and corridors, and after the explosion returned to our classes. Repeated and constant disruption made learning difficult and the school broke up early that year in June for the summer holidays, only those pupils taking the School Certificate Exams remaining.

My mother had a friend, Harriet Chamberlain, who had been bombed out of her coffee shop during the Blitz and had moved to Blackpool, where she ran a boarding house with her daughter René. It was decided that my cousin Joan and I would go and stay there and we were provided with beds on the landings, the bedrooms being occupied by two Jewish ladies and their small children. So began my fourth and final evacuation from London, surely a record!

It was another beautiful summer and I soon found a job helping a donkey man on the sands. Each donkey man had a pitch for his half-dozen donkeys which moved along one place each day. There were (and still are, I think) three piers in Blackpool, each with an adjoining beach and the most profitable pitches were by the North Pier, close to the expensive hotels, which at that time were mainly occupied by wealthy Europeans who had managed to escape the German occupation, and American Army Officers from nearby camps who, with their troops, were awaiting to serve on mainland Europe.

I would join the donkeys at their pitch each morning, help the children into the saddle, and lead the donkey up and down the pitch for their ride.

My donkey man was a crippled Liverpudlian, who would disappear as soon as the pubs opened. 'Doesn't matter what you do, lad, so long as you don't let them go into watter!' were his last words until he returned in the afternoon, when I would be rewarded with sixpence or a shilling, after I handed over the takings. The well-to-do parents at the North Pier end of the sands would ask me to return their children to them at their deck chairs (their gold teeth glinting in the sunlight) at the end of the ride. The resulting tips would exceed my reward from the donkey man!

Joan and I returned to London in time for the beginning of the school term in September but we faced a new threat, the V2 rockets, the first arriving on 8 September, followed by two hundred each month. They were completely silent until they exploded. One morning I was walking along Essex Road on my way to school when a rocket exploded in the grounds of Whipp's Cross Hospital, rather less than a quarter of a mile away. Mr Berry, one of the masters, nicknamed 'Wiggy', was a few yards in front of me and I was able to confirm the aptness of his nickname, the blast blowing off his wig. I was very lucky, for the blast also blew in the windows of the gym at the back of the school where I and my classmates would have been an hour later.

Much has been written in recent years about the morality of the thousand bomber raids on German cities, particularly Dresden, but I can say that if the customers in the shop were a barometer of public opinion at the time, the citizens of the East End were overjoyed.

Victory in Europe on 8 May 1945 really brought our war, my war, to an end, although victory in the Far East was more than a year away. We celebrated with street parties and ours must have been one of the best, because my father produced some fireworks which he had hidden away during the war, no doubt confident that, come what may, they would be used at our victory celebration.

There was a General Election in July and, surprisingly, Winston Churchill, who had led the nation to victory, was replaced by Clement Atlee, heralding a new era. Gordon and I stood in the crowds at the subsequent State Opening of Parliament. In spite of rationing, which continued until 1954, and with most things still in short supply, there was a general air of optimism for the future.

CHAPTER 5

Higher education

THE END OF THE WAR IN EUROPE COINCIDED with my move into the upper school and preparation for the School Certificate Examination rather less than two years away. Time for leisure was inevitably curtailed. I had been in the habit of visiting the local cinemas three or four times a week, using the free passes which came in return for advertising the weekly programmes on billboards outside the shop. I became quite an authority on films of the 1940s and their stars, but as homework increased my cinema attendances decreased. My father's eldest sister, unmarried Auntie Nell, was a keen opera-goer, regularly attending performances at the Sadler's Wells Theatre. Perhaps she thought that my cultural exposure was rather narrow, limited as it was to the cinema, and for a season or more she invited me to accompany her to the Sadler's Wells. I remember particularly Benjamin Britten's opera *Peter Grimes* being staged, I think for the first time, which I did not much like. I much preferred the Gilbert & Sullivan operettas. My theatre attendances since have been rather sporadic, usually linked to the celebration of anniversaries.

Then the time came for me to choose the subjects for the exam, bearing in mind a possible future career. I had been a member of the St John Ambulance Brigade Cadets and I suppose that had stimulated to some extent my interest in a career in medicine. Furthermore I was most comfortable with the sciences, which would ultimately be required for entry to a medical school, but poor at languages, and so the choice was relatively easy. Maths, English Language and Literature, one foreign language and one science were compulsory. I opted for further science and history and geography, both of which I enjoyed.

When the results of the exam were announced in the summer of 1947, I was on holiday with my mother, staying with one of her old friends from the Bedford Institute, Kathleen Pearson, in Northern Ireland. Four Distinctions and four Credits seemed to me a satisfactory if modest outcome (there were only three grades in those days – Pass, Credit and Distinction). A lasting memory of that holiday was scrawled across the partition of a railway carriage on the journey from Belfast to Armagh, 'This is Ulster where an Orangeman is welcome.' The significance only became apparent in later years. I had never before appreciated the antipathy between Protestant and Catholics until one day, whilst walking along a street in

Armagh with Kathleen and my mother, we passed a group of nuns on the opposite side of the road. I was a little surprised when Kathleen said, 'You know they all think that we are going to hell, don't you?'

'How do you know what they are thinking?' I replied.

'Well, they are Catholics and all Catholics think that all non-Catholics are going to hell!'

Fortunately religion did not dominate the visit, although we did attend a Quaker meeting. No one led the worship and the members of the congregation 'spoke when the Spirit moved them.'

We managed to visit the Giant's Causeway and saw the Carrick-a-Rede rope bridge and appreciated the beautiful Antrim Coast. Sadly I have never returned to Northern Ireland, apart from a brief visit to lecture in Belfast.

What at first sight seems a modest school certificate result was surpassed by only three other boys and resulted in the award of three prizes at the next Prize Day. I had won a prize or a certificate of merit most years, receiving them from such luminaries as Lord Mount-Evans (a member of Scott's Antarctic Expedition and a distinguished First World War Naval Officer), R. A. Butler, the architect of the 1944 Education Act, and Derek McCulloch (Uncle Mac of BBC *Children's Hour*). But this prize-giving was rather special. 1948 was the 50th Anniversary of the school's foundation and Professor P. B. Moon, Professor of Physics at Birmingham University, a distinguished atomic scientist and recently elected Fellow of the Royal Society, and an old boy of the school, was presenting the prizes. Furthermore two of my prizes were prestigious memorial prizes awarded for special merit and named in memory of old boys who fell in the First World War. I remember that Professor Moon's speech was quite amusing and he mentioned that whilst at school he had often complained about the amount of work he had to do but now realised how necessary it was if Leyton boys were to succeed. My mind wandered fifty years into the future to the school centenary and I wondered who might be invited to present the prizes on that occasion. Perhaps another successful old boy, even me! Sadly there was no celebration in 1998 in spite of the headmaster's confident prediction that the school was well able to meet the challenges of the next fifty years. Few would have anticipated the subsequent abolition of grammar schools in the name of equality of opportunity, for surely that is what they provided. The Leyton County High School for Boys was turned into a comprehensive school. The merit boards were removed from the walls on either side of the Assembly Hall and the names of the old boys who had gained distinction in the examinations and university entrance were no longer there to inspire future generations.

Professor Moon was not the only LCHS old boy to be elected a Fellow of the Royal Society. Giles Skey Brindley, my senior at school, where he was known as Giles Skey, was also made an honorary Fellow of the Royal College of Surgeons, and it was then that I became aware of his achievements. Sir Philip Wilkinson, also senior to me, left school aged 16 to work as a bank clerk and retired as the Chief Executive of the Nat West Bank. Russell Burgess and I were in the same form. He was awarded the MBE for his work as music master at Wandsworth Comprehensive School where he founded and conducted the internationally acclaimed Wandsworth School Choir. Sir John Lill, the concert pianist, was my junior, whilst Sir Derek Jacobi, the actor, arrived at the school as I left, just as I had arrived when Frank Muir left. Jonathan Ross, the current TV personality, was a later pupil and I am sure there were many other distinguished old pupils, both before and after my time at school.

I was awarded another memorial prize the following year but most rewarding of all was the headmaster's personal prize for leadership. I had wholeheartedly embraced the freedom of the Sixth Form. I became a school prefect and one of the three librarians taking turns to run the library after school each evening. I persuaded the headmaster to have the school tennis courts reinstated, with interesting consequences. The work was carried out by the Borough Council workforce, more familiar with resurfacing the roads and so the surface was cambered, the level of the net being some six inches above the base line, which gave the school tennis team, which I captained, a rather unfair advantage over their opponents accustomed to playing on a level surface! I was a regular member of the school football team and would become captain the following year, and I became assistant stage manager for the school plays. Mr Hawkins, the chemistry master, appointed me his laboratory assistant with the responsibility of setting up the apparatus for the class experiments among other duties, a paid appointment (15/6*d.* per week), which I was surprised to find on my retirement was taken into account in calculating my state pension!

Perhaps it was my contribution to the life of the school that led to the award of another memorial prize but it was the headmaster's prize for leadership that I particularly cherished. It was perhaps a little surprising therefore that I was not made school captain or vice-captain on moving into the Upper Sixth Form, the roles being awarded to two pupils staying on for a third year. I learned some years later from Mrs Cattel-Jones that the senior master had opposed my appointment. I could only assume it was because of *something I said*. I remember that he often accused me of always wanting the last word in any argument or discussion and I think that was true, but it was not until many years later that I realised how irritating that could be. As consolation a new post of sports captain was created for me, which was perhaps more surprising. Although I captained the school football, handball, and tennis teams and played table tennis for the school, I was not much good at cricket or athletics but with the assistance of the school secretary, Mrs Jones, I did produce a duplicated school sports magazine to complement the twice-yearly official school magazine, reporting the up-to-date sports results. I also re-established the award of school and house colours for the various sports and so perhaps all this, rather than general sporting prowess, justified the creation of an overall sports captain.

I was certainly interested in most sports and had attended many of the events of the 1948 Olympic Games at Wembley Stadium. I remember particularly the late Fanny Blankers-Koen, the Dutch housewife who won three Gold Medals, and the graceful Jamaican athlete, Arthur Wint, who won the 400 metres Gold Medal and later qualified at Bart's where I was to meet him, when he was Jamaican High Commissioner in London many years later, when his daughter qualified. I was told by one of his student contemporaries that he spent most evenings playing Bridge in the bar, smoked quite heavily and spent very little time training! How different from today.

Mr John Cummings became headmaster at the beginning of my last term at school. He was a wartime Commando Officer badly wounded in the abortive attempt to capture Mussolini, losing the use of his left arm and hand. He had been a county rugby and tennis player and an Army boxing champion and so school sports and the school sports captain acquired a higher profile than before. However, I believe that my extra curricular activities were, at least in part, responsible for my achieving no more than average results in the Higher School Certificate. The four basic passes were sufficient to meet the requirements for entry to a medical school but I do not think I would have gained a place had there not been a separate entrance examination for the medical faculty at University College London.

I had applied for admission to all the London medical schools but not elsewhere because of the need to live at home for financial reasons, and to the best of my recollections many of the applications were not even acknowledged. I do remember, however, that St Thomas's Hospital replied, suggesting I take a commission in a non-medical regiment and apply after National Service, which seemed a little unrealistic. Bart's did not offer me a place, but reassured me that it did not mean that I was unsuited for a career in medicine, but that there were thirty applicants for every place.

That I could well believe. The UCL entrance examination was held in the vast hall in the Liverpool Victoria Insurance building in Southampton Row, a building I was to pass on innumerable occasions over the years on my way to and from the College of Surgeons. There must have been several hundred candidates taking what I suppose would now be called an aptitude test. One of the questions I remember was 'Devise an experiment to test the relative sweetness of sugar and saccharin.' I proposed determining the amount of sugar or saccharin required to neutralise the acid taste of slices of lemon. My performance in this written examination resulted in a later interview and the offer of a place, consequent only on four basic passes in the forthcoming Higher School Certificate. It is a matter of some interest that some universities and colleges, disillusioned by the falling standards of the current A level exams, are introducing similar independent tests for admission to the medical and some other faculties at the present time.

The UCL entrance test was part of a research programme conducted by Minnie Johnson on the selection of medical students. The results were published in *The Lancet* in the early 1950s and it would be interesting to bring that research project to fruition by following the careers of the successful candidates over the last fifty years, bearing in mind the recurrent interest and subsequent studies on student selection.

My last term at school ended after the High School Certificate exams with a trip to Denmark as captain of football and handball teams (handball was the Danish national game). We played teams from schools in Odense, Aarhus and Copenhagen and stayed with Danish families. The Danes were so full of gratitude for the part that British Servicemen had played in their recent liberation, that the reception we received was overwhelming. When we left for home after three memorable weeks we were laden with gifts of food, for rather surprisingly, although food rationing continued in the UK, there was no rationing in Denmark. I have retained my affection for the Danes over the years and have visited the country on more than one occasion professionally to lecture and operate and I recall the words, in perfect English of course, of one of my surgical hosts, 'The only difference between the Danes and the English is we can speak Danish.' On one of these visits I mentioned the very happy memories of my school trip, and the surgeon I was visiting managed to locate the boy I had stayed with in Odense, Hans Christian Anderson's birthplace, in spite of the fact that Paul Martin Christiansen is the commonest name in Denmark. He now lived in Aarhus and after a short flight in a light aircraft we met again twenty years after that memorable school exchange.

The 1949 university intake was the first since the end of the war in which ex-Servicemen and women, as well as school leavers, were admitted in equal numbers. Previously former members of the armed services were quite rightly given priority through the Forces Education Training Scheme (FETS). Most had been commissioned officers and as the scheme provided grants based on their previous rank they were generally quite well off. Joe O'Neill had been a Group Captain in the RAF and arrived each morning by taxi! Most were married and the social events were perhaps less boisterous than tradition might lead one to expect. I do remember,

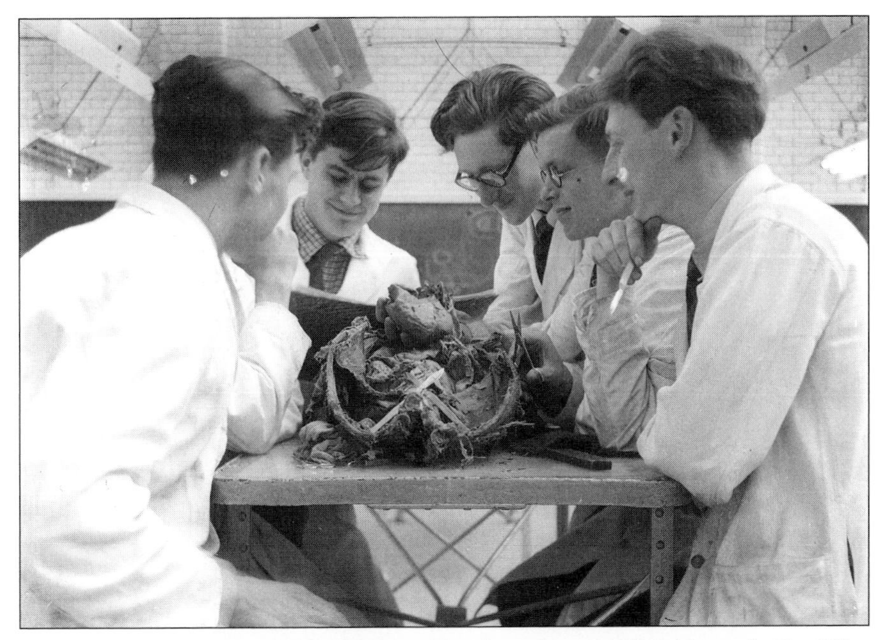

Dissection circa *1950–51. From left to right: the author, Radford (obscured), Ratcliffe, Pead, Read and Nelms*

however, that a Belisha Beacon used to mark pedestrian crossings appeared in the Common Room during a Rag Week and was converted into a standard lamp.

I could not have made a better choice of medical school had I been given a choice. The Department of Physiology was world renowned for research and teaching and at that time every Chair of Physiology in the United Kingdom, with the exception of Oxford and Cambridge, was occupied by someone who had passed through the department. Professor G. L. Brown (later Sir George Lyndor Brown), Professor J. Z. Young, and Professor Bernard Katz, were all Fellows of the Royal Society and Bernard Katz was later to be knighted and awarded the Nobel Prize to join another Nobel Prize winner, A. V. Hill who, although retired, continued to work in the College. The heads of department were all eminent in their respective fields and teaching was well organised but on traditional lines. Every morning was spent in the dissecting room following the 9 o'clock lecture and before the midday lecture, and the afternoons were spent in physiology, pharmacology and biochemistry laboratories.

There were six students to each dissecting table, allocated in alphabetical order of surname. I shared a table with John Nelms, 'Ginger' Pead, Ray Radford, Gordon Radcliffe, and John Read, all of whom are in the accompanying photograph. I took the photograph using the delayed action

The author at his home-made drop-leaf desk in the alcove cupboard in his bedroom 1950–51

device on my camera, which was placed on an adjoining dissecting table, and I inadvertently obscured Ray when I took up my position on the left. We spent so much time dissecting together that we became good friends and in addition, Ray, John Nelms and I spent an extra year together studying for a B.Sc. degree in physiology.

'Ginger' Pead and Gordon Radcliffe had already completed their National Service in the RAMC. 'Ginger' became a consultant pathologist and, sadly, committed suicide. Gordon entered general practice in the Midlands and died at an early age. John Read became a consultant orthopaedic surgeon and so, not surprisingly, we have met frequently over the years. John Nelms, who became a physiologist initially in Rhodesia but after independence at the RAF Institute of Aviation Medicine, died in his early fifties. Ray stayed in the Navy after completing National Service and trained as an anaesthetist, eventually retiring with the rank of Surgeon

Commodore (all naval doctors are called surgeons) and served as commanding officer of the naval hospital at Haslar and Dean of the Naval Medical School. We still keep in touch and in the year 2000 organised a reunion, tracing sixty-five of the seventy-two in our original student intake. Seventeen had emigrated, probably because of the poor prospects of permanent appointments in both hospital and general practice in the 1950s and 60s. Fourteen were known to have died, including two suicides and two road traffic accidents.

Conscious of my poor showing in the Higher School Certificate exam, I did not initially avail myself of the many extra-curricular opportunities offered by a university education, attending each day assiduously from nine until five and working in my bedroom in the evening at a folding desk which I constructed in a cupboard in the alcove beside the fireplace. It was really a continuation of school but with a longer journey to and fro by bus and tube each day, but after a couple of terms I was persuaded to play tennis in the College second team and, the following year, to join the hospital football team.

Most medical students in London received their training in the medical schools attached to the great teaching hospitals, which of course were single faculty institutions. The separation of medical students from the main body of undergraduate students was deplored by educationalists and eventually led to the incorporation of the pre-clinical schools into the four multi-faculty colleges. Although UCL was a multi-faculty college and regarded as the ideal environment for the education of doctors, there was in fact very little inter-faculty mixing, other than among the minority of students living in a Hall of Residence. The intensity of the medical curriculum, with the all important second MB examination after five terms rather than the eight terms for most final degrees, was in part to blame. Team sports provided one of the few opportunities for mixing with fellow undergraduates but I doubt that incorporation of the traditional medical schools into multi-faculty colleges has made much difference.

My hard work was rewarded following the second MB examinations, when I was awarded a Medical Research Council Scholarship to spend an extra year in the pre-clinical school, leading to a B.Sc. (Hons) Degree in Physiology putting me on a par with the Oxford and Cambridge students, most of whom had come from Public Schools, whom I joined for the clinical course at UCH. I do not remember feeling particularly disadvantaged by my state education and I think by this time, although I may still have had traces of my cockney accent, my grammatical mistakes were no longer an embarrassment. My attitude to work was now more relaxed and I continued playing football and tennis in the hospital teams and pursued an earlier interest in photography, photographing hospital events and

Prizewinning photograph of the Coronation decorations in the Mall at night, 1953

providing photographs for the student magazine, and even for publication in photographic magazines, winning a prize for a photograph of the Coronation in 1953, reproduced on this page.

Among the many social events held in the College were the regular dances, or 'hops' as they were called, on Saturday evenings, as well as more formal events. Patricia Plumb, a friend of my cousin Joan whom I had known since 1939, was a very proficient medal-winning ballroom dancer, and she proved to be a very congenial and attractive companion with a similar background to my own. She had left school at the age of 14 to work in the offices of a firm of West End solicitors, eventually becoming the senior partner's personal secretary, and in September 1953 we were married, with John Nelms as best man. With so many married contemporaries, particularly among the ex-servicemen, marrying whilst still a student was not quite as unusual at that time as it might be today. Her salary was a

Pat a year after our marriage, 1954

welcome addition to the State Scholarship I had been awarded for the clinical course.

Though my academic career was undistinguished, I did win the Sir Thomas Lewis prize for clinical research in collaboration with my friend Ray Radford, and this proved to be a regular topic for discussion at the numerous job interviews in the years to come. I qualified in 1955 with the Conjoint Diploma (LRCP MRCS), one of the three non-university licensing qualifications then in existence. The Conjoint could be taken in separate parts at three-monthly intervals and so the majority of students at that time took this exam as an insurance policy in case of failure in the MB, which meant a six-month wait for a resit. It was a wise decision on my part because I failed surgery in the subsequent MB. In spite of this disappointment I was appointed to a prestigious post in my own teaching hospital as house physician to Dr Blake Pritchard and Dr William Goody, but once again a separate internal hospital examination came to my rescue. There was a time when passing 'finals' led to immediate registration with the GMC

Christmas in hospital, 1953. Sister Grace Schofield. From my bed

and the right to 'put up one's plate' as an independent practitioner, but by now a pre-registration year, six months' medicine and six months' surgery, was compulsory and an integral part of medical education.

I started the job on 1 December and Christmas was soon upon us. It is a wonderful time to be in hospital, as I had first discovered when I elected to have a torn cartilage removed from my knee over the Christmas holiday a couple of years earlier. The usual ward routine was a little more relaxed and before coming on duty on Christmas Eve the nurses would use their charms on the ever-generous Covent Garden porters, returning with bountiful supplies of greenery to decorate the wards. They did not want for helpers and there was no shortage of medical students willing to hold the ladders whilst they decorated the curtain rails and the Christmas tree. I took the accompanying photograph from my bed on Christmas morning. Sister Schofield led in Father Christmas riding on the backs of Philip Fulford and Duncan Craven, house surgeons disguised under the blanket as a reindeer. The gentleman in the centre of the picture was visiting a patient and was quite determined to be in the photograph.

It's quite amazing how much talent is to be found among medical students and in the weeks before Christmas rehearsals began for the Fallopians, a name passed down from year to year to the concert party responsible for the Christmas show. As far as I know this was their only production each year and I can remember such titles as *It's Quicker by Tube*

Hospital Christmas show

(rather appropriate I thought) and *Work is the Curse of the Drinking Man.* The moustachioed jellied eel vendor in the accompanying photograph is Tony Morgan, who followed me to UCL and UCH from the Leyton County High School and became a general practitioner in Ascot. On another occasion the Fallopians staged *Moulin Rouge* and Larry Valentine, another of my contemporaries, spent the whole evening on his knees as Toulouse-Lautrec. I suppose the height of sophistication was not achieved until a few years later when Jonathan Miller came down to UCH from Cambridge where he had starred in the Footlights revues.

Dr Blake Pritchard and Dr Goody were neurologists and so the emphasis on this unit was on diseases of the nervous system, although all the firms admitted general medical emergencies. Knowledge of neurological disorders proved to be very valuable in my ultimate specialty, for disorders of the nervous system manifest themselves in the musculo-skeletal system, the province of the orthopaedic surgeon. In the course of the next six months there was a widespread move to integrate psychiatry into mainstream medicine and it was decided to use a few beds in one of the wards for psychiatric patients. Someone had to be responsible for their day-to-day care and who better than the Neurological HP and so I found myself working for Dr Roger Treadgold and Dr (later Sir) Desmond Pond, later to become President of the Royal College of Psychiatrists. I am afraid I was rather naive and believed the patients when they told me that the milkman was trying to poison them or that their next-door neighbours went upstairs and downstairs at exactly the same time as they did, but on one occasion I did contribute significantly to a patient's welfare. On clinical examination I found that the patient had focal signs which proved to be due to a benign brain tumour. At the end of the job, Dr Treadgold offered to provide me with a testimonial but warned me that a testimonial from a psychiatrist was not always helpful.

I successfully negotiated MB surgery at the next attempt and I had the great good fortune to be appointed to a second house job at UCH as house surgeon to Mr Cecil Fleming and Mr H. R. I. Wolfe. Many would say that UCH was slow to embrace surgical specialisation and the consultant surgeons had all been appointed as general surgeons with a particular interest in one of the specialties. This provided excellent general experience of the common surgical conditions at undergraduate and early postgraduate level. Cecil Fleming's speciality was orthopaedics and by the time I became his house surgeon he no longer undertook general surgery. More important, he was a well-respected man of great integrity and influence and chairman of the hospital Medical Staff Committee.

At 10 a.m. on 1 June 1956, on completion of six months as a house physician, I became a house surgeon. As I entered the ward, Sister Schofield took me by the arm and with some urgency led me to the bedside of a patient who could hardly breathe. He had had an extensive operation the previous day for a cancer of the jaw and his airway was now obstructed. Thrusting a scalpel into my hand she directed me to cut here, cut there, and in minutes I had performed a tracheostomy! I realised then just how much junior doctors in particular relied upon the wisdom and knowledge of experienced ward sisters, and how foolish it would be to disregard their advice. A few days later Cecil Fleming asked me if I had had any leave.

'Afraid not, Sir,' I replied.

'Ask David Phillips [the registrar] to stand in for you for a week.'

'Thank you very much, Sir.'

'Purely self-interest,' was Cecil's reply. 'I didn't think you'd last the next six months!' There were no locums, no extra duty payments and the ethos of the voluntary hospitals remained. The welfare of the patients was paramount and there seemed to be no lack of enthusiasm for the infant NHS, in spite of the misgivings of some senior consultants who had previously worked in an honorary capacity.

No doubt at the inception of the National Health Service the BMA negotiated the terms and conditions of service for all grades of medical staff, but the conditions applying to junior staff, whether negotiated or not, seemed to be a relic of the voluntary hospital system. When I took up my first house appointment at UCH the salary of £425 a year, of which £125 was deducted for compulsory board and lodging, was at least an improvement on the voluntary hospital days when house appointments in the teaching hospitals were usually unpaid. There was, however, no official time off and no paid holidays, so theoretically one worked 168 hours a week with direct and continuous responsibility for the patients under one's care, as well as on-call commitments for emergency admissions. No more than twelve hours could be spent away from the hospital without a consultant's permission, which one was rather reluctant to seek. By now I was the father of an infant daughter and on Sundays, when possible, I would leave the hospital after an early morning ward round with one of my fellow housemen covering for me, to spend a day at home. There was no married accommodation at that time. Nevertheless I was at last doing what I wanted to do from my early teens, something for which I had spent six years training. I was now caring for patients, albeit with supervision, but the initial responsibility was mine. They were my patients and, whatever time of the day or night, it was my duty to care for them. This was good for me and good for them for I followed their progress throughout their treatment day-by-day and witnessed their complications should they occur; the patients enjoyed continuity of care, safe in the knowledge that their doctor knew everything about them. Such personal involvement never occurs again.

Of course I and my contemporaries did not work 168 hours a week. If our wards were quiet and if an in-patient crisis seemed unlikely, we would arrange for a colleague to stand in for an hour or two while we visited a nearby cinema or restaurant (the hospital food was rather poor). The debt would be repaid in kind later.

We had a particularly keen group of students on the firm, the majority of whom lived in the student hostel and I was quite prepared to summon them from their beds to see the emergency admissions. This did not go down well with the night superintendent, Sister Gell (I think) who, unbeknown to me, complained to Cecil Fleming.

'I hear you have upset the night superintendent, Lettin.'

'Have I, Sir?'

'Keep up the good work' was his encouraging response. On this occasion it was not *something I had said* but something I had done that had caused a potential problem.

There were five surgical firms, each of which was on call for a week at a time for emergency admissions. If operative treatment was required it was carried out as soon as practicable, whatever time of the day or night. Daytime clinics, ward rounds, and elective operations went on even though one might have been up half the night. During a particularly busy night we operated on a Covent Garden porter with a strangulated hernia. On the ward round the following morning he said, ' 'Ere doc, there's a bloke on at night who looks just like you and he wasn't 'arf busy last night!'

'I know, and that bloke was me,' I said.

He was somewhat surprised by my reply and advised me to join a union!

I subsequently suggested to Cecil Fleming that it would be much less exhausting if each of the five firms was on duty one day and night a week and one weekend in five, and this proposal was accepted by the Medical Staff Committee and represents, I suppose, my first attempt to initiate change.

The filming of *Doctor at Large* was a pleasant distraction in the summer of 1956. Scenes for *Doctor in the House*, the first of Richard Gordon's doctor books to be filmed, were shot at UCL and UCH in 1953 when I was still a student and I remember that the hospital rugby team were co-opted for one scene, a rugby match. Because it was thought too dangerous for Dirk Bogarde to take part, one of my fellow students, John Jenkins (later to become a Consultant Urologist) acted as his double. Another of my friends, Bernard Cooke, asked Shirley Eaton, who played the part of the landlady's seductive daughter, to accompany him to the annual students ball but, alas, she declined the invitation!

It is difficult to believe that Gower Street, a busy thoroughfare parallel to Tottenham Court Road, was closed for a week or so for the filming of *Doctor at Large*. The hospital and University College were on opposite sides of the road and the classic portico of the college with the large front quadrangle was used as the fictional St Swithin's Hospital. The director and the producer sat on the front steps of UCH in the folding chairs which seemed to be part of film-making the world over. My wife was now working as a locum secretary, leaving our baby daughter in her mother's care and had a splendid view of the filming from an office window immediately above the front steps of the hospital. I, like other members of the staff, popped out onto the hospital steps whenever we had a spare moment, but how terribly boring film-making seemed to be, with each scene being shot time and time again and the actors standing around doing nothing for most of the time. A couple of elephants corralled in the front quad of the college munching hay patiently awaited their turn to perform for the cameras. I doubt whether there have been elephants at UCL before or since.

On one occasion I chatted to James Robertson Justice, the slightly larger than life actor playing the part of the redoubtable Sir Lancelot Spratt. 'Do you know Snorker Barrington?' he asked. Snorker had retired long before I became a clinical student, but his eccentricities were legendary. He was a Fellow of the Zoological Society and often conducted student-teaching rounds at the zoo in nearby Regent's Park.

'He taught me to scrub up in the private wing theatres when we here before filming *Doctor in the House*,' the actor confided. 'and he taught me a few new swear words as well!'

Snorker had been brought dead into casualty about six months before, having choked on a sandwich in a nearby pub.

Much of the simpler operative surgery was carried out by the registrars (an intermediate training grade between house surgeon and consultant). They were also, as the name implies, responsible for the administrative paperwork of the firm, particularly the patient discharge summaries. David Phillips of the Fleming-Woolf firm was hopelessly behind for some reason and both the consultants would send him off to work on the summaries during the operating lists. This meant that I became first assistant at the operations and after suitable instruction I was allowed to perform many of the simpler procedures, for example for varicose veins, piles and bunions, almost unheard of in a teaching hospital, which whetted my appetite for a surgical career.

Mr H. R. I. Wolfe (known as His Royal Ighness) was also surgeon to the Hospital for Tropical Diseases, which had a relationship with the London School of Hygiene and Tropical Medicine in Keppel Street, not far from UCH. One evening at about 6 p.m. I was called to the telephone and asked by someone from Keppel Street for the whereabouts of Mr Wolfe. 'I'm afraid he's on holiday,' I answered.

'Who's his deputy?'

'Mr David Bailey.'

David Bailey was the Resident Assistant Surgeon, a sort of super senior registrar who deputised for all the consultants in their absences. I called him to the phone and overhead the ensuing conversation.

'Why do you want Mr Wolfe?'

'Well, you see, we've got a chimpanzee with what we think is an intestinal obstruction.'

'Why don't you get a vet?'

'Well, the chimp is a very valuable part of an important research project, and it is more likely to survive if operated on by Mr Wolfe, who has helped us out before, or another surgeon.'

'Have you X-rayed the abdomen?'

'No, we don't have the facilities here.'

'Well, you'd better bring the chimp to UCH.'

They brought the chimp, cradled in the arms of an animal technician, on the back seat of a car and in the meantime David had warned the duty radiographer to expect the chimp. There were several patients waiting for X-rays and she thought it unwise for the chimp to wait with them and, indeed, for them to see what was going on, and firmly closed the waiting-room door. The chimp was carried past the door and placed on the cold X-ray machine, whereupon it let out a piercing and unnerving scream, to the consternation of the waiting patients.

The X-ray confirmed the diagnosis and an operation was imperative, but as there were no facilities for surgical operations at Keppel Street, it would have to be done at UCH. The main theatres were occupied and so David phoned the superintendent at the private wing. 'What's the patient's name?' she asked.

'Well, actually, it's a chimpanzee called Bobo,' he replied.

'Is this some kind of a joke? There'll be no chimpanzees in the private wing of UCH.'

Eventually she relented, providing the chimp was not admitted to a bed. After the operation it returned to Keppel Street with its attendant and David visited it every day to supervise its uneventful post-operative recovery.

The X-rays went through the usual reporting procedure and the report signed by the senior radiologist read, 'Abdominal X-ray of a West African child suffering from Coeliac Disease,' much to the amusement of those who saw it. The senior radiologist was not well liked. It is not generally realised that, whilst it is permissible for anyone to operate on a human being, it's illegal for even a fully qualified surgeon to operate on an animal without the appropriate Home Office licence. So this operation was, needless to say, hushed up.

On another occasion a fourteen-year-old boy attended the casualty department on a sunny Sunday morning claiming to have been bitten on the arm by a snake in the nearby Regent's Park Zoo and he certainly had two puncture marks on the forearm. The zoo authorities initially claimed that it was quite impossible because the zoo was closed on Sunday mornings but it seems the boy had entered the zoo the previous afternoon and had spent the night there. In order to leave the following morning he had attempted to climb over a wall and disturbed a snake basking in the sun. A tourniquet was applied to the arm and anti-venom was brought from Guy's Hospital in a speeding police car. Traditionally snakebites were treated by making two incisions through the puncture wounds at right angles to the line connecting them, and then washing out the venom. The consent of the boy's parents was required before undertaking any surgical procedure but he refused to divulge their whereabouts and the tourniquet could not remain in place indefinitely. It was decided to operate with the boy's consent alone and he finally agreed, providing the procedure was undertaken without an anaesthetic so that he could watch! It was evening before the boy's parents were located in Gloucestershire. By then his arm was very swollen and the next day his kidneys were failing, but he eventually made a full recovery. He apparently had a snake pit in his garden and this whole episode was reported extensively in the *Daily Mirror* under the heading, 'Snake Boy bitten in Zoo.'

I lasted the six months and in spite of the long hours and lack of free time I regard my pre-registration year as one of the most enjoyable of my life. The experience gained in that one year, especially the second six months, was invaluable. Sadly, and to the detriment of their training, such concentrated experience is no longer available to the newly qualified, and as a consequence it is currently proposed that the pre-registration period should be increased by a further year.

At the completion of my six-month surgical appointment I received a very nice letter from Cecil Fleming, telling me that he thought there was a future for me in surgery if I liked to take it and that I should keep in touch with him. I decided without hesitation to follow his advice but National Service came first.

CHAPTER 6

Surgical training

COMPULSORY NATIONAL SERVICE WAS SOON TO COME to an end and already the Royal Navy would only accept applicants for three-year short service commissions. On Cecil Fleming's advice I applied for a two-year National Service commission in the RAF, and so my boyhood ambition to join the Navy was unrealised. On the 6 January 1957, my 26th birthday and a bitterly cold day, I travelled north to Wharton in Lancashire to begin preliminary training and, perhaps rather unsurprisingly, among the thirty or so new recruits were three of my medical school contemporaries, including John Nelms. One or two of our number decided to make a career in the RAF and others had short service commissions but the majority had elected to serve for the minimum two years. We were billeted four to a Nissan hut heated with a rather inefficient coke stove but we had the particular privilege of a shared batman.

As medical officers we were all commissioned as Flying Officers and issued with a standard battledress uniform with a beret, but most of us bought caps when Gieves the military outfitters called to measure up the 'regulars' for their much nicer traditional officers' uniforms. Unfortunately the battledress with which we were supplied rarely fitted in every respect. If the trousers fitted, the tunic didn't and vice versa, and the ill-fitting parts of the uniform were taken away to be altered. As part of preliminary training we were not exempt from 'square bashing' and we certainly looked a motley crew with part battledress and part civilian clothes marching up and down on the parade ground in full view of the impressionable 'other ranks' recruits. The shambles was exacerbated by Dr Livingstone from Glasgow, who was one of those uncoordinated individuals whose arms move forward at the same time as the legs on the same side rather than the opposite side. This was particularly unfortunate for me because we lined up in alphabetical order and so whilst marching in one direction I could hardly avoid Livingstone's heels and in the opposite direction he mine. We were drilled by a warrant officer who was obliged to issue his commands more politely than might otherwise be the case but he became so exasperated that we were taken by lorry to a quiet country lane where our rather unenthusiastic drill was unobserved.

Before leaving for the next stage of our training at Farnborough I made a nostalgic visit to nearby Blackpool but, of course, there were no donkeys in January. Our time at the Institute of Aviation Medicine was rather more conducive and relevant to our service in the RAF, in spite of the need to learn whether F. Med. 1 or F. Med 4, for example, was the appropriate form on which to requisition hypodermic needles. We did learn precisely where to site field latrines and that we could condemn cracked crockery if we thought it a health hazard in spite of any opposition from the commanding officer.

The most desirable postings in the Royal Air Force were awarded to those on short service commissions and so after preliminary training, I was posted to the Central Medical Establishment (CME) in London. The routine examination of service and civilian air crew and officer recruits to assess their fitness to fly was humdrum, but I lived at home and with the living-out allowance in addition to the 18/6*d.* per day the pay was a great improvement on my recent NHS salary. I also had time to study for the Primary Fellowship examination of the Royal College of Surgeons, the first hurdle to be cleared in a surgical career.

Dr Frank Stansfield a lecturer at the Royal College of Surgeons ran an evening course at St Mary Abbot's Church Hall in Kensington every evening from 6 until 8 p.m., with a short break at the halfway mark, and sometimes on Saturday mornings. CME was in effect an RAF station, albeit a rather specialised one, where in addition to the routine medical examinations, the senior RAF specialists conducted outpatient clinics on a regular basis. The station had two Vauxhall Vanguard staff cars at its disposal, based on the annual mileage covered, but it was perilously close to losing one of them. The Adjutant (a retired officer) was very keen to keep the mileage up and as a consequence I was chauffeured to St Mary Abbots for the evening lectures, much to the dismay of Stansfield's other pupils congregating outside the church hall. There was also a physiotherapy department at CME and I was often accompanied by a very attractive physiotherapist who lived in nearby Notting Hill, which exacerbated their mock rage. Often when I was in uniform Stansfield would proudly announce that he had been a squadron leader during the war and there was speculation of the rank he would have by now attained had he remained in the RAF. He was very much a railway enthusiast and would take the opportunity to travel to any threatened railway line, particularly if it was the final journey. I telephoned him at home on one occasion after missing one or two of the evening lectures to ask if there was a lecture on the following Saturday morning. I apologised and hoped I was not interrupting anything important. 'Not at all,' he reassured me. 'I am only reading Bradshaw.' This, of course, was the famous book of railway timetables. 'The lecture starts at Mancunian Time' which he expected me to know was 10 a.m. If anyone arrived late during a lecture he would look at his watch and announce, 'We are just going through Bletchley Junction' or some other station on the route.

Anyone who failed the exam was allowed to attend the next course of lectures free of charge, provided they informed Dr Stansfield of the questions they had been asked in the oral part of the exam. These he would record and before the next exam he would tell us each of the examiners' favourite questions. The lectures were patronised mainly by potential surgeons from Australia, New Zealand and South Africa and my much modified but still discernible cockney accent caused some confusion among them, the South Africans, for example, thinking I was an Aussie and the Aussies quite certain that I was South African, or perhaps even a New Zealander. There are similarities between the Cockney and Australian accents, which leaves me to speculate that most of the transported convicts probably came from London.

When I took the examination one of the examiners was Sir Gordon Gordon-Taylor, an eminent surgeon who had spent some time in Australia during the war and was very well disposed to Australian candidates. He asked me if I was Australian and I was tempted to say yes but no doubt the follow-up questions would have established the truth, probably to my disadvantage. It was certainly no disadvantage, however, when Sir Gordon asked me the nerve supply of the gluteus maximus muscle. 'The inferior gluteal nerve, Sir.'

'What's unusual about that?'

'It's a large muscle supplied by a small nerve, Sir.'

'Good. Now tell me the name of a small muscle supplied by a big nerve,' as predicted by Frank Stansfield, and I was glad I knew the answer.

Less than 1 per cent of the candidates passed the Primary at the first attempt and the overall pass rate was only 13 per cent. The examination certainly eliminated the less determined as well as the less able and I was fortunate to pass at my second try, which gave me a distinct advantage on completion of National Service.

All the officers at CME were medics so we had to inspect the non-commission personnel on parade at 8.30 a.m. every morning. This took place on the flat roof of the building until the Ministry of Works decided it was unsafe and so the parade was transferred to the basement where the filing cabinets were stored. The staff lined up a row at a time between the filing cabinets, with little room for the inspecting officer, which often led to great hilarity and was not conducive to military discipline; the parades were eventually reduced to one each week on pay day.

Two leading aircraftmen (LACs) remained on duty in the building overnight and at weekends, but the duty officer who held the key to the safe was non-resident. I was called in one weekend to decode a message (the code book was locked in the safe) expecting something quite dramatic, but it was merely an order to lower the flag to half-mast as a member of foreign royalty had died.

The CO Group Captain, Ossie Williams, could never understand why I volunteered to be on duty over every public holiday until I explained to him that this entitled me to leave in lieu, which I was saving up for final revision before the exam. He didn't himself have a great deal to do and spent a great part of his time casting his fishing line through the open window of his fourth-floor office into Cleveland Street below. Another eccentricity was the wearing of spats in winter but not, of course, when he was in uniform. We had no mess at CME but the officers were allowed to order wines and spirits from the NAAFI stores at discounted prices. I was appointed mess officer, collecting the monthly orders and distributing them and passing on the money, a not particularly arduous task but quite instructive, allowing me to sample a variety of bin ends I might not otherwise have tasted.

I was released from the RAF three months early to take up the post of casualty surgical officer at UCH. This was essentially a nine to five job in which I treated minor surgical conditions attending on a casual basis, and assessed the more serious emergencies, for possible admission. There were twelve cubicles, six on each side of the room into which the casual attendees were called in turn from the adjacent waiting room by Sister Kirk. I progressed from one cubicle to the next, checking the students' findings and recording my own on the casualty card and instituting treatment, stitching wounds, opening abscesses and undertaking minor operations. When patients complained about being kept waiting, the eccentric Sister Kirk would immediately provide them with a footbath, whether or not there was anything wrong with their feet. As she said, 'No one's feet were really clean and anyway it made them think that something was being done!' On one occasion I noticed that she was pouring disinfectant into all the sinks and washbasins. I asked her why. 'Dr Edith Summerskill, the Minister of Health, is bringing her husband here with a cut finger and so at least we must make the place smell like a hospital,' she replied. Dear Sister Kirk, I still have the toasting fork she gave me for Christmas 1958.

Sprained ankles were a common problem and there was no generally accepted method of treatment, which ranged from doing nothing to immobilisation in plaster. Elastoplast strapping was the most common treatment but local injection of Hyalase, which dispersed the painful haematoma and swelling, seemed to have advantages. I conducted a trial comparing one with the other and found that pain-free walking was restored significantly quicker with Hyalase. The need to X-ray every injured ankle to exclude a fracture was frequently questioned and in this same study I found that careful clinical examination could be relied upon to exclude a broken bone. The results were published in the *British Medical Journal* but sadly made little impact on clinical practice.

I completed the six-month casualty appointment at the end of April 1959 and needed a general surgical registrar post to gain experience and prepare for the Final Fellowship Examination. At that time two years' general surgery was an almost universal requirement before undertaking training in any of the major specialties. Although general surgery was beginning to break up into various sub-specialties, the young surgeon was expected to acquire a broadly based general training. My initial applications were unsuccessful but at one interview I was offered a locum at Tilbury Hospital without any prospect for the definitive job which had been awarded to a New Zealander who was working his passage over as a ship's doctor, like many other Commonwealth trainees at that time.

Tilbury Hospital was situated next to the docks and the big P&O liners could be seen from the windows, through which gentle puffs of smoke from their funnels occasionally drifted. There were two surgical teams on call on alternate nights and weekends and the members of the team of which I was part were all locums. Even worse the house surgeon was a student from The Middlesex Hospital and had recently failed his Finals. He kept a pet red setter in the hospital, which accompanied him on the ward rounds. When I objected, he made it clear that if the dog went he went too and I knew that would mean more work for me. The locum consultant had recently been appointed to a consultant post in London where he lived and needless to say was rather reluctant to travel out from London to deal with emergencies unless it was absolutely necessary, and I was reluctant to call him. With the aid of Hamilton Bailey's *Emergency Surgery*, and advice over the telephone, I learned on the job and fortunately nothing untoward happened in my short stay.

What might have proved to be the most valuable experience of my time at Tilbury occurred one evening on board one of the P&O liners docked alongside the hospital with a skeleton crew on board. The medical officer invited me to join him and the very junior deck officers remaining on board for dinner. The conversation turned to the instruction the young officers received on self-defence, to enable them to protect themselves in the event of unprovoked attacks in the seafront bars of the Antipodes. 'Never fight fair, pick up the bar stool and impale the aggressor on the legs.' This, I thought, might prove to be more useful in the future than the experience I had gained in the operating theatre, but fortunately I have never been called upon to put the manoeuvre into practice.

After a couple of weeks I moved onto Billericay Hospital where my responsibilities included not only general surgery but also orthopaedics, gynaecology and ENT. Once more I was largely unsupervised as I am sure most junior doctors were in those days. In later years whilst serving on the Council of the Royal College of Surgeons, I played a significant part in bringing to an end this extreme form of learning by experience. I remember to this day the face of a wonderfully co-operative little boy about eight years old who had had his tonsils removed one afternoon. That evening he had a severe bleed. The simple measures I tried to staunch the haemorrhage failed and each time I phoned the consultant, a man with an overseas qualification who lived in West London, it became clear that he had no intention of coming to my aid, and the measures he advised I had already tried. I remember thinking that as long as I can keep blood going in (by transfusion) as fast as it is coming out, he's not going to die. Fortunately the bleeding eventually stopped.

Whilst at Billericay I received a telephone call from David Bailey, the former Resident Assistant Surgeon (a post from pre-NHS days) at UCH, who was now a consultant general surgeon at Barnet General Hospital. His registrar suffered from Hodgkin's Disease which at that time was almost always fatal. He had been admitted to hospital with a relapse and David thought it unlikely that he would recover. If the post became vacant it would be a rotational appointment with UCH. Although initially I would be a locum, I would be in a strong position for the subsequent appointment, but in any case David Bailey was an excellent surgeon and a conscientious teacher and I jumped at the opportunity of working for him, whether or not I ultimately got the job. Sadly David's prediction materialised, but for me, of course, it was a stroke of good fortune.

There were three surgical teams, the senior of which was on call one night a week and the other two teams on two nights, and all three one weekend in three. David Bailey carried out a full range of what was then regarded as general surgery: not only gastro-intestinal surgery but vascular surgery, breast and thyroid surgery, some chest surgery and urology, and even emergency cranial surgery for head injuries. We were on call on Tuesdays and Thursdays, on the afternoons of which we had our elective operating lists and for the first couple of hours I would assist David or he would assist me, each week introducing a different operation of gradually increasing complexity into my repertoire. We would then separate, each continuing with our own lists in adjoining operating theatres, I carrying out the simpler procedures after David was satisfied that I was competent to do so, but even then he was invariably available for help and advice should it be needed. Surgery is a practical specialty and surgical competence can only be acquired by operating oneself. This was indeed the ideal way of learning.

The hospital was very busy and the local general practitioners had been given an undertaking that their patients would always be admitted in an emergency, if necessary, with the result that there might be ten or more extra beds down the centre of the surgical wards. I would be called to the A&E Department between operations to examine the surgical emergencies and if operative treatment was necessary that would be carried out on the operating list, either between the elective operations or at the end. David would usually leave in the early evening but return after a meal if necessary. I would continue into the early hours of the next morning with a break, perhaps for a meal in the nurses' dining room with the house surgeon, at about midnight. There was never a question of cancelling an operation. If the patient had been prepared for operation it was carried out, no matter how late the hour and sometimes the sun was rising by the time we had completed the afternoon list and the added emergencies! The surgical registrar was obliged to do a ward round with the night sister before going to bed, which was a rather bizarre experience as dawn was breaking.

It was not unusual to admit ten or twelve emergencies when we were on call and perhaps half would be taken to theatre after consultation with David Bailey, either in person or on the telephone. I wish I had kept a record of my operative experience as trainees are now obliged to do, but before I moved on to UCH I looked through the operating theatre register and discovered that I had removed 108 acute appendices in the six months I was at Barnet, besides, of course, many other operations.

There are many who believe that efficiency must suffer after long hours in theatre and that mistakes must inevitably occur. This was certainly not my own experience. Concentration is maintained during the more exacting parts of the operation with a degree of relaxation during the more routine phases, for example whilst sewing up and, of course, between operations. During a party one becomes tired about midnight but then gets a second wind enabling one to continue until dawn. It is much the same in the theatre and, of course, the Armed Forces but it is only possible in one's youth. Neither I nor any of my contemporaries resented the long hours, for we were gaining valuable experience and acquiring the skills for our lifetime's work.

The pace was less intense back at UCH where I acquired some experience in neurosurgery and thoracic surgery, as well as further general surgical experience. The one in five rota introduced during my pre-registration year enabled me to spend more time studying for the Final Fellowship Examination but I was allowed to take only one week of my annual leave to revise for the exam. Unfortunately my mother died in UCH, a few days before I took the exam, from liver failure caused by primary biliary cirrhosis, a familial condition inherited through the female line. Although unrelated to alcohol consumption, it seemed rather perverse in view of her lifelong abstinence. The liver's inability to deal with the breakdown products of digestion resulted in recurrent episodes of coma and the collection of fluid in the abdomen. Repeated treatment in hospital temporarily relieved the condition but with each successive admission it became less effective.

During one admission about a year before she died, my father was admitted to UCH while I was casualty officer. He had always been a very heavy smoker, a source of considerable irritation to my mother, and he had suffered particularly during the last great London 'Smog' when so many people died. In spite of heavy smoking, he seemed generally healthy. He was small but muscular and in his youth had been a good all-round sportsman and a particularly good gymnast. The family still have several of the prizes that he won. I remember having to practise handstands and head-stands at home when I first became a pupil at the LCHS and although he was then in his forties, he had no difficulty in giving me a practical demonstration. Unfortunately X-ray revealed an inoperable carcinoma of the bronchus, to which of course there is an inherited predisposition. Two of his brothers died from the same cause and, had I smoked, I would no doubt have suffered a similar fate. He died within a few days and my mother was too ill to attend his funeral, something that troubled her for the remaining year of her life.

It is sad that they really had no time to enjoy their short retirement and managed only one holiday together, benefiting little from their very frugal lives. Like my mother, my father bought few clothes and he possessed only one suit, made of blue serge, which was worn on special occasions. When he dressed for a family wedding on one occasion, he noticed that the moths had been at work on his trousers, leaving several small holes which appeared as white dots on the front of his thighs. Having no other suit, he spread shoe blacking onto his long underpants so that the holes did not show.

I failed the exam, a not unusual occurrence when the overall pass rate was usually around 30 per cent, but happily I succeeded at the next attempt. There were four parts to the final Fellowship at that time: the written paper, the clinical examination, operative surgery, and surgical pathology vivas. The clinical examination was the most important and excellent marks in the other parts of the examination could not compensate for a poor performance in the clinical. The volunteer patients were sent to the examination halls in Queen's Square by the examiners, who were consultants at the various hospitals in London. Some patients did their best to be helpful and as soon as a candidate reached the bedside would begin: 'I know how important this examination is to you, doctor, and I will do everything I can to help.' They would then proceed at breakneck speed to relate most of the inconsequential details of their complaint, which took up valuable time and was not at all helpful. At the other extreme, the response to the candidate's opening question, 'What are you complaining of?' would bring the brusque response, 'I'm not complaining of anything, Doctor.' The alternative cheery opener, 'What's the problem?' would bring the equally brusque, 'That's for you to find out.' One way or another the candidate would need to demonstrate his clinical skills to the satisfaction of the examiners.

By now I had made up my mind that I would specialise in orthopaedic surgery and at the next available opportunity I moved back to the firm where I had been a pre-registration house surgeon. Cecil Fleming advised me to apply for a registrar post at the Royal National Orthopaedic Hospital (RNOH), one of the foremost specialist postgraduate hospitals in the country and, indeed, the world, with a galaxy of consultants, led by H. J. Seddon (later Sir Herbert), the Director of the Postgraduate Institute of Orthopaedics, each of whom specialised in one of the developing orthopaedic sub-specialties.

The Appointments Committee decided that I had insufficient orthopaedic experience to be a registrar and advised me to apply for the more junior post of Senior House Officer (there were no pre-registration house officers). I was duly appointed house surgeon to Mr Philip Newman and Mr Charles Manning, the latter Deputy Director and Deputy Dean of the Institute who, like Cecil Fleming and David Bailey, would play a very significant part in my life.

The original wards at the country branch of the hospital at Stanmore where I was to spend the next six months had been built in the early 1920s in over a hundred acres of delightful grounds, mainly for the treatment of children with bone and joint tuberculosis and polio. They had been supplemented by prefabricated wards during the war and now accepted patients with a wide range of orthopaedic problems. Philip Newman specialised in the treatment of low back pain in which I developed a continuing interest and Charles Manning ran the scoliosis unit, treating children with spinal deformities. The post was resident but residence was compulsory only when on duty, although I also slept in after operating lists. I was able to live at home and travel back and forth each day from the house we had inherited, on the death of my parents, in Chigwell some twenty miles away. It was not sensible to move closer because of the possibility of having to move to another hospital in another part of the country at the completion of the six-month appointment.

Postgraduate training at this time was rather haphazard, unplanned and lacking in continuity, and of no specific duration. The aspiring specialist moved from one freestanding post to another every six months as SHO, or a year as a registrar, in an attempt to gain experience and in the hope of securing a senior registrar position of longer duration; he or she remained a so-called junior doctor with no security of tenure until the eventual appointment to a permanent consultant post when judged to be ready for independent practice, often around the age of 40.

On completion of my first appointment at Stanmore I was appointed to a registrar post at the RNOH where some attempt had been made to provide continuity of training, although not in a pre-planned and progressive manner but at least moving between surgeons with different interests every six months. I spent the first six months at the town branch in Great Portland Street gaining general experience and experience in the management of bone tumours before moving to the Barnet General Hospital where the emphasis was on the treatment of fractures and on hand surgery with a one in two on-call rota. Here I gained my first experience of dealing with a major accident when a coach full of holidaymakers was involved in a head-on collision with a heavy lorry on the A1 before it was made into a dual-carriageway.

The accident happened just as the morning fracture clinic was coming to an end, and the first casualties arrived as I was about to go to the mess for lunch. There were thirty or so injured passengers and as I knew that most of the junior staff would also be making their way to the mess I asked for their help. It was now possible for each doctor to concentrate on one patient and before long all the casualties had been assessed and initial investigations and treatment had been instituted. It was then that I noticed that the two obstetric and gynaecology consultants were standing in the middle of the accident department, studying a rather thick document which proved to be the hospital major accident plan, and they were supposed to be in charge. All hospitals have major accident plans but fortunately major accidents are relatively rare and the best plans are soon forgotten as staff change. There really is no substitute for common sense and a number of readily available doctors, if possible each initially taking personal responsibility for a single patient. On this occasion two patients proved to have quite severe head injuries and were immediately transferred to the neurosurgical unit at the Whittington Hospital but fortunately the remainder could be dealt with and, as far as I remember, there were no deaths.

At the end of the year my appointment was renewed and I moved back to Stanmore, gaining further general experience before promotion to senior registrar after further interview. My immediate future was now settled and there would be no need to move house until the ultimate appointment to a consultant post which was very important from a family point of view, because our elder son Nicholas was autistic and his education was a problem. He was born after a very protracted induced labour over Easter, 1958, during my National Service. From the beginning he was a very unhappy, miserable baby, with very severe eczema and icthyosis, another skin condition, where the superficial layers form hard plaques like fish scales which fail to separate, and on the scalp become imbedded in the hair, which eventually separates with them. In addition he developed severe asthma, but it was not until much later, when he was late walking and late talking, that we realised there was something seriously wrong. His behaviour was very repetitive and he would spin coins with great facility and spin plates on edge and keep rows of table knives spinning. He would place items of furniture at just the right distance from a wall to enable a tennis ball to bounce from side-to-side as it fell to the floor. Most remarkable of all, before the age of three, he could play simple tunes on the piano after hearing them on the radio or television. We discovered that he had perfect pitch and could instantly identify and reproduce a musical note on the piano. Autism was something we were unfamiliar with but now such behaviour is instantly recognisable, although the severity of the disorder varies. Nicholas would probably have had what is now called Asperger's Syndrome, a less severe form of the condition.

By the time he was six years old his attendance at primary school had been so infrequent that arrangements were made by the school medical officer for him to attend a school for the physically handicapped. Although the staff were supportive, this proved equally unsuitable but by chance one of my school contemporaries, Barry Edwards, and his wife ran a private nursery school, 'Woodcroft', which also accepted young children with learning difficulties. Nicholas and a second son, Jonathan, born in 1962, both attended and it would have been very disruptive for them to have moved at this time.

Within six months I was invited by Mr H. J. Seddon (soon to become Professor Sir Herbert Seddon) to be his first assistant on the professorial unit at both branches of the hospital and the lecturer at the Institute of Orthopaedics. I had earlier begun an experimental research project in my spare time, to investigate the effects on the healing of fractures by compressing the bone ends together, prompted by a lecture given by Professor Maurice Müller who had developed this technique in Switzerland. My teachers were rather sceptical about his work and I realised that it would be impossible to assess the effects of compressing the bone ends together in living patients because of the difficulty in determining the precise point at which a fracture unites. This appointment allowed me a day a week to continue my research.

It was impossible to produce a standard fracture in an experimental animal and I devised a method for dividing the tibia in adult New Zealand white rabbits, under a general anaesthetic of course, at exactly the same point along its length and then immobilising the divided bone with miniature plates and screws with and without compression, or in plaster in a plaster of Paris cast. After a lethal injection the bones were removed and

X-rayed, then, after removal of the plates, the strength and rigidity of the healing bone was measured and the microscopic appearance of the same specimens was determined in groups of animals at various intervals of time between three days and three months after the 'fracture'. This had not been done before and as far as I am aware has not been done since. The strength and, more importantly, the rigidity of the healing fractures returned more rapidly to the plated bones than to those treated in plaster and the process of repair was found to be quite different, but there was no significant difference between the bones treated by simple plating and those treated by plating with compression. I was subsequently awarded the Robert Jones prize and gold medal of the British Orthopaedic Association and the Mastership in Surgery of the University of London for this work. Over the years, the internal fixation of fractures has increased at the expense of more traditional methods of treatment and this experimental work provided the scientific basis, but was never really recognised.

Compression plating was being popularised by the Swiss Association for Osteosynthesis (AO) led by Professor Maurice Müller who invited me to present my findings at the AO instructional course in December 1965. This was the first time I had lectured abroad and Sir Herbert suggested I should visit orthopaedic units in Paris and Lyons on my way to Switzerland.

Paris at the beginning of December was cold and wet and I was on my own, lodging in a room near to the Church of St Sulpice, and the dismal sound of the bells striking the hours haunts me to this day. Professor Merle d'Aubigné was Le Patron in charge of the orthopaedic department at L'Hôpital Cochin and, in common with continental practice, was in charge of all the members of the staff of his department no matter how senior they might be, unlike professors in the United Kingdom where the professor happens to be just another consultant but appointed by the university to organise teaching and research. Exasperated by my poor French, he and his rather superior secretary-cum-theatre assistant, and, it was rumoured, his mistress (apparently a common combination in France) who had been educated in England, reluctantly spoke to me in English. I attended his outpatient clinics and watched him operate from the gallery above the theatre. On one occasion I found myself sitting next to an elderly lady who introduced herself and clearly took pity on me. She was quite happy to talk in English and felt very privileged to be allowed to watch the professor operate, a reward for her financial contribution to his research funds. She was the widow of Monsieur Talbot, the founder of the motorcar manufacturers of that name, and she invited me back to her apartment for lunch. Her chauffeur-driven car had fur carpets, I remember, and I felt reluctant to step on them. The apartment was even more opulent and her white-jacketed butler served pre-dinner drinks whilst we awaited the arrival of her daughter, married to a London gynaecologist, who just happened to be flying over for lunch.

The junior members of the staff were more friendly, particularly Jean Zuckerman, the Chef de Clinic who had spent a year in the orthopaedic department at Oxford. He invited me to his rather less grand apartment for a meal and also to dinner in the doctors' mess, La Salle de Garde, on the evening he was on duty at the hospital. I was rather surprised to find the walls covered with erotic, if not pornographic, murals, which I gathered was the tradition in French hospitals.

Before leaving Paris I mentioned to Merle d'Aubigné that I was on my way to the AO course in Switzerland. 'I've been invited to be guest of honour, but I don't need that little Swiss watchmaker to teach me to how treat fractures' was his comment.

I spent a few days in Lyons where the atmosphere was rather more congenial; Professor Albert Trillat had previously spent some time working at Stanmore with Sir Herbert Seddon. I could not proceed immediately to Switzerland for the AO course as planned and returned to London for just twenty-four hours to attend the interviews for a travelling fellowship to North America, but I was not one of the successful applicants. I returned to Davos with Pat, presented my research and enjoyed the valuable theoretical and practical instruction on this extremely popular and well-run course, determined to incorporate the techniques into my surgical repertoire. Maurice Müller invited us to spend a few days at his hospital in St Gallen before we returned home in time for Christmas.

Sir Herbert Seddon was an international authority on the treatment of brachial plexus and peripheral nerve injuries, and polio, but after two years I decided it was time to acquire more general experience, particularly of children's orthopaedics. But first I was sent to the Luton and Dunstable Hospital for further experience of accident surgery before moving on to Great Ormond Street, both senior registrar posts linked to the RNOH training programme. One sunny Sunday afternoon a man was brought into the A&E department of the Luton and Dunstable Hospital after cutting off his big toe with a rotary lawnmower. It had been difficult to start and, with each pull on the rope, his foot moved closer to the cutter deck and inadvertently his toes went underneath. The mower suddenly started with the inevitable result. The patient was worried that the loss of a big toe would affect his walking. I hoped that he would be reassured when I explained that the big toe was not essential for normal activities, adding that it might be essential for a monkey climbing trees in bare feet. Unfortunately he considered that I was being flippant and reported me to the hospital authorities and the local newspaper. He was the Mayor of Luton. Undoubtedly *it was something I said.*

George Lloyd-Roberts was a charming and greatly respected Old Etonian paediatric surgeon at the Hospital for Sick Children, Great Ormond Street, one of that well-known family with members in most professions from banking to broadcasting. He had a slight speech impediment and pronounced the letter R as a W. He mentioned one day that he was from the military branch of the family and I asked why he had not followed the family tradition. 'Well, as an NCO in the Cadet Corps at Eton,' he replied, 'when I ordered "Fwont Wank Wight Dwess" everybody laughed.'

George expected his senior registrars to write a paper with him while they were working at GOS and I was no exception. I produced the facts and figures and George wrote the text in the course of two or three evenings when I joined him in the bar at the old St George's Hospital, Hyde Park Corner. While I was working at Great Ormond Street I was appointed to the consultant staff at Bart's. After congratulating me he said, 'I don't know if you've done the wight thing accepting. I was always advised never to work south of the wiver or north of the park.'

CHAPTER 7

Consultant appointments

CONSULTANT APPOINTMENTS AT LONDON TEACHING HOSPITALS still enjoyed the reputation and prestige acquired in the voluntary hospital days, and even twenty-five years after the foundation of the NHS were much sought after. The hospitals were centres of excellence, well staffed and well equipped, and enjoyed considerable independence. I had been led to believe that I might be chosen to succeed Cecil Fleming at UCH but I was unsuccessful. I had previously applied for a vacancy at Guy's Hospital, with a similar outcome, and I now contemplated applying for vacancies in non-teaching hospitals outside London but Sir Herbert Seddon would not hear of it.

Charles Manning, who was a consultant at St Bartholomew's Hospital as well as the RNOH, suggested that I wait for a forthcoming vacancy at Bart's. The teaching hospitals had a tendency to prefer their own graduates, Bart's more than most, and I was not optimistic, but nevertheless I decided to apply when the vacancy was advertised. As usual, the names of three referees were required with the formal application and I asked Charles Manning to be one of them. He pointed out that he would be a member of the selection committee and would be able to express his views in person. He suggested that I should ask the same people that I had asked before, all of whom, by chance, were Bart's men, including Sir Herbert Seddon.

The deliberations of statutory advisory appointments committees are supposed to be confidential but there are always leaks and I had been advised by my friends at UCH never to ask Sir Herbert again, but Charles insisted that I must, for if I did not it would look suspicious as I had been his first assistant and I must go and 'have it out with him'. This was easier said than done. It was unheard of to question a reference, particularly as it was supposed to be confidential, and Sir Herbert was a rather intimidating figure. I agonised. How should I go about it? I made an appointment to see him and told him that I wanted to apply for the vacancy at Bart's. He agreed that I should but did not fancy my chances because 'they always appoint Bart's men'. I asked him if he would support my application, emphasising the word 'support' rather than merely asking him to be a referee.

'I emphasise the word "support", Sir,' I said. 'I understand that you did not give me a very good reference for the UCH job.'

'What do you mean?' he replied. 'It was one of the best references I have ever given anyone but I did say you were a bit difficult to get on with, but I'll leave that out this time!'

Was it something I'd said?

It was still the custom at Bart's to write individually to every member of the consultant staff, informing them of the intention of applying for a consultant post and asking 'if I might call on you' – a quaint phrase, reminiscent of a more leisurely age. Only two or three responded in the affirmative and in due course I was short-listed for interview. The Statutory Appointments Committee included representatives from the hospital (including Charles Manning), the Regional Board, the University and the Royal College of Surgeons, chaired by the Chairman of the Board of Governors who was the immediate past Lord Mayor of London. With five other candidates, all of whom I knew, I was interviewed in the Guild Room and then we waited anxiously for the outcome. Eventually we saw the chairman leave, to attend another engagement, we were told, and then we were informed that the Committee had been unable to agree on an appointment. This was an extraordinary outcome and no one could say what would happen next. A few days later David Trevor, one of my referees, asked me if I'd ever upset Nobby Clarke. The inference was obvious. Sir Henry Osmond-Clarke, a small rubicund Ulsterman with a goatee beard, had represented the Royal College of Surgeons at both my previous interviews when, interestingly, both successful candidates had Irish connections. I had of course met him on several occasions and he had congratulated me warmly on my presentation in Switzerland the previous year when he had been guest of honour at the AO Course, but he was rather like that with everybody.

The role of the external assessors was primarily to ensure that the successful candidate was appropriately qualified and suited for the job and unless there were such doubts, the choice of the hospital representatives was usually accepted. I subsequently learned that Bart's wanted me and Charles Manning would not give way. There was certainly no doubt about my training and my qualifications, the Mastership of Surgery, unusual for an Orthopaedic Surgeon, the Robert Jones prize and gold medal of the British Orthopaedic Association, and several publications. I imagine that the Bart's staff felt rather affronted that their choice of a colleague had been thwarted for what they perceived to be no very good reason and so the short-listed candidates were invited to an unofficial interview at Bart's.

The beautiful pine-panelled Guild Room was packed to overflowing and I remember people sitting on the windowsills as I sat at the end of the green baize-covered table, overlooked by Reynolds' well-known painting of Percivall Pott. Although the RNOH was a specialist orthopaedic hospital, there were consultants on the staff from associated specialties, three of whom were also by coincidence consultants at Bart's whom I obviously knew quite well. I imagine that they had been well briefed by Charles Manning, for after I had answered a few questions from around the room, Campbell Connelly, a neuro-surgeon at both hospitals, said: 'I understand you are rather difficult to get on with.'

This, of course, was the comment which Sir Herbert had made in his reference for the post at UCH and which he had undertaken to omit from his current reference. Osmond-Clarke was the only link between the two references, having sat on both appointment committees.

'Well, I am rather straightforward and I tend to say what I think,' I replied, and then added: 'I think I get on well with my contemporaries and I am a member of a rather exclusive orthopaedic club, the Innominate Club, the membership of which is by invitation only.' Then after a short pause I added: 'But then I was one of the founder members.'

There was laughter all round and I cannot recollect if there were any further questions. *Was it something I said?* Early in the New Year the same official selection committee was reconvened and the same candidates were called for interview but it appeared to be a mere formality because within thirty minutes I was appointed.

Sir Henry was obviously aware that I knew that he had opposed my appointment at the first interview and invited me to his consulting rooms for pre-dinner drinks. After congratulating me on my appointment he confessed that he had been unsure at the first interview that I was the right person for the job because Bart's had never appointed a grammar school pupil to the consultant staff. This I subsequently discovered was quite untrue.

The Royal and Ancient Hospital of St Bartholomew was founded in 1123 by Rayhere, a member of the Court of Henry I who, while ill on a pilgrimage to Rome, promised St Bartholomew in a vision that if he recovered he would found a hospital in London for the treatment of the sick poor. The hospital was built in Smithfield, a corruption of Smoothfield, an area used for jousting and tournaments, just outside the City Wall, where it remains to this day. After the dissolution of the Monasteries by Henry VIII, the King was prevailed upon by Sir Thomas Gresham, the Lord Mayor, to refound the hospital with a secular Board of Governors under the control of the City Fathers. When they visited or 'viewed' the hospital for the first time in 1546, they found the buildings 'in grievous state of repair' and thereafter every year on the second Wednesday in May the buildings have been inspected on what has become known as 'View Day'.

I took up my appointment on 9 May 1967, the day before View Day, and I and my fellow Orthopaedic Consultants, John Aston and Charles

Manning, and our junior staff, all in morning suits, lined up with the nursing staff in one of our three wards in the beautiful Georgian buildings and were 'viewed' by the members of the Board of Governors, carrying their staves of office, led by the Beadle with the mace. The Beadle read out the names of all the patients in the ward, together with the district or town in which they lived, most if not all coming from the surrounding boroughs, and then asked them if they had any complaints. Needless to say there were none. He then asked first the nursing staff and then the medical staff the same question, and the answer was the same. The procession then moved on to the next ward, where the ritual was repeated. What a beginning.

The role of surgery in the treatment of rheumatoid arthritis was increasing and before taking up my appointment I was given three months' leave to visit hospitals specialising in this field in the United Kingdom, Denmark, Sweden and Finland, so that I could better collaborate with Dr H. Wykham Balm a physician specialising in the medical treatment of this condition at Bart's, a collaboration that was to bear fruit.

The Norfolk & Norwich Hospital was my first stop, where Ken McKee an old Bart's man, had developed, in collaboration with John Watson-Farrer, the first successful total hip replacement, which had been available for general use for a couple of years. John (later Sir John) Charnley had also introduced an artificial hip joint at around the same time, with a plastic rather than a metal cup, but the original plastic material had proved unsatisfactory and the early patients required re-operation when more durable plastic became available. Charnley was also concerned about infection and developed a 'tent' in which the patient and only the surgeon and one assistant were enclosed. They also wore all-enveloping theatre suits with helmets from which the air they breathed was continuously replaced. It was important for a young surgeon entering on a consultant career to experience the techniques and the innovations first hand. In addition Charnley had an agreement with a company marketing his implant, limiting its sales to those who had assisted him. I was not persuaded to adopt the Charnley implant and his operative technique, but the principle of positive pressure ventilation was subsequently incorporated in all orthopaedic operating theatres and the low friction arthroplasty, as it was called, is still in worldwide use.

In Edinburgh I visited Douglas Savill, a pioneer in the surgical treatment of rheumatoid arthritis, and then I went to Glasgow where Professor Roland Barnes had established an excellent undergraduate teaching programme, the features of which I later incorporated into teaching at Bart's. Liverpool was perhaps the cradle of British orthopaedics where Hugh Owen Thomas, the son of a Welsh bone setter, and his nephew Sir Robert Jones, had flourished at the end of the nineteenth and the beginning of the twentieth centuries. The medal, which I had recently been awarded, was established in his memory and I duly paid homage to the great man at the Royal Southern Hospital where he had worked.

I then set off for Scandinavia, first to Copenhagen, where the unit specialised in the treatment of juvenile rheumatoid arthritis and where I was able to renew my acquaintance with that attractive city and Paul Martin Christiansen, as I have previously mentioned. Swedish surgery in general and orthopaedics in particular had attained a standard to be admired. Charles Manning advised me not to book accommodation in advance during my trip because I might find it more worthwhile spending more time in one centre than perhaps I had planned. There were very helpful accommodation offices at all the main railway stations and I made my way to the Central Station in Stockholm, only to be told that the world table tennis championships were in progress and all the hotels in the city were full. The very helpful young lady suggested I should have a meal at a nearby restaurant while she tried to find me a room. On my return, the only accommodation available was in the bridal suite of a splendid hotel overlooking the many islands on which Stockholm stands, with their myriad of twinkling lights. What a waste. Pat was at home! I previously asked the girl at the railway station what she would have done had she not been able to find me a room. 'Take you home with me,' she replied.

The weather was appalling when the time came for me to leave for Helsinki and all flights were cancelled, except one Russian flight to Leningrad calling at Helsinki on the way. I decided to take it and found that there was only one other passenger, which added somewhat to my apprehension. Furthermore, all the signs were in Russian and the crew were unable, or unwilling, to speak English. The other passenger, however, did and was anxious to know who I was, where I was going, and why. He thought I could only be going to Finland for one reason – timber – and he thought my name was probably Latvian in origin.

The working day in Scandinavia starts early and the work is usually finished by mid afternoon. In Helsinki it seemed to start even earlier, with lunch at about 11 a.m. One of the Finnish surgeons offered to show me the city and another invited me to his house for dinner the same evening. I did not realise that the city tour included a family meal at his home at about 5 p.m. and it would have been ungracious to refuse his hospitality. I did not mention that I had also been invited to dine with Pentii Salenius, with whom I have remained in contact over the years, recently visiting him in Helsinki. Another substantial meal was awaiting me when I arrived. I remember particularly the Kereliyan fish pie, made by scooping out the middle of a loaf of bread and filling the cavity with various pieces of fish before cooking. I declined a second helping but felt I had to eat the reindeer meat!

Pentii was very proud of the sauna installed in the basement of his house. I do not relish a sauna at the best of times, never mind so soon after two large meals, but after all I am British and I felt that a stiff upper lip would see me through. If the Finns could stand the heat then so could I. A cold shower afterwards was such a relief and happily there were no birch twigs, but I was glad to return to my spartan accommodation at the YMCA.

I was taken by car to Heinola, about seventy miles from Helsinki through the still snow-covered forests. The hospital was devoted entirely to the treatment of rheumatoid arthritis and staffed by a physician, Dr Laina, and a surgeon, Dr Kauko Vainio, who relied almost entirely on long-stay visiting doctors for help. I shared a self-catering flat in the hospital with a Norwegian surgeon who, inevitably, spoke excellent English. The hospital was unusual in many ways. It was jointly funded by the trades unions and by the Government and was open to trade unionists from all over the country, and, surprisingly, there were no anaesthetists. Vainio did even quite big operations with nerve blocks and local anaesthetic but was not yet undertaking hip joint replacements. Whilst I was there the snow melted almost overnight and by tradition the staff went down to a sauna on the shores of a neighbouring lake before immersing themselves in the ice-cold water. I was not among them.

Professionally the future looked rosy but on my return I found Nicholas's asthma was much worse and he had nearly died during an attack, prompting our excellent GP, Dr Michael Heavens, to treat him with steroids, with all the possible attendant complications. He had been wheezing when I left on my trip and was wheezing on my return. The asthma was an increasing problem and severe attacks were often precipitated by visits to friends' houses, even though they took care to shut away their pets and on more than one occasion we returned home, with them bringing the meal that they had prepared. On one occasion we had to abandon a holiday on the south coast because the environment seemed to precipitate and perpetuate an attack and we were reluctant ever to return.

Needless to say every available treatment was tried but it proved impossible to carry out the usual allergy tests because of the condition of his skin. The flexures of his knees and elbows were perpetually raw with scratching, and topical ointments were of little value; large doses of anti-histamines made him sleepy without reducing the continuous itching. Emollient creams scarcely affected the icthyolic fish-like scales which made his shins in particular look like a crocodile handbag. As they separated from the scalp, so the hair came with them but fortunately his face was spared. Nicholas was reluctant to eat, barely gaining weight, but was making reasonable progress with the 'three Rs' at Woodcroft School, with additional private tuition at home in the evenings from Pamela Davey, originally at Chigwell Primary School but now full-time at Woodcroft. Worse was to come.

At the beginning of December, Jenny was preparing for the Grade 5 piano examinations and had begun violin lessons when she complained that she could not use her left hand properly. She developed severe neck pain and could only sleep sitting up. On Sunday 10 December she was admitted to Bart's (we were burgled whilst we were taking her to hospital) under the care of the consultant neurologist, Dr Aldren Turner. His senior registrar, Molly Painter, by coincidence one of my contemporaries at UCH, made a tentative diagnosis of polyneuritis but Jenny considered that perhaps Molly-neuritis might be more appropriate. It reminded me of a conversation over the dinner table when she was about six years old. I was talking about David Matthews. 'Who's David Matthews?' she asked.

'Oh, he's a plastic surgeon,' I replied.

'You're sure you don't mean a rubber surgeon?' was her somewhat unexpected and amusing rejoinder.

A couple of days later special X-rays revealed a tumour in the upper part of the spinal cord, which I realised was almost certain to be inoperable. That evening I was due to travel to Havant in Hampshire to give a lecture to the local medical society at the invitation of another of my contemporaries, Bob Thomas, a local GP, and to stay with him overnight. I did not feel much like going but I knew that whatever the outcome, it could not be worse than Bob and his wife had endured a year or two before when their twin daughters had been killed on a pedestrian crossing on their way to school. No matter how badly you may think life has treated you, there are always those who have overcome greater suffering. I decided to go but in retrospect it now seems unkind to have left Pat alone that night.

We prayed in the little church of St Bartholomew's the Less within the gates of the hospital whilst the operation to remove the tumour was carried out the following week, but our worst fears were realised. The malignant tumour could not be removed.

The whole family spent Christmas at Bart's, the boys playing with the model train layout donated to the neuro-surgical ward by Peter Sellers, and early in the New Year Jenny began a course of radiotherapy; on the evening of 7 January (the day after my 37th birthday) we arrived at the hospital to find that she was completely paralysed. We slept on the floor in her room for the next three nights and I recorded in my diary that on 8 January she momentarily stopped breathing at 8 p.m., midnight, and at 4 a.m. On each occasion the duty anaesthetist was called and the immediate crisis was resolved but each time he asked us if he should resuscitate her. This was a decision that neither Pat nor I was prepared to make, believing it should be a dispassionate professional decision by her carers, not an emotional one.

She herself was clearly aware of the gravity of the situation. 'I'm going to die, aren't I daddy?'

'I will not let you die,' I replied with conviction.

With massive doses of steroids her breathing improved over the next twenty-four hours and on 10 January we returned home. In the meantime, Pat's parents had moved in to look after the boys and each day Pat accompanied me to the hospital and spent the day at Jenny's bedside. My colleagues unobtrusively made it possible for me to start work a little later in the morning and to leave earlier at the end of the day to have a meal with the boys, before returning to be with Jenny in the evening, as well as relieving me of emergency commitments.

The radiotherapy continued but without any improvement in the paralysis; we prayed for a miracle. As a child I had said a personal prayer followed by the Lord's Prayer with my mother at my bedside every evening and I had continued to do so into my adult life. Now the prayers had an added intensity but every Sunday morning we met John O'Connell, the greatly respected but rather gloomy neuro-surgeon who shattered our hopes, telling us there was no hope of recovery. This we knew in our hearts but to this day I do not believe that patients and their relatives really want to hear the absolute truth, leaving them without hope, though politically correct current practice is to tell them everything.

When the course of radiotherapy ended we were determined to take Jenny home but John O'Connell was reluctant to agree, believing that it would break 'the family'. But the family was already broken. Patients unable to move develop pressure sores, unless the pressure is relieved by regular changes of position, a task undertaken by the nursing staff every four hours or so. How could we manage this at home? A Stryker Frame was the answer. The frame, on wheels, essentially consists of two firm mattresses mounted in metal frames and whilst the patient is lying on one the other is clamped on top with the patient in between, rather like the filling in a sandwich. The frame and the patient are then turned through 180° before the upper frame is removed, leaving the patient prone until the process is repeated in reverse four hours later. With a daily visit from the district nurse who managed the mid-day turn and general skin care, we could manage the routine – one of us getting up at night for the 4 a.m. turn. All went well until one day the nurse forgot to put on the upper frame and turned Jenny onto the floor. Our splendid GP immediately left his morning surgery on receipt of Pat's call and together they laid her on the floor without the help of the distraught nurse. The ambulance took her to Bart's where X-rays excluded any bony injuries. She returned home and the routine continued.

In a curious way it was a happy time because, perhaps for the first time, I spent more time with her than I had ever done before and I really got to know her. She had always wanted a pony and John Griffiths, a General Surgical colleague at Bart's and a keen rider, arranged for us to buy Robin. At first we kept him at the bottom of the garden but after several escapes onto the neighbouring golf course and into other gardens, we were obliged to find more secure grazing in a nearby Convent after he had trodden on a policeman's foot early one morning, attempting to resist arrest. The rather officious policeman intended to charge me with some misdemeanour but the station officer, with perhaps more common sense than might be shown nowadays, decided that if I bought the policeman a new pair of boots, all would be forgotten.

Every evening her school friends visited, usually bringing the pony to the house where it stood on the terrace with its head through the window. There was much laughter. Jenny learned to mouth paint and the picture hangs in our bedroom. I remember her headmistress visiting during Wimbledon fortnight and earnest conversation taking place on the merits of the participants. It was a sunny summer but the tumour was gradually extending into the base of her brain, resulting in repeated vomiting and necessitating continuous intravenous fluids. She looked forward to becoming a teenager and had a lovely party with her friends to celebrate her 13th birthday with a brand new bridle for the pony and some smart new shoes, but we knew that she would never be able to use them. Sadly, she died a month later at 11.30 p.m. on 20 July. Could we have done more? Should we have done more? Should we have taken her to North America where miracle cures can supposedly be bought but, of course, never work? There was now no need to agonise. A great burden had been lifted from our shoulders.

Jenny had made it all very easy for us. She never complained and never mentioned dying again, but she must have known it was inevitable. I longed to ask her friends if she had ever mentioned it to them, but could not bring myself to do so. If by chance any of them should read this book, I would still like to know.

Charles Darwin delayed the publication of *The Origin of Species* for ten years, after the death of his daughter, at a similar age, because he was unable to reconcile his traditional religious beliefs with his scientific reasoning. Her death destroyed his belief in an almighty omnipotent God and my hitherto, perhaps tenuous, faith suffered a similar fate.

Nicholas was now eight years old and had outgrown Woodcroft and once more we were faced with finding a suitable school. Dr Kenneth Soddy, the child psychiatrist at UCH who had first told us that Nicholas was autistic and who had supported us over the years, suggested he went to a boarding school specialising in the education of children with behavioural disorders. Pat was reluctant to agree but we visited the school and, although I was prepared to follow expert medical advice, Pat was even more opposed to the idea. It was just as well. A few years later we read in the newspapers that the headmaster had been convicted of sexually abusing his pupils.

Dr Soddy suggested the Gatehouse School as an alternative, a Montessori school run by Mrs Wallbank, the wife of the Reverend Newall Wallbank, the rector of St Bartholomew's the Great in Smithfield. The school began life in the gatehouse of the church but was now so popular that it had moved to larger premises in an old warehouse in Clerkenwell and later moved to Hackney near Victoria Park. Mrs Wallbank believed that every class should have one or two children with disabilities, a view now widely held but seemingly failing both the able and the disabled in State Schools. It needs very special teachers to make it work and Mrs Wallbank was very special. I am sure that she never doubted that whatever action she took or whatever decision she made was anything but the right one and in this she was guided by God. Self-doubt was alien to her. The system and Mrs Wallbank clearly suited Nicholas, although he would never admit it and he remained at the Gatehouse until he left school at the age of 16, capable of earning a living. Like most autistic children he had one very special talent, music, which Mrs Wallbank encouraged. Besides his ability to play the piano by ear, producing tuneful melodies of his own as well as reproducing the music of others in a variety of styles, he taught himself to play the guitar, both acoustic and electronic, to a very high standard. In his teens and early twenties he often played with semi-professional Country & Western groups. In view of the 'drug scene', we were relieved that for whatever reason he never became a full-time musician.

'Move house, have another child, immerse yourself in your work' was the advice freely proffered after such a cataclysmic event as Jenny's death. We moved from Chigwell to a period farmhouse in the nearby village of Chigwell Row, just inside the green belt, with a large garden, an orchard and a paddock. Jenny and her pony would have loved it. A third son, Timothy, had been born the previous year. We hoped, of course, for another daughter, but perhaps it was just as well it was a boy – comparisons would have been inevitable.

By coincidence, on the day Jenny died a part-time consultant post at the RNOH was advertised in the *BMJ*. Consultants contracted to work a number of four-hourly sessions each week for the National Health Service, up to a maximum of eleven if they wished to be paid a full-time salary, nine or less if they wished to retain the right to private practice. The sessions were frequently at different hospitals, often with separate employing authorities. I had six sessions at Bart's and three locum sessions at the Queen Elizabeth Hospital for Children in Hackney, which had recently become part of the Hospital for Sick Children, Great Ormond Street, and I hoped that I might be appointed to the permanent post in due course.

The Queen's was a small friendly hospital close to my roots in the East End and the work was enjoyable and rewarding. There was almost always a child from one of the three Dr Barnardo's units located in suburban Essex at the weekly outpatient clinic, always accompanied by a nurse and a physiotherapist. The majority of Barnardo's children were no longer orphans, but had been rejected by their (usually one-parent) families because of severe physical disability, frequently needing orthopaedic treatment. Dr Iris Knight, the medical officer whose disabled daughter I had treated whilst working for Sir Herbert Seddon, suggested that it would save a great deal of staff time and money if I visited the units every month or so, in an honorary capacity, to examine the children, so eliminating the trips to hospital. This proved to be very rewarding and I was most impressed with the care the children received. I have remained a strong Barnardo's supporter ever since. However, although I enjoyed the work, the opportunity to join the staff at the RNOH could not be missed.

Before being called for interview, I was dismayed to find that Sir Henry Osmond-Clarke was again the College representative on the appointments committee.

'He burnt his fingers once,' Charles Manning reassured me. 'He won't do it again.'

Subsequently, Sir Henry wrote me a nice congratulatory letter, part of which I quote:

> 'I certainly have no qualms about your future. You are and will continue to be a real spokesman for, and credit to, British orthopaedics.
> Very sincerely yours,
> H. O-C.'

I took up my appointment at the RNOH on 1 January 1969 with two sessions at Stanmore and one at Great Portland Street. George Lloyd-Roberts, the Consultant Orthopaedic Surgeon at Great Ormond Street, asked me to continue at the Queen's until a definitive appointment was made, so now I was effectively working twelve sessions a week, in addition to my visits to Barnardo's, whilst trying to establish a private practice – dashing from one hospital to another in my second-hand Mini Cooper S.

The freely proffered advice had been fully implemented. We had moved house, had another child, and I was indeed immersed in my work, which now centred on Bart's and the RNOH, but still included the Queen's and Barnardo's.

Chapter 8

Bart's

Surgeons' apprentices and physicians' pupils and latterly medical students have been taught at Bart's since the refoundation of the hospital. The traditional three-year clinical course was common to most medical schools at the time of my appointment – a systematic course of lectures at 9 a.m. each day, some laboratory teaching, and periods of attachment to general medical surgical and obstetric firms to acquire at the bedside the clinical skills required for the practice of medicine. Knowledge of the emerging specialties was acquired in a rather haphazard and almost involuntary fashion by attending outpatient clinics and ward rounds. Furthermore, the content of the formal daily lectures was entirely unrelated to the clinical attachments on the wards.

With the encouragement of my colleagues and the support of the Dean, I introduced a six-week orthopaedic attachment providing an opportunity for each group of ten or twelve students to clerk and examine orthopaedic inpatients, attend teaching ward rounds, outpatient and fracture clinics, and assist in the operating theatre. A comprehensive course of lectures for each week covering elective orthopaedics and trauma was delivered by members of the department and repeated for each new group of students, effectively eight times a year, culminating in a multiple-choice examination, long before in-course assessments became fashionable. The teaching was unashamedly vocational, now decried by the educationalists in favour of problem-based 'DIY learning', although currently there is a view that the baby may have been thrown out with the bath water. I must admit in retrospect that some of my teaching was by 'humiliation', which I now regret, but I wanted it to be entertaining in order to encourage the students to attend. Perhaps I was trying to emulate Sir Lancelot Spratt. 'Of course you don't need to know that to run birth control clinics' was certainly something I said more than once to any unfortunate young lady unable to answer one of my questions. The boys loved it, of course, and the students in general certainly enjoyed the attachment. In two surveys carried out over the years by Brian Jolly, then a member of the Department of Medical Illustration and subsequently Professor of Medical Education at UCL and Adviser to the GMC and now at Melbourne University, it was found to be the most popular part of the clinical course.

Unwittingly I acquired an 'anti-women' reputation, which was not helped when trying to explain at a careers workshop why there were so few women consultant surgeons. There are many more junior posts than senior posts, but medicine is perhaps unique in that only the consultant posts are permanent. Not all junior officers in the Army, for example, would expect to become generals but they would expect to retain the rank they had achieved until they retired. In medicine, in the absence of promotion, one falls off the ladder and many women decide at this stage that the rigours of surgical training are incompatible with normal family life and move into less demanding specialties, or give up medicine altogether. Although true, it was politically unacceptable to say so and it is surprising that Professor Dame Carol Black, the President of the Royal College of Physicians, has had the courage to draw attention to the problem some twenty years later.

The relationship with the students was not limited to their orthopaedic attachment. Weekend sports usually brought a student or two to my Monday morning fracture and injury clinics and, perhaps as a matter of their self-interest, I was invited to be president or vice-president of all the major sports clubs at one time or another; I was elected an honorary member of the very elitist Vicarage Club, and the Wine Committee made me their president. Furthermore, I was nominated by the students to represent them on the committee allocating the various house jobs.

The Wine Committee ran the student bar in the Medical College and organised the social events, dances, a summer show *The Smoker*, and the Barbecue Ball, the social event of the year. Much of the profit was used to finance the old people's Christmas Dinner, held in the Great Hall every year. The elderly from the surrounding districts who had been patients (many born in Bart's) were waited on by the students at a traditional Christmas meal, with musical entertainment, dancing and singing. The complimentary tickets were always in great demand for this splendid event, which I always found most enjoyable.

Christmas was a wonderful time in hospital as I had discovered both as a patient and a junior doctor. Elderly patients particularly often welcomed the opportunity to be admitted over the Christmas period and their names were put on a special waiting list for admission to avoid wasting beds. There was never a shortage, for many would otherwise have spent Christmas alone. Before coming on duty, nurses in uniform would visit Covent Garden Market on Christmas Eve to collect material to decorate the wards, as they had done a UCH and I expect most other hospitals, and in the evening went from ward to ward singing carols by lantern light. A wonderful sight and sound.

Traditionally the consultants visited their wards with their families on Christmas morning and carved the turkey. The students from each of the various firms, the 'Kids' Firm', the 'Gynae Firm' and so on, would each produce their own ward show and tour the wards after lunch on Christmas

Day. Such shows were a feature of all the teaching hospitals in one form or another and frequently included vulgar medical jokes, and members of the consultant staff were usually lampooned, much to the amusement of the patients and their visitors.

At Bart's, the best of the Christmas ward shows were incorporated into the *Pot-pourri* which was staged at the Cripplegate Theatre in the Barbican on the last three evenings of the old year. Nicholas and Jonathan whilst at the Gatehouse School took part in the inevitable nativity play a few days before Christmas and so our family Christmas began with the nativity play in the Church of St Bartholomew the Great and ended with the *Pot-pourri*. Sadly, supposedly to save money, many wards now close over Christmas and the staff are obliged to take part of their annual holiday. Sadly television has supplanted the ward shows.

The popularity of the orthopaedic teaching stimulated a gratifying number of students to become orthopaedic surgeons and postgraduate surgical training was by now becoming better organised. In 1968, the Royal Colleges of Surgeons in the British Isles adopted a scheme of Higher Specialist Training to begin after basic training in surgery in general. Aspiring orthopaedic surgeons, for example, would in future spend four years, at least two at senior registrar level, in recognised posts acquiring experience of emergency and elective orthopaedics in equal measure, in both adults and children. This almost invariably involved moving from one hospital to another, to free-standing posts of defined duration as in the past, although local arrangements sometimes existed for direct exchanges between senior registrar posts within a teaching hospital, rarely with posts in district hospitals. There were no proposals, however, for continuous planned, progressive training, allowing trainees to move seamlessly from one post to the next at regular intervals over the four years. Furthermore, the transition from registrar (an internal appointment) to senior registrar (a statutory appointment) after further interview was a formidable obstacle, often delaying progress and the acquisition of new skills unnecessarily.

I devised and implemented a rotational training programme, with the approval of the regional Postgraduate Dean, based at Bart's, in which the trainees were appointed to registrar posts with a senior registrar appointments committee, enabling them to move from post to post every six months for training purposes and from registrar to senior registrar, without further interview, in a regular fashion, acquiring the required experience without repetition. The following year a similar programme was introduced at the RNOH but this was far more complicated because of the larger number of trainees and involved the creation of eight separate rotational programmes, in collaboration with seven of the London undergraduate teaching hospitals.

Before implementation, Department of Health approval was sought and at a meeting at the Department I was surprised to find that Terry Geffen, the senior registrar when I was a house physician at UCH, was now the senior medical officer in charge of manpower at the Department. Both he and the civil servant involved, Mr R. Cattran, thought that the number of training posts, which was strictly controlled, were somehow being increased surreptitiously, but in reality existing posts were merely being incorporated into comprehensive coherent and structured training programmes. Mr Cattran said that he wanted to 'work it all out with his matches' but formal approval never arrived and the scheme was nevertheless implemented. I suppose Mr Cattran's letter of 3 January 1974, reproduced below, implies acceptance, although it rather misses the point. The posts were not being redistributed, but integrated into formal rotational programmes.

3 January 1974

Dear Mr Lettin

REDISTRIBUTION OF REGISTRAR AND SENIOR REGISTRAR POSTS

Thank you for your letter of 12 December which (due no doubt to the vagaries of the Christmas post) reached me only on the 27 December. I am sure that in relation to RNOH we will need to look at the question of redistribution in the light of the training needs in the specialty and your letter is very helpful in giving us an up-to-date picture of how the rotational training arrangements work. I will have copies made for other members of the Department's team.

With best wishes for the New Year,

Yours sincerely

R Cattran

Vacancies on the programme were much sought after for the certainty and security they provided, but the schemes were not generally supported by the surgical establishment, fearing that the near certainty of promotion would lead to complacency and a falling in standards. In fact the successful applicants were of the highest calibre and between 1968 and 1996, fifty-six trainees from the Bart's training programme became consultants in the UK – an average of two a year, three of whom have been elected to the Council of the Royal College of Surgeons (one becoming President) and four elected president of the British Orthopaedic Association. Others have served the profession in many different ways and eventually comprehensive training programmes of this type became College policy.

My association with the Queen Elizabeth Hospital and Dr Barnado's came to an end when Mr John Fixsen was appointed to a consultant post between the Queen Elizabeth and Bart's, although I subsequently accepted another honorary appointment at St Luke's Hospital for the Clergy, which

I held until my retirement, serving on the Medical Committee with a period as chairman.

His Grace, the Archbishop of Canterbury, Robert Runcie, was the guest of honour at the Medical Committee dinner on one occasion, but was not amused when I recounted the story of the parish priest who had been a friend of a previous Archbishop at Theological College and invited the Archbishop to preach at his small village church. The Archbishop was rather surprised by the small size of the congregation. 'Did you tell them I was coming?' he asked, as they left the church.

'No, but I'll damned well find out who did,' replied the vicar.

Was it something I said? The following year the Archbishop entertained the staff on a very memorable visit to Lambeth Palace, where we were able to enjoy both the Palace and the gardens in his company, and listen to an informal and inspiring address.

I now limited myself to adult orthopaedics and particularly the surgical treatment of rheumatoid arthritis, joint replacement, and low back pain. As a result of an early publication on 'The Diagnosis and Treatment of Lumbar Instability' a rewarding association developed with Dr James Cyriax, a well-known medical manipulator and Consultant Physician at St Thomas's Hospital, and his colleagues, which continued until I retired. Dr Cyriax was a very cultured man and in spite of his consultant appointment at St Thomas's he was never elected a Fellow of the Royal College of Physicians, remaining a member – a diploma gained by examination – all his life. Perhaps this was the result of what many in the medical establishment of the time regarded as his unorthodox methods of treatment, but he certainly attracted a multitude of patients, particularly those suffering from low back pain. He nevertheless recognised the limitations of his treatment and as a result of my paper on this subject and a subsequent presentation at a symposium on low back pain at his invitation, he regularly referred patients to me for consideration of surgical treatment.

He lived in a rather extraordinary house in Albany Street near Regent's Park where King Edward VII is reputed to have kept one of his mistresses. I particularly remember a bedroom without windows, the walls and ceiling painted with a uniform dull green wash. The four corners of the room were cut off, essentially making the room eight-sided but of course the cut-off corners were only the width of a door and indeed one of the corners was the door, but the uniformity of the surfaces and the paint made it impossible to determine which one. Furthermore, the only furniture was a bed placed diagonally across the centre of the room and it was not difficult to imagine waking up in the night and feeling quite confused. The bathroom was constructed as a grotto and shaped like an open shell with the walls entirely covered with shells of every description.

This was perhaps the happiest time of my professional life. The Gatehouse School moved to Victoria Park, which enabled Nicholas and Jonathan to travel unaccompanied to school on the underground. The Montessori system suited Nicholas but Jonathan preferred more conventional teaching and moved to Chigwell School at the age of eleven, where he was eventually joined by his younger brother Tim. Meanwhile the development of Intal for the treatment of asthma proved to be of great benefit to Nicholas, enabling him to stop taking steroids, which were beginning to affect his growth. His skin, however, continued to be a problem.

At Bart's I very much enjoyed my involvement with the medical students, both academically and socially. It was perhaps the heyday of Bart's rugby with several Oxford and Cambridge Blues and at least one international player in the team. The Hospitals Cup matches in those days merited reports in the national newspapers and I remember a visit to John Hunter's birthplace outside Glasgow, now a museum, and on signing the visitors' book I suppose I must have added St Bartholomew's Hospital as my address; I was very surprised when the Curator said, 'I believe Bart's won the Hospitals Cup this year.'

The consultant staff would cancel their hospital commitments so that they and the junior staff could join such festive events (the managers would not allow it these days.). Naturally I was on hand to treat any injuries and on one occasion I remember one of the Bart's team sustaining a fracture just below the knee as he tripped and fell whilst running onto the pitch before the game started. Needless to say the reserve, not expecting to play, had already consumed several pints of beer, but nevertheless played a magnificent game. On another occasion the students did not let me forget that I was a UCH graduate when Bart's scored what I believe was, and probably still is, a record 98 points against my old hospital. UCH were of course a soccer-playing and not a rugby-playing medical school. Fortunately the UCH soccer team subsequently managed to redress the situation with a less dramatic score.

The Bart's tennis team was no less successful. All six members were County players at one time and a Cambridge Blue could not command a regular place in the team, which was captained by a former junior Wimbledon Champion, Nick Perry. As a consequence, the annual staff/student tennis match was rather one-sided and in spite of the introduction of a handicapping system, I cannot remember winning a single match as one of the staff second pair. Bart's black tie affairs sometimes tended to be a bit boisterous and on one occasion I was obliged, as President of the soccer club, to ask an unruly student to leave. To his credit he later apologised to me for his behaviour and I am happy to say he is now a consultant orthopaedic surgeon in South London.

In 1973 we celebrated the 850th Anniversary of the foundation of St Bartholomew's Hospital and the celebrations were preceded by a visit from

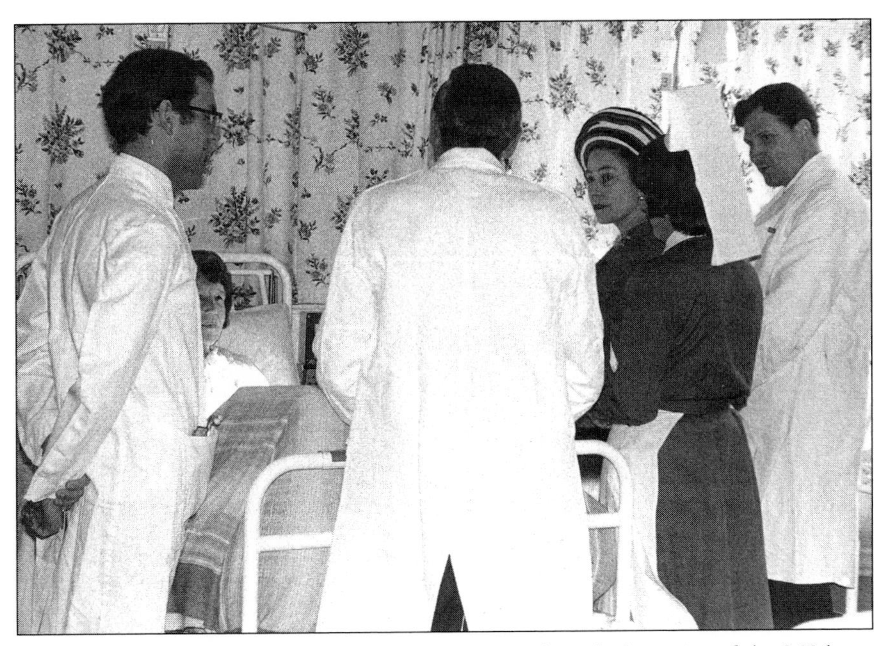

The Queen visiting Bart's after the Old Bailey bomb at the beginning of the 850th Anniversary celebrations, 1973 (photo Bart's)

Her Majesty the Queen on 21 March. A few weeks before, the first of the terrorist bombs exploded outside the Old Bailey and 130 casualties arrived at the hospital, most of whom were cut by flying glass. Thirty were admitted to the hospital, some to the orthopaedic wards. The patients were delighted when the Queen stopped by every bed to speak, not only to the injured but also to every patient, as she was conducted around the orthopaedic wards where she is seen in the accompanying photograph with Charles Manning, Jonathan Wilkinson, the Senior Registrar, Sister Griffiths, and me on the extreme right. This was the first of several occasions on which I was privileged to meet her.

The celebrations began a week later with a champagne supper served in the Livery Hall and the new crypt of the Guildhall, soon to be followed by a Tudor feast held in the Great Hall of the hospital on 30 April. The authentic Tudor food was accompanied by musicians, singers, dancers, jugglers and acrobats and, like the rest of the participants, Pat and I were in Tudor costume. The Bartholomew Ball, inevitably called the Meat Ball, was a less formal affair on 5 May, held within the Meat Market which was suitably decorated for the occasion. The Victorian building was designed to keep the meat cool and fulfilled the same purpose for the revellers dancing to the Ray Ellington and the Monty Sunshine Bands.

On each evening of the following week the students put on a play especially written for the occasion by George Blackledge, a houseman and

The author and his wife at the Tudor Feast, part of the 850th Anniversary celebrations, 1973

recent student, on a large stage constructed on scaffolding in front of the Henry VIII gate, with seating for one thousand people erected opposite in Smithfield. Bartholomew Fair had been an annual event in Smithfield from the eleventh century until it was banned in the nineteenth century, and small theatre groups set up stages and entertained the fair-goers. The play, called *The William Harvey Revolutionary Circus*, was based on the fair and the audience were the fair-goers. William Harvey, who discovered the circulation of the blood, was probably the most famous Bart's doctor and he served King Charles I during the Civil War. The play told the story of his life and times, a mere seventy years in the long history of the hospital.

The ancient fair lasted three days but the authentic re-creation of the fair, a vanished part of the pageantry of the City, lasted for just one day and was opened by the Lord Mayor, Lord Mais, 'according to ancient custom at eleven of the forenoon'. Smithfield and the streets around and a large part of the market itself were occupied by stalls and by demonstrations of ancient crafts. The stallholders and all those hawking their wares were in appropriate period dress. A large ox was roasted on a spit and food and drink was in abundance. The festivities continued into the afternoon on the historic lawns of the Medical College in nearby Charterhouse Square adjacent to the ancient house of the Carthusian Monks. There were roundabouts, helter-skelters, Punch and Judy shows, rides on pony carts, on model trains and on wagons drawn by magnificent shire horses from nearby

Whitbread's Brewery; there was Morris dancing, wrestling, falconry, pie men and gingerbread men, bell ringers and a beauty contest judged by Edward Woodward the actor, and still the picture is incomplete, but all is recorded on cinefilm, later transferred to video, which I presented to the Bart's archives.

No one would have believed that the future of the hospital would soon be in doubt and, indeed, the hospital would have been closed but for a change of government in 1997. A dinner in the Great Hall to mark the 875th anniversary was organised by the Finsbury Labour Party, with the local MP and Secretary of State for Health Frank Dobson as the principal guest. He received a standing ovation during his speech when he stated that if he achieved nothing more in his political career he would be satisfied that he had saved St Bartholomew's Hospital from closure. His resemblance to King Henry VIII, who refounded the hospital, did not go unnoticed.

Visitors to the Tower of London were the victims of the next terrorist bomb in 1975. I had just begun my weekly Wednesday afternoon outpatient clinic on my duty day when Keith Tucker, the senior registrar, reported the arrival of the first casualties from the Tower, and the patients waiting to be seen were sent home. Hospitals have a pre-arranged emergency plan but details are invariably forgotten in the heat of the moment. As a result of my previous experience at Barnet, I summoned all available junior doctors to the A&E Department. As each patient arrived the next available doctor was instructed to examine the patient, noting the findings and completing the requests for appropriate investigations. I then assessed the priorities for X-ray and operative treatment as each of the eight operating theatres became available. There were head, face, eye, chest and abdominal injuries, as well as burns, and inevitably nearly all thirty patients had broken bones. A New Zealand family was particularly hard hit. Mother was very badly burned and father had a broken leg. One of the children had a shaft of wood from one of the gun carriages driven through his body like a spear, but miraculously none of his major organs were damaged. Another boy had a leg amputated, but they all survived and before returning to New Zealand the High Commissioner invited the medical staff involved in their treatment to a reception at New Zealand House. Regrettably other commitments prevented me attending. A young German boy had the back of his skull blown off, damaging the underlying visual cortex but fortunately the resulting blindness was only temporary. Sadly, his mother was killed by the explosion.

By 8.30 that evening all the patients were in the designated receiving ward which had been cleared according to the pre-arranged plan and Miles Irving (now Sir Miles) the general surgeon on duty and I did a ward round on the injured. The importance of a multi-disciplinary hospital was only too apparent and the specialists in each field had been on hand, but the prevalence of bone injuries meant that the overall management was co-ordinated by the orthopaedic staff, particularly by the Senior Registrar, Keith Tucker, over the following weeks. It is not often appreciated how the routine work is disrupted, not only at the time of a major incident but for many weeks after, as injured patients return to theatre for further procedures and elective admissions are postponed.

The explosion had taken place in a confined space and all the injured patients but one had perforated eardrums and on the ward round the following morning that patient had disappeared. He was thought to have planted the bomb. Leaving the immediate area of the explosion but unable to escape, he had the presence of mind to join the injured. He must have had some reason to leave the hospital overnight without a word.

A committee was established to prepare for possible future incidents, on which I represented the medical staff. The representatives of the police, fire and rescue services were surprised to learn that I would not necessarily be the surgeon the next time, for whilst these services are essentially waiting for an emergency to occur, the hospital staff are going about their normal duties, with emergencies added to the day's (or night's) work, on their duty days. We decided that in future, if a medical presence were requested at the site of a major incident, the senior medical registrar on duty was to attend to decide if a mobile team was needed. If so the team would be led by the senior obstetric and gynaecology registrar, leaving the senior general surgical registrar and senior registrars in the various specialties in the hospital to treat the casualties. The Moorgate train disaster occurred in the underground tunnel and the police radios were inoperable. The obstetrician in charge of the mobile surgical team, Glyn Evans, called for Entonox, a painkilling gas frequently used for women in labour. His request was passed by word of mouth through the tunnel to the surface and to a police motorcyclist who took the message back to Bart's, by which time 'Send Entonox' had become 'Send empty box', which was interpreted as a euphemism for coffin and so cardboard coffins were despatched. Whilst the members of the rescue teams were relieved at frequent intervals, no one thought about relieving the medical team who remained in the tunnel for eighteen hours. Glyn Evans received the MBE.

The Cannon Street rail crash and the Baltic Exchange bomb made fewer demands on the staff of Bart's, and although Bart's had been the main receiving hospital for major incidents on more occasions than any hospital in the United Kingdom outside of Belfast, the Accident and Emergency department was reduced to a minor injuries unit, and plans made to close the hospital completely. Although the hospital was spared, it is no longer a general hospital capable of dealing with a major incident in the City, a decision which in the present uncertain times may be regretted.

The Times 28 April 1993

Sir, the latest terrorist bomb in the City of London must call into question the wisdom of closing the accident and emergency department at St Bartholomew's Hospital, or reducing its capacity to treat no more than minor injuries.

Simon Jenkins (April 28) speaks scornfully of the hospital 'howling to be kept open for next time'. In the last twenty years Bart's has been the major receiving hospital for those injured by the Old Bailey, Tower of London and Baltic Exchange bombs, as well as the casualties from the Moorgate and Cannon Street rail crashes. The number, nature and severity of the injuries have been different each time.

Although the City is largely empty at the weekends, 41 people were injured and one died in the recent explosion. After the Old Bailey bomb in March 1973, 130 arrived at Bart's within the hour. Many with minor injuries walked, but in similar circumstances today is it likely that they would walk to the Royal London Hospital in Whitechapel? Transporting the injured by ambulance or even buses through crowded streets would delay possible life-saving treatment. The first hour, 'the golden hour', is all-important for the survival of the severely injured.

The Royal London Hospital helicopter is valuable but cannot land in narrow City streets and can evacuate no more than five casualties at a time.

The arrival of many casualties, however minor the injuries, requires a large number of doctors, ideally one to each patient, to assess and document injuries and decide priority of treatment, arrange X-rays and give antibiotics and tetanus toxoid injections. These doctors are, in the first instance, the resident house officers and only the larger hospitals have a sufficient number. It takes time to bring in staff from home and from other hospitals.

Experience has shown that it is difficult even for a major teaching hospital with many surgical teams to deal with more than 30 patients with major injuries. There is a limit to the number of X-ray machines, operating theatres and operating teams and ancillary staff available. Flying glass requires vascular surgeons to repair severed arteries and ophthalmic surgeons to deal with eye injuries, neurosurgeons to treat head injuries and surgeons to treat the chest. Plastic surgeons would be required, if not immediately, later to treat burns.

Those close to the explosion will have perforated ear drums and orthopaedic surgeons will be required to treat the inevitable injuries to bones and joints. All these injuries may be present singly or in combination.

This latest bomb re-emphasises the need to maintain a service to those who work and live in the City of London which has existed uninterrupted for 870 years.

Yours faithfully,
ALAN LETTIN (Vice-President, British Orthopaedic Association)
St Bartholomew's Hospital
West Smithfield, EC1

Evening Standard

Jo Revill (Mrs Bottomley and a special kind of madness, 25 May) is quite right to draw comparison between the Royal Victoria Hospital in Belfast and St Bartholomew's in London.

But neither exists solely to treat casualties of terrorism or major disasters. Both have a daily responsibility to care for those in need who arrive at their doors.

As an example, 46 emergency patients were admitted to Bart's last weekend, when the City is supposedly empty. Fourteen required operations, eight for broken bones. The Royal London was similarly inundated.

Available beds were soon exhausted and there were no empty beds at our sister hospitals at Homerton. Six beds previously closed for financial reasons were reopened, but even so, five patients spent Saturday night in the accident and emergency department until patients could be discharged the next day.

Problems did not end there. Patients expecting to be admitted for elective operations this week have had them postponed because there are no beds for them, though staff are available.

This situation is not uncommon. It is difficult for people to believe that there is over provision of resources in the capital. A waste of resources, yes; over provision, no.

Alan Lettin, Senior Consultant orthopaedic surgeon, St Bartholomew's Hospital, Smithfield, EC1

The fortunes of the hospital and the medical college were inseparable and the traditional vocational training for a career in medicine was already under threat in 1968 when the Royal Commission chaired by Lord Todd recommended integrating the London Medical Schools with multi-disciplinary institutes for financial, academic, and social reasons. Bart's and the London would be the Medical Faculty of Queen Mary College and its location in East London was an added political attraction. Mixing medics with the other students would make them better doctors, so it was said.

Lord Todd addressed the staff in the Great Hall at Bart's extolling the relationship between UCL and UCH as the ideal university education for all doctors. I pointed out that in my own experience as a science and a medical graduate at UCL and UCH, there was no academic integration with the wider student body and social integration was limited to the Halls of Residence and the sports fields. These comments were not well received. *Was it something I said?* But now the hospital itself was under threat, in spite of the fact that it and its medical school were the cheapest and most cost-effective in London. The Thatcher Government was determined to limit expenditure on health care and Sir Bernard Tomlinson, a retired neuro-pathologist from Newcastle, recommended the closure of the hospital and the merger of the Medical College with the (by now) Royal London Hospital and Queen Mary College, relying on statistics from the Kings Fund which were later repudiated by its then director himself.

Adrian Marston, a fellow College Council member, and I met Sir Bernard and his civil servant to present the Royal College of Surgeons view on the impact the closure of a London teaching hospital would have on postgraduate surgical education and training. Our views were dismissed and it was apparent that Sir Bernard knew little about the needs of London and the suburban population, and naively assumed that there was spare capacity in the surrounding district hospitals to treat the patients that up to now had been treated in the centre, with the consequences that are all too evident today. Even so he led us to believe that he had no intention of destroying centres of excellence.

The proposal to close Bart's was accepted by the Government in spite of a vociferous 'Save Bart's Campaign' backed by the *London Evening Standard* and a petition of a million and a quarter signatories and representation from a multitude of medical and scientific institutions at home and overseas. Support from the City Corporation was rather disappointing, perhaps because the Corporation was concerned that its own rather anomalous position as a unique local authority might be at risk if it opposed the Government's proposals. One influential member of the Corporation with links to a property developer saw the potential of developing the hospital and the redundant Central Post Office buildings adjacent to the hospital as a massive single redevelopment project on a prime site in the city, but the beautiful Georgian buildings around the square were Listed Grade I and this made permission for their development unthinkable. There was talk of turning them into a museum or an annexe to the London School of Economics or the City University, but this came to nothing.

At about the time of the Tomlinson Enquiry, British Rail was planning the re-development of the extensive goods yards and redundant buildings around King's Cross mainline station. The land on which the railway complex had been built in the mid-nineteenth century had been owned by St Bartholomew's Hospital and had been sold to the Railway Company for £68,000 on the condition that if in the future it was not required for railway purposes Bart's could buy it back for the same amount. When the voluntary hospitals were effectively nationalised at the inception of the NHS, they retained their endowments vested in Special Trustees. The site was now worth many millions of pounds and needless to say the Bart's Special Trustees naturally wished to acquire the property on the original terms; equally British Rail were not prepared to let it go. Inevitably the issue went to court and the Judge ruled in favour of Bart's but British Rail appealed and the appeal was successful, on the grounds that the Act of

Parliament, which established the NHS, superseded all other legal arrangements. Should the Special Trustees go to the House of Lords? British Rail offered to pay all their legal expenses to date if they agreed to relinquish their claim. Perhaps unwisely they accepted this offer for when St George's Hospital moved to a new hospital from Hyde Park Corner, the Duke of Westminster regained the property, which presumably must have been subject to the same legislation. Had the Special Trustees succeeded in their action the enormous proceeds from the development of the King's Cross site might have been used to preserve Bart's as an independent private hospital.

John Major acknowledged in a private conversation some years later at Barber-Surgeons Hall that the decision to close Bart's had probably been a mistake and cost the Conservative Party many votes in the 1997 General Election. As a consequence of that election the hospital was saved from complete closure but remained only as a sad shadow of its former self. We can perhaps take comfort from the fact that nearly 500 years ago Henry VIII failed in his attempt to close the hospital and, following its refoundation, it went from strength to strength to become one of the foremost centres of medical education, research, and the treatment of the sick.

Chapter 9

RNOH

Prosperity and poverty went hand in hand in Victorian England but the social conscience of the more affluent members of society began to stir, leading to the foundation of hospitals in many towns and cities for the treatment of the sick poor. Among them were three small hospitals in London treating musculo-skeletal deformities, which were eventually amalgamated at the turn of the nineteenth century to form the Royal National Orthopaedic Hospital in purpose-built premises lying between Great Portland Street and Bolsover Street close to Regent's Park.

Many of the patients were children suffering from tuberculosis of the bones and joints and from poliomyelitis. Bed rest, good food and fresh air were the mainstay of treatment, which often lasted for several years. In 1922 the RNOH opened a country branch at Brockley Hill, Stanmore, initially in a private house, with later purpose-built wards opening onto open verandas on to which the beds were wheeled for the all-important sunlight and fresh air, even in the coldest winter months. They remain in use to this day together with the 'temporary huts' built at the onset of the Second World War, supplemented by modern operating theatres and outpatient facilities including a new outpatient centre opened by His Royal Highness the Duke of Gloucester in 1977.

I had of course received most of my orthopaedic training at the RNOH and the hospitals with which it was associated and I was delighted to return as a member of the consultant staff, with one outpatient session at Great Portland Street and an operating list and a ward round at Stanmore. Professor John Scales, the director of the Department of Bio-Engineering, was a pioneer in the application of engineering principles to medicine and indeed was the founder of bio-engineering as a separate discipline. His boundless energy, enthusiasm and innovation were recognised by innumerable awards from institutions around the world. He had very generously allowed me to use the facilities of the department to determine the strength and rigidity of the healing experimental fractures when I was undertaking my research into fracture repair, and soon after my appointment to the consultant staff he invited me to collaborate with him in the development of artificial joint replacements, a major part of the work of the department. It was not, however, the only work taking place, for John Scales was instrumental in the development of porous wound dressings in collaboration

The author (right) with HRH the Duke of Gloucester at the opening of the Patient Centre RNOH (photo RNOH)

with Smith & Nephew. The development of the low-loss airbed was his most innovative idea. A hovercraft floats on a cushion of air generated by the machine itself. John Scales utilised the principle in reverse. A patient suffering from pressure sores or severe burns, for example, floats on a bed of air generated from the bed below. In the initial tests, pigs were floated on jets of air, resulting in several amusing cartoons in the London evening papers. Eventually the time came for tests on humans and, in common with most experimental scientists, Johnny volunteered to be the first. Initially he would float in a box and who better to provide a custom-made box than the local undertaker.

'Where will we find the deceased?' the undertaker dutifully enquired in the sombre tones reserved for such occasions.

'Oh, no one's dead,' replied Johnny in a rather jocular fashion. 'It's for me.'

'If this is some sort of joke, it's in very bad taste,' responded the undertaker with more than a little irritation, yet to be convinced that the request was genuine. Eventually, after a somewhat lengthy explanation, a coffin was supplied.

Joining the joint replacement programme fitted in well with the surgical treatment of rheumatoid arthritis, which I had been asked to undertake at Bart's and which I would subsequently undertake at the RNOH. An artificial hip replacement was already in use but, unlike the Charnley and the McKee devices named after the principal originators, this hip joint was called the 'Stanmore Hip' in recognition of the fact that several people working at Stanmore were involved in its evolution, and all the subsequent implants that were developed at Stanmore bear the same name.

An artificial knee joint had been produced in 1952 to replace the knee joint and the bone immediately above and below the site of a malignant bone tumour in a 19-year-old woman, who refused amputation, the first operation of this kind in the world. Over the next fifteen years twelve similar custom-made knee replacements were used in similar situations, with gratifying results. In 1968 we modified the design for more general use to replace arthritic knees and, after careful follow-up of twelve original patients, the joint became commercially available five years later and remained in use for several years before being superseded by other designs.

Every operation is to some extent an experiment, with no guarantee of a successful outcome, and every new surgical innovation poses a dilemma – how many operations should be done before the procedure is considered safe for general use and how long the delay before one can be confident that, as time passes, there will be no untoward complications? In spite of the most careful monitoring of every form of medical or surgical treatment there will be failures, for which no one can be blamed and for which compensation is not due. Without such trials progress would come to an end.

The hip and knee joints are most frequently in need of replacement but the shoulder and the elbow are sometimes severely damaged in rheumatoid arthritis, often in both arms, leading to difficulty with everyday tasks. Dr Wykham Balm, my colleague at Bart's, suggested to me that an artificial shoulder joint was needed and so the Stanmore shoulder replacement was developed and at the time of its introduction into clinical practice in 1969 was the first of its kind in the world. Inevitably this led to several publications and invitations to lecture, and sometimes to operate in many parts of the world, often with unexpected consequences. 1973 was a particularly busy year. Whilst attempting to improve the view for a closed circuit television audience watching a total shoulder replacement at a provincial hospital in Holland, I inadvertently punctured a major vein, blood flooding into the wound, but thankful for my early general surgical training I was able to satisfactorily repair it. I arrived in Rotterdam the next day to carry out a similar operation and on my way to the hospital to see the patient my host, Professor Wouters, casually mentioned that he'd ordered an extra six units of blood. *Was it something I did?* Fortunately this time the extra blood was not needed.

Later that year I was invited to demonstrate the operation in San Francisco. My anaesthetic colleagues in London would routinely lower the blood pressure for most operations, to minimise blood loss. When I asked the American anaesthesiologist if he would do the same he told me that he had done it once but the patient died, which did nothing for my peace of mind. I was alone in the changing room after the operation when an American general surgeon came in and, after the usual friendly greeting, soon established that I was an orthopaedic surgeon from London.

'I suppose you've come over to learn how to do one of those new-fangled hip replacements?' he confidently enquired.

I pointed out, somewhat to his surprise, that total hip replacement had been invented – if that's the right word – in the United Kingdom twenty or so years earlier.

My good friend Harlan Amstutz had in fact carried out the first total hip replacement in the United States in the mid 1960s on his return to New York after a year at the RNOH. He was now Professor of Orthopaedics at the University of California in Los Angeles and I was on my way to make a presentation there on total shoulder replacement.

The components of most artificial joints are anchored to the bone with acrylic cement, the exact composition of which was a closely guarded secret at this time, and Harlan had received special permission from the United States Food and Drugs Administration to use the cement, which was made by a small company based in Old Hill Place, Stamford Hill, in North London. I remembered the address particularly because the provision merchant who had supplied the shop in my childhood had his premises there. The FDA would not licence the cement for general use without knowing its composition.

In collaboration with Peter Cole, my anaesthetist at Bart's, and Hugh Phillips, the registrar, I carried out some research on the reasons for a frequent fall in blood pressure when the cement was introduced into the bone. We received a small grant from the American owner of the company manufacturing the cement and he told us that if he had divulged the precise nature of its composition it would inevitably have been leaked to one of the large American companies and he would have been unable to afford to defend his patents. He was eventually bought out by one of them and the cement was then released for general use in the USA.

Perhaps my most bizarre experience occurred in Bruges. When I arrived at the hospital (almost as old as Bart's) I was told that the patient whose shoulder I was to replace had died overnight but to avoid disappointing the large audience (who I discovered later had paid to see the operation and listen to a lecture on total knee replacement the same evening), I was asked if I would operate on the corpse. I had used preserved cadavers in the dissecting room to develop operative techniques but I had never operated on a fresh dead body in the operating theatre with all the aseptic ritual of a real operation. The surgeon and both the nursing and medical assistants scrubbed and gowned, the skin was prepared and the body towelled, and the sterile instruments were handed to me by the theatre sister, a nun. The only things missing were the anaesthetist and blood.

Pat had accompanied me on this trip and whilst I was 'operating' she had taken a trip on the canals and was surprised on her return to find several rather green-looking individuals outside the theatre doors, the representatives of the company marketing the joint.

The RNOH attracted many overseas visitors, one of whom was Luptja Serafimov, an experienced surgeon from Skopje in Yugoslavia, whom we invited to spend Christmas Day with us at home in 1965 or 1966. We remained in contact and subsequently his wife Tania spent six weeks with us to improve her English. The communist regime at that time would not allow him to accompany her for any part of her stay, presumably for fear they might defect. In 1974 he was the Secretary of the Yugoslav Orthopaedic Association and responsible for organising their annual congress. Perhaps to counterbalance the obligatory presence of several Russian surgeons, John (later Sir John) Charnley, Robin Ling, Roger Dee, Chris Attenborough and I were invited to present papers on our various implants.

The conference was held in Ohrid, a beautiful old town situated on the shores of Lake Ohrid on the border with Albania and Greece, through which ran the ancient Roman highway from Rome to Constantinople. We travelled from Skopje, the capital of Macedonia, in two Mercedes cars and on the way stopped to view an old monastery. John Charnley had just acquired one of the early video cameras and he and I were taking photographs when a policeman approached us, pointing to a sign high on the wall indicating that photography was forbidden. John Charnley managed to slip away and I was left protesting my innocence when Serafimov arrived and a heated argument with the policeman followed. Fearing that Serafimov might be arrested I handed over the film from my camera to the policeman and subsequently discovered that photography was forbidden, not for security but for commercial reasons, to promote the sale of official postcards and slides.

The Yugoslav delegates were not particularly punctual and the conference began with the five Englishmen sitting alone in the lecture hall for about an hour before anyone else arrived, but we eventually presented our papers. The episode with the policeman had unnerved one or two of our partners who persuaded their husbands to leave early, which was a pity because the banquet at the end of the meeting was extraordinary. The British Orthopaedic Association banquets are quite sedate, black-tie affairs ending at about 10.30 p.m. but the Yugoslavs were dancing and singing between courses, folk dancers were performing and eventually everyone seemed to be dragged onto the dance floor for what I can only call communal dancing. Pat and I went to bed at about 2 a.m. and were rather surprised when Luptja Serafimov arrived on time at 9 a.m. the following morning, a Sunday, to take us for a pre-arranged drive through the surrounding countryside before visiting his wife's family for lunch in Ohrid.

'What happened to you last night? You should have stayed. It was really beautiful as the sun came up over the lake.'

He and most of his fellow Yugoslavs had not been to bed at all.

We stayed on for a few days in Ohrid and the lake and surroundings were really beautiful, a mixture of east and west, Muslim and Christian, markets and mosques. The water was warm enough to swim comfortably and so clean and clear. We paid a visit to the local hospital on the shore of the lake and I had a curious feeling of déjà vu on catching my first glimpse of the patients, all of whom, without exception, were wearing blue and white broad striped pyjamas or nightgowns. Where had I seen this before? Eventually I remembered that the inmates of the Nazi concentration camps had been similarly dressed.

Serafimov arranged for a car to take us back to Skopje after our short stay and our driver drove down the outside of a long line of traffic, waiting at a crossroads in a small provincial town on the way. When we reached the front of the line, a policeman motioned the driver to pull into the kerb on the other side of the crossroads. The driver and the policeman, neither of whom spoke English, disappeared, leaving us sitting rather apprehensively in the back of the car. About an hour later the driver returned carrying two large sacks of walnuts. He handed a few to Pat and to his obvious surprise she produced a pair of nutcrackers from her handbag and began to shell them. He must have thought that the English were prepared for every eventuality but in fact the nutcrackers had been bought in a market in Ohrid as a last minute souvenir for Pat's mother.

The invitation to lecture and to operate at home and abroad did not come about exclusively as a result of my collaboration with John Scales at the RNOH. The Australian Association of Manipulative Medicine invited me to address their conference in Sydney in 1975 on the recommendation of James Cyriax. The Australian and New Zealand postgraduate organisations are quick to pick up the names of overseas visitors and at their invitation I spent an eventful six weeks, unfortunately in their winter, visiting not only Sydney but Melbourne, Brisbane, Adelaide, Auckland, Christchurch and Dunedin. In addition to presentations on low back pain and, inevitably, shoulder replacement (I carried out the first in the Antipodes in Melbourne), I lectured to undergraduate and postgraduate students. I had met many of the surgeons before in England, where they had received part of their training, some as my registrars, and it is always a delight to renew old acquaintances. It also gave me the opportunity to talk about the new arrangements we had introduced at the RNOH, with the approval of the Department of Health, for overseas trainees, setting aside two registrar posts each specifically for trainees from the Commonwealth who would be appointed by their orthopaedic associations, relieving them of the necessity of competing for posts on arrival in this country.

Unfortunately there was not much time for sightseeing, perhaps one day in three – one day for travelling, one for talking, and one for sightseeing. I then managed to visit the magnificent Sydney Opera House with John Beer who had been an SHO at Great Portland Street, and I saw the sand and the surf of the Gold Coast whilst in Brisbane. A cousin in Adelaide insisted that I should spend a day with her, visiting the vineyards in the Borossa Valley, but more Australian sightseeing had to await later visits.

The cold in Dunedin, with a hot water bottle in the bed in the small hotel where I stayed, was well worth enduring for the magnificent scenery on a beautiful sunny winter's day driving along the Otago peninsula to see the albatrosses. The scenery reminded me so much of Scotland and Dunedin was well named. In Christchurch and Auckland the domestic architecture was generally rather dull. Most of the houses of the suburbs had corrugated iron roofs and inside the houses the noise during heavy rain could not be ignored. There is no natural roofing material in New Zealand and the corrugated iron was transported as ballast in the ships returning from Europe in the early days of colonisation.

I needed no persuasion to return to Copenhagen with Pat just before Christmas 1975 to speak to the Danish Surgical Society about joint replacement generally. This visit was memorable for two reasons: first the beautiful Christmas decorations in the shops and streets, far more elaborate than we had ever seen in London, and second the customary banquet at the end of the meeting. The principal speech was delivered in Danish and was extremely amusing, for although we could not understand a word of it we were carried along on the uproarious waves of laughter, laughing ourselves like everyone else.

The topics for these various presentations were not only replacement of the shoulder, although this was often the main reason for the invitation, but also included knee and elbow replacements, low back pain, and even the management of major accidents. The invitation to visit the Madi Military Hospital in Cairo was rather different. The Egyptian authorities paid our hotel and our fares. It was not until we arrived that I realised that I was expected to conduct daily outpatient consultations for fee-paying Egyptian civilians, which I suppose covered the cost of our visit. A trip to the Pyramids was easily arranged but we were led to believe that we would also have the opportunity to visit the Valley of the Kings, Luxor and Aswan. These arrangements, however, seemed rather nebulous and it occurred to me that there was probably a quota of private patients to be seen before the visits would take place. After a couple of weeks a visit was arranged and we flew to Luxor and were accommodated in a caravan park on the banks of the Nile. Unfortunately I was struck down by a 'gippy tummy', perhaps related to the hospitality we had received the evening before at the house of one of the Egyptian Army surgeons. Fortunately we found ourselves in the company of a physician from Glasgow, Dr Watson-Buchanan, on a similar mission to our own, and he had had the foresight to bring appropriate medication, which he rather parsimoniously shared with me. Fortunately I made a sufficient recovery, sustaining myself on biscuits and Seven-Up, to enjoy the marvellous antiquities. We flew on to Aswan, landing in a military airfield with no obvious facilities for civilian passengers, where a couple of coaches waited to take us to the nearby town. Unfortunately Watson-Buchanan's luggage was missing and I felt obliged to help him find it. We went in different directions and by the time I returned to where the coaches had been parked, they had disappeared. It later transpired that Watson-Buchanan had found his bags and had left on one coach, with Pat on the other – both thinking that I was on the other coach. The airfield was deserted and a rather run-down single storey building masqueraded as the airport terminal. Inside, a couple of employees sat drinking coffee, not the least interested in my predicament. There was no transport to the nearby town, no prospect of a taxi or even a camel. I did not know the name of the hotel where we were due to stay. Just as I was beginning to despair, a small military plane landed and a visiting neuro-surgeon from the United Kingdom recognised me and I was able to take advantage of the car that had been sent to collect him.

It was not the usual practice to be paid for contributing to scientific meetings, although expenses for overseas visits were usually met. Brief mention has already been made of the Innominate Club and in 1979 we were invited to provide the speakers for meetings in Barcelona and Madrid. We had all now been consultants for ten years or more and between us could speak with experience, even authority, on a wide range of orthopaedic topics. I was somewhat surprised, as the treasurer of the club, to be handed literally armfuls of Spanish banknotes at the end of the meeting. Philip Yeoman accompanied me to my hotel room. The lift had no inner doors and the draught from the shaft as we ascended blew the notes out of my arms and we must have been a comic sight as we plucked them from the air, rather like the Lavender Hill Mob following a burglary in the film of that name. I think there were eight members on this trip and on reaching my room we divided the notes into eight piles, going round and round putting one note on each pile. At the end there were four or five notes over so we decided to divide them between the two Scottish members because they had travelled the farthest.

That evening, Pepe Palacious, the Professor of Orthopaedics in Madrid, invited us to a wonderful outdoor banquet at his villa just outside the capital and musicians in traditional dress walked among the guests. Quite suddenly there were fireworks everywhere and we dived into the bushes for cover. Pepe then 'knighted' us for our bravery with replica Toledo swords, which he then presented to us, leading to more than a little difficulty at the airport on the way home.

The War of Independence between east and west Pakistan, which resulted in the establishment of the Independent Nation of Bangladesh in 1971, inevitably caused many muscolo-skeletal injuries with long-term disability. An American missionary-doctor, Ron Garst, was largely responsible for establishing the Rehabilitation Institute and Hospital for Disability (RHID), an orthopaedic hospital and rehabilitation unit in Dacca, which developed into a four-hundred bed orthopaedic hospital very similar to the RNOH at Stanmore. 'Ginger' Wilson, a consultant at the RNOH, recommended to the Ministry of Overseas Development that a joint venture should be established to train orthopaedic surgeons in Bangladesh. Over the years under the auspices of World Orthopaedic Concern (WOC) surgeons from many parts of the world have volunteered to support Bangladeshi orthopaedic surgeons for varying periods of time by operating, teaching, and visiting outlying hospitals.

A close affinity between the surgeons of Great Britain was fostered by Geoffrey Walker, an early volunteer and one-time president of WOC (and incidentally a founder member of the Innominate Club.) 1981 was the Year of the Disabled and with the agreement of my employing authorities and the Department of Overseas Aid, I volunteered to spend three months in Bangladesh. The High Commission guesthouse provided accommodation for various specialist volunteers and the excellent recreational facilities were used at the weekends by the many ex-patriot families working on long-term aid projects. The 'house boys' looked after the residents most efficiently and it was not difficult to understand why the British so enjoyed life in the days of Empire. Former Gurkha soldiers protected the guesthouse and after some preliminary training from the Gurkha drivers, I was able to drive myself to and from the hospital each day but was warned never to stop if I had the misfortune to be involved in an accident on the busy streets, for fear of immediate, if unwarranted and unjust, retribution.

I arrived a few days after severe storms and floods, a frequently recurring disaster in Bangladesh, had devastated large areas of the country and the casualties were making their way to the hospital as best they could, often with very severe injuries, flying sheets of corrugated iron from the flimsy shacks often amputating or partially amputating limbs and causing severe injuries to other parts of the body. Often there was little that could be done. More trying, however, were the self-inflicted injuries resulting from the injudicious treatment from the so-called barefoot doctors practising native medicine in the country villages where orthodox medicine scarcely existed. Incredibly a painful limb was often treated by the application of a tourniquet, which would be left in place for hours or even days. The pain must have been excruciating and, of course, the limb rendered lifeless, with amputation the only treatment. The outcome was accepted as the will of Allah. Sometimes little blocks of wood were inserted under the skin of a painful extremity, inevitably resulting in infection and suppuration (comparable I suppose to the laudable pus of eighteenth and nineteenth century European medicine), often leading to persistent discharging sinuses.

The DC electricity supply of Dacca, which had originally been installed by the British Administration in the 1930s, was being converted to 250-volt AC by Ewbank, a British company from the south-east of England, financed by overseas aid. The engineers needed to have the electricity flowing through each section of overhead cable by nightfall, otherwise it would be stolen by the next morning. Even so, little boys would climb the electricity poles and attach wires to the cables to provide free electricity to the homes and shops below. Needless to say they frequently fell, sustaining not only fractures but also quite severe electrical burns. There were no plastic surgeons at that time in Bangladesh and so it fell to the orthopaedic surgeons to treat burns as well as fractures. A particularly vicious form of punishment – throwing corrosive acid into the face (meted out, it seemed, to unfaithful wives) – left extensive scarring and often blindness. Again there was little that could be done. Sadly many of the Bangladeshi surgeons on completion of their orthopaedic training chose to seek lucrative posts in the Middle East, the exception being the very talented Professor Salek Talukdar.

A brand new multi-storey hospital had been financed by the Czech Republic at the provincial town of Barisal, a fourteen-hour journey by river on the *Rocket*, a paddleboat built on the Clyde and transported out in parts and assembled locally in the 1920s. It was still going strong and because of its shallow draft, it was capable of travelling nearer to the shore than the more modern gifts from Japan, cutting the corners, so to speak, on the river bends and providing a faster service. The journey along the River Ganges provided an opportunity to see the rather flat but nevertheless attractive and interesting countryside with many small riverside towns and villages. I arrived in Barisal soon after midnight and the local orthopaedic surgeon met me on the quayside and took me to the Roman Catholic Seminary where I would be staying. I soon began to wonder why I had volunteered to come to Bangladesh. Only a thin straw mattress covered the wooden slats of my bed and, no matter which way I turned, comfort and sleep eluded me, but I contented myself with the thought that many endured far worse without complaint.

Cows still grazed on the greenfield site on which the new hospital had been built and no attempt was made to clear them from the main reception area, but fortunately they seemed disinclined to take the lift to the operating theatres on the top floor. There was sufficient conventional theatre clothing available for the surgeon and his assistant only. The medical students watching the operations covered their mouths and noses with the lapels of their outdoor white coats and, whether as a gesture to Allah or asepsis, they removed their shoes. Equipment was in similar short supply and I found myself having to break the wire I had used to fix a fracture of the kneecap by bending it back and forth until it snapped, because there were no wire cutters.

Although the Czechs had installed modern X-ray equipment, this had long been out of action and there was no one locally able to repair it. The Czechs themselves seemed reluctant to return, either to repair their X-ray machines or to restore a pure hospital water supply, but fortunately a British company was undertaking that task. The only X-ray machine for both in-patient and out-patient use was a Second World War portable American army machine, similar to the one I had used to X-ray my experimental rabbit fractures. The X-rays, as a consequence, were of poor quality and availability restricted. It is customary to take X-rays of a fracture, for example, in two planes but for reasons of economy only one was allowed. Fractures of the neck and the femur were common as they are elsewhere in the world but the surgeons and their trainees, with only one view, could not be sure that they had adequately reduced the fracture or placed the internal fixation device into the correct position. It was a matter of chance. The patients would soon return to their villages and would never be seen again and the eventual outcome was likely to remain unknown. At my first out-patient clinic I was presented with a single X-ray of a broken ankle.

'Where's the other view?' I asked.

'Here, sir, you only have the AP or the lateral, not both' was the reply.

In spite of these difficulties the technical skills of the surgeons were quite high but it was clear that there was no point in introducing them to the latest western techniques, and the methods of treatment of the early twentieth century were more appropriate. Penicillin and streptomycin were provided by WHO free of charge but were usually in short supply, either because they were used indiscriminately or perhaps diverted for private use. Anything was available at a cost, but at a cost most could not afford. Anaesthetic gases and intravenous fluids, for example, could be obtained from a shop opposite the hospital and were often paid for with the proceeds of selling the corrugated iron from the roof of the patient's shack, their most valuable asset.

Before I left Dacca for Barisal the High Commission told me that I must inform them by telephone when I decided to leave Barisal and they would arrange for me to be met on the quay in Dacca, and under no circumstances should I leave the boat without the Gurkha escort. When the time came I asked the hospital administrator to let the High Commission know what arrangements I had made and later asked him if all was in order.

'I couldn't get through, Sir. There was no answer.'

'But the phone at the High Commission is staffed twenty-four hours a day.'

'Very sorry, Sir. There was no one there.'

That evening at dinner I mentioned my predicament to the principal of the Seminary, a French Canadian who had been in east Pakistan and Bangladesh since the Second World War.

'There's only one place in Barisal from which you can make a call to Dacca,' he confided, 'and that's from the tobacconist's shop opposite the hospital.'

'Why?' I asked.

'Nothing happens here without a bribe. You pay a bribe to the tobacconist, he pays a bribe to the telephone operator and so on down the line.'

To emphasise the point, he told me that the Canadian High Commissioner had to bribe the appropriate Bangladeshi official to get Canadian aid into Bangladesh!

On the return journey to Dacca I struck up a conversation with a well-educated Bangladeshi. The topic of aid soon came up and I mentioned the re-wiring project.

'It would be much better if you gave us the cash.'

'I very much doubt it' was my reply. He just grinned.

Bribery and corruption were part of everyday life, part of the culture, and it seemed there was a set tariff for everything, even for a bedpan.

On ward rounds I was accompanied by a member of the junior staff to translate. Mothers invariably stayed with their children, sitting on their haunches on the floor against the wall at the head of the bed, almost as if they had been folded up, with head on knees, enveloped in their voluminous garments. On my approach to the bedside they would look up imploringly and, if through the translator they were told that I could do nothing for their child, they might grab me around the legs to stop me walking away. It was a most harrowing experience. It was impossible to be without sympathy, not only for the patients but for the population as a whole. With no significant natural resources and jute, the only significant export product, superseded by synthetic materials for rope making, linoleum no longer a fashionable floor covering, and recurrent devastating storms and floods, it is not surprising that those with initiative escaped to the West. Life in the squalor of Bethnal Green around Brick Lane, which my parents and grandparents and so many others worked so hard to leave behind them, is infinitely better than life in Bangladesh. Yet no matter how desperate the conditions the population of the Third World cannot all be accommodated in the West.

The RNOH itself was not without its problems and although the Board of Governors on which I had served for six years survived the 1974 re-organisation, it was abolished in 1982 and the hospital became part of the Bloomsbury Health Authority. Two years later, by which time I was chairman of the Medical Staff Committee, the town branch of the hospital was closed and the in-patient facilities were transferred into two wards at The Middlesex Hospital. Before long the doors of one were padlocked and chained, leading to newspaper, radio and television interviews critical of the authorities. Before long the main hospital at Stanmore was under threat and specialist hospitals in general were out of favour. The Second World War hutted wards needed replacement but the suggestions to rebuild at Chase Farm or Northwick Park Hospitals were strongly resisted.

With a small subcommittee I produced a well-reasoned report for rebuilding at Stanmore, which was supported by a working party chaired by Professor Leslie Le Quesne, the Deputy Vice-Chancellor of London University, and also by an independent firm of consultants. Hugh Dykes, the local MP, arranged a meeting with Kenneth Clarke, the Secretary of State, but this did nothing to increase confidence in the Minister or his advisers, who seemed to have little idea of the workings of the NHS. It was the Limb Fitting Centre and the Spinal Injuries Unit, both purpose-built at Stanmore in an orthopaedic environment, and above all the Graham Hill Rehabilitation Centre with its powerful and influential friends, that saved the day. The creation of the Royal National Orthopaedic Hospital Trust as a result of the 1992 re-organisation restored the hospital's independence, although the Institute of Orthopaedics remained part of University College. Specialist hospitals now seem to be in favour again and, twenty years on, the Royal National Orthopaedic Hospital is to be rebuilt on the Stanmore site.

I continued to fulfil my clinical responsibilities at The Middlesex Hospital but with only three beds at my disposal and a part share in a pre-registration house officer, changing every six weeks, I elected to take early retirement in 1994.

Chapter 10

The Worshipful Company of Barbers

The worshipful company of barbers is one of the oldest and most prestigious livery companies in the City of London and came into existence some time before the appointment of its first Master, Richard le Barber, in 1308. It was the custom of individuals with a similar occupation to form guilds or fraternities, initially for religious and charitable purposes and later to regulate their particular trade or craft.

Following the departure of the Roman Legions in AD 406 the practice of medicine and surgery was largely in the hands of the monks and the clergy for there were few with sufficient learning to read the ancient texts. The letting of blood, or venesection, formed a significant part of medical practice in medieval times and indeed for several centuries later. In 1163 Pope Alexander III forbade the shedding of blood by those in Holy Orders, an edict not to be ignored, and as a consequence the clerics were no longer able to perform the limited surgical procedures of the time or to bleed patients. They henceforth confined their activities to the healing art of medicine and handed to their barbers, with whom they had a close relationship because they shaved their tonsures, any tasks involving the shedding of blood.

Initially the barbers undertook their surgical activities under supervision but it was not long before they were carrying out their new responsibilities on their own. They had become Barber-Surgeons. From the beginning there was a degree of specialisation among the barbers, some limiting their activities to shaving and the trimming of beards, and others carrying out simple surgery, particularly on the battlefield, and bloodletting, but few limiting their activities to surgery alone. There were, however, a small number of specialist surgeons in a separate guild who vied with the barbers for the control of surgery in the City of London – power swinging from one to the other until finally they were united by Act of Parliament in 1540, an event depicted in Holbein's famous painting of Henry VIII and the Barber-Surgeons which hangs in Barber-Surgeons Hall, seen in the background of the photograph of the Court of Examiners on page 153.

Over the two following centuries the roles of the barbers and the surgeons became increasingly distinct. The better educated and more prosperous surgeons became dissatisfied with the union and in 1745 the barbers and the surgeons separated, the surgeons forming the Company of

Surgeons, which became the Royal College of Surgeons in 1800. However, the barbers retained the hall which remains Barber-Surgeons Hall. Today, few of the livery companies regulate their historic crafts and trades and apart from civic functions in the City of London which include the election of the Lord Mayor and the Sheriffs, the most important reason for their continued existence is their charitable work. The Barbers' strong connection with medicine and especially surgery continues, with its financial support for medical and surgical causes.

Dinner in the Hall following the regular Court Meetings provides an opportunity for members of the company to enjoy the fellowship of medical and non-medical members and their guests. I had the great good fortune to be invited to dine in the Hall by Sir Lionel Denny, a past Lord Mayor and past Master of the Company, when his portrait, painted by Terence Cuneo, was unveiled, and to sit next to the artist at the table. This most enjoyable evening led to my admission to the Freedom of the Company and to the Freedom of the City of London in 1974. A year later I became a full member of the Company as a liveryman. All liverymen are Freemen of the City and it is the liverymen who annually elect the Lord Mayor and the Sheriffs in the Guildhall, amid great pomp and ceremony, in which the Masters of the livery companies proceed wearing their gowns and insignia.

The close proximity of Barber-Surgeons Hall to St Bartholomew's Hospital enabled me to attend most of the Company functions, and in particular Court dinners to which I usually invited a member of Bart's or RNOH junior staff. The opportunity to dine in the splendour of Barber-Surgeons Hall with its many historic treasures on display was particularly appreciated by trainees from overseas, giving them the opportunity to meet eminent members of the Company and often equally eminent guests.

The after-dinner speeches at the Court dinner follow a set pattern. Usually a member of the livery, chosen perhaps as a potential candidate for future high office, proposes the health of the guests but in particular the principal guest, usually someone of importance – perhaps a personal friend or acquaintance of the Master. The other guests singled out for special mention would include the Masters of four or five livery companies with whom hospitality is regularly exchanged and finally noteworthy personal guests of the livery. I found myself performing this daunting task on more than one occasion, hoping to be informative, amusing, and above all brief. The principal guest replies and among the best remembered, of course, are the politicians, for speaking is their stock-in-trade, and the Barbers gave me the opportunity of meeting, for example, John Major, Willie Whitelaw, Enoch Powell, Ann Widdecombe and Charles Kennedy, all of whom proved to be entertaining speakers. I remember talking to Enoch Powell, a former Minister of Health at the time the 'internal market' was introduced in spite of universal opposition from the medical profession.

'You have to take the profession with you,' he said, 'otherwise you will fail.' This was a prediction that ultimately materialised.

Lawyers as a general rule speak well, although occasionally disappoint. Over the years I can recall the Master of the Rolls disabusing us of any notion of a connection with a car of that name and the Commons Sergeant assuring us that he was neither common nor a sergeant! City financiers, captains of industry, generals and admirals, and diplomats have rarely failed to entertain – always ending their speeches in the time-honoured fashion with the toast 'the Worshipful Company of Barbers root and branch may it live and flourish forever' coupled with the name of the Master, to which the Master replies, bringing the evening to a close.

The social highlight of the year is the Ladies Livery Dinner when the livery entertain their ladies and the Lord Mayor and the Sheriffs and their ladies and the high-ranking City officers to dinner. Other social events to which ladies are invited often include places of interest, usually with a Company connection, and talks and presentations in the Hall, particularly the Sir Lionel Denny lecture in memory of that distinguished Barber.

The livery companies in general are regulated in a similar way. The twenty-four members of the Court of Assistants of the Barbers Company elect a Master and three wardens from among their numbers annually on the second Thursday in August, as required by the Act of Parliament which separated the Barbers and the Surgeons in 1745. The wardens, and indeed the assistants in general, can anticipate being elected Master in order of seniority in the absence of any unforeseen circumstances. I was delighted to be asked in 1983 if I would be prepared to be elected to the Court and to give an undertaking ultimately to agree to become Master in due course. I had no hesitation in accepting but it meant relinquishing other commitments. I was about to become Secretary of the Orthopaedic Section of the Royal Society of Medicine but unfortunately the meetings of the Section clashed with the meetings of the Court, and reluctantly I resigned, a decision which was not well received. Initially, membership of the Court of Assistants is not particularly onerous but with each passing year membership of various committees increases the amount of time spent on company affairs.

The company is not among the wealthiest of the livery companies and as a very junior member of the Court I recollect the debate which followed a bequest of £100,000 by past Master Sir John McNee. Past Master Henry Thompson, a very generous supporter of the company himself, argued that it should be assigned to the general funds to support the upkeep of the Hall but Past Master Raven, also a friend of Sir John, believed that he would have wanted it to be used for charitable purposes, in which case there would be no tax to pay, thereby increasing its value to the company. In the end it was divided in such a way that the general funds and the charitable funds received an equal share after taking tax into consideration. The income from the charitable part of the bequest was used to finance scholarships for students in each of the twelve London medical schools to study for an intercalated B.Sc. degree, a decision which I strongly supported. Sir John's attractive Chinese carpet on the Court room floor reminds us of his generosity.

In 1984 Harvey White, a consultant surgeon whom I had known as a member of the junior staff at Bart's as well as a patient, sought to admit his daughter as an apprentice, one of the three ways of joining the company, the others being by patrimony or by redemption. Patrimony dates from the time when a son frequently followed his father into a trade and accordingly a child born to a liveryman at the time of its birth had the right to become a Freeman, but not automatically a liveryman by patrimony. Although there were several women who had gained the freedom in this way, in spite of there being a female monarch, a female prime minister and a female lord mayor, Harvey White's request was refused after a rather divisive Court meeting. The Barbers remained a male preserve for the next twenty years but in 2004 the Court decided that henceforth women should be admitted to the livery on equal terms with the men.

Perhaps the most significant event for the company since the rebuilding of the Hall after the destruction of the previous Hall in the Blitz resulted from the demolition of Lee House, a post-war office block on the opposite side of Monkwell Square, and its proposed replacement by a much larger and, in particular, much taller building, to be known as Alban Gate, which would have overshadowed the Hall. The foundation stone of the present Hall was laid by Sir Lionel Denny in 1966, the year in which he was Lord Mayor, and followed several years of negotiations with the City Corporation which involved the granting of restrictive covenants to the Company, limiting the height of neighbouring developments. The Corporation seems to have overlooked these covenants when granting planning permission for the demolition of Lee House and the building of Alban Gate. I and other members of the Court believed that Sir Lionel would have safeguarded the interests of the Barbers in the negotiations twenty years earlier and were proved right when the title deeds were scrutinised. MEPC, the developers, offered the Barbers £130,000 to release them from the covenants but the company's advisers considered two million pounds a more realistic figure. Kenneth Bagnall QC, a liveryman specialising in planning law, considered two million pounds inadequate. MEPC had already started to demolish Lee House and Kenneth Bagnall threatened an injunction to bring all work to a halt. MEPC agreed a figure of three million pounds to allow the work to continue. This made an enormous difference to the company's finances and particularly allowed a considerable increase in charitable grants and donations and the budget for hospitality, raising the company's profile in the City. Most of all it allowed the company to appoint a full-time clerk, the person responsible for the day-to-day management of the company's affairs. Colonel Andrew Harfield, a retired Royal Marine Commando, was the inspired choice of the Selection Committee.

The increased wealth of the company resulted in an avalanche of applications to the Charity Committee, which nearly overwhelmed Andrew. By now I was the Upper Warden and the Master, John Smethers, asked me formulate with Andrew proposals to simplify the award of grants to avoid the Charity Committee (of which I was a member) spending hours approving or rejecting requests for relatively small amounts of a hundred pounds or so. We decided that there should be one or two main beneficiaries and smaller sums should be available for education and medical charities, particularly with City connections, and occasionally impecunious hairdressers! The Court subsequently decided that the two principal beneficiaries should be the Phyllis Tuckwell Hospice in Farnham, Surrey, founded by Past Master Sir Edward Tuckwell in memory of his first wife, and the Royal College of Surgeons to meet the salary of the Barbers Reader in Anatomy, restoring the Barbers' historic role in the teaching of anatomy.

John Smethers also suggested that Andrew Harfield and I should revise the standing orders and particularly the criteria for election to the Court and ultimately of the Master, a task which was completed when I became Master in 1990. In many livery companies seniority is the main criteria – 'Buggins's Turn'. The Court agreed that no one over the age of 60 should normally be elected, bearing in mind that they might not be up to the rigours of becoming Master in their late sixties. Regular participation in Company activities, professional achievements and personal attributes were the main considerations.

My year as Master proved to be one of the most enjoyable of my life. I was by now an elected member of the Council of the Royal College of Surgeons and my clinical commitment to Bart's and the RNOH of course occupied most of my working day. In an effort to limit the NHS budget, cuts in services were being implemented at this time and I lost one of my two weekly operating sessions at Bart's, which by coincidence was the afternoon on which Barbers Committee Meetings were held. I stayed in the Master's Lodge from Monday to Friday, a mere five minutes' walk from Bart's, saving a couple of hours travelling time each day, time which was well used. With the never failing support of Andrew Harfield I believe that none of my many commitments suffered, apart from my private practice, a small price to pay for a memorable and privileged year.

Besides chairing or attending the various Committee Meetings, I presided over the six Court Meetings during the year, beginning with the Election Court, the formal ceremony in which the Master and wardens swear ancient oaths of office before proceeding, badged and gowned, for the election service in St Giles, Cripplegate. Every Court Meeting is followed by a Court dinner and, though there are several excellent medical after-dinner speakers I could have called upon, I limited myself to two, the first, Professor Harold Ellis and the last, Sir David Innes Williams. As a representative from the City, Sir Philip Wilkinson, the Chief Executive of the Nat West Bank and an old boy of my school, was an excellent choice and another old boy (by virtue of the wartime association with the Sir George Monoux School) Douglas Insole, the former test cricketer and chairman of the Test & County Cricket Board, represented sport. I had hoped that Frank Muir, another former Leyton County High School pupil, would represent the Arts but unfortunately he was working overseas. Peter Cull, the Director of the Department of Medical Illustration at Bart's and a talented artist, was an equally talented speaker and proved to be a worthy alternative. He subsequently became a liveryman. Three of the liverymen I asked to propose the toast to the guest subsequently became Masters of the Company.

On two or three evenings each week, accompanied by the Clerk who made sure that I was in the right place at the right time appropriately dressed, I dined as a guest of the livery companies with whom we regularly exchanged hospitality. Visiting most of the livery company halls, I often found myself responding to the toast on behalf of the guests, sometimes at short notice. During my year in office I made no fewer than forty-two speeches at one function or another, using a few stories from the pages of that invaluable publication *Pass the Port* which I adapted to suit the occasion.

Occasionally Pat was included in the invitation, particularly on those special occasions when the Lord Mayor, Sir Alexander Graham in 1990/1991, for example, would be in attendance and at the annual banquet that he himself gave for the Masters, Prime Wardens and Upper Bailiffs of the companies at the Mansion House. On these occasions she would stay overnight at the Hall. The annual Guilds Service at St Paul's Cathedral, the Service of Remembrance, the Buckingham Palace Garden Party and the Lord Mayor's show were other memorable events but it was not until a surgical colleague from Bart's and fellow Barber, Sir John Chalstrey, became Lord Mayor in 1993, that I rode in an open carriage in the procession itself to the Law Courts and witnessed his formal installation by the Lord Chief Justice.

Meeting the Queen Mother on her visit to Barber-Surgeons Hall in 1991

Her Majesty Queen Elizabeth the Queen Mother, our patron, celebrated her 90th birthday in 1990 and her many commitments prevented her from visiting Barber-Surgeons Hall that year (she came to lunch the following year) but she invited me and the Wardens to pre-lunch drinks at Clarence House. I presented her with No. 1 of a limited edition of Barbers' bowls, commissioned to commemorate the 600th anniversary of the election of a Master the year before and I also showed her the silver candelabrum made by Grant Macdonald, the eminent silversmith, to celebrate her birthday, hoping that she would not think that this was also a gift! Pat and I presented a similar candelabrum to the company the following year, to mark my year as Master.

We were surprised that the Queen Mother stood throughout our visit. I remember particularly the flower arrangement on the grand piano. She, a keen gardener, seemed surprised when I identified the pink-flowered branches of *Prunus subhirtella* 'Autumnalis', the autumn-flowering cherry, only because we had a similar tree in our own garden. She took me over to the window to show me the tree in the garden from which the branches were cut. During the conversation that followed, it became apparent that her Majesty believed that King George VI had been a Barber but I felt it wise not to correct her. On this occasion it was not *something I said*! The following year I sat next to the Queen Mother at lunch when she visited the Hall and once more gardening was the topic of conversation, particularly the lack of rain.

'When I put a spade into the soil at the weekend it was as dry as a bone,' she confided. An amazing lady, still gardening at 90!

Most of the events during a Master's year in office recur each year but some, like the visit to Clarence House and the 90th Birthday tribute on a beautiful summer evening on Horse Guards, were unique. The City of London's Welcome Home Parade by Britain's Gulf Forces was another unique occasion. Unfortunately it was a rainy day but the Masters of the companies with service connections, ours with 257 Field Hospital RAMC Volunteers, were assured a seat in a covered stand. Our support for this unit included a visit to their summer camp, which was held at Caister Camp near Chester, where the regular RAMC were assembling before departing to the Gulf. At a Mess Party an RAMC Major approached me.

'You're a member of the SAC, aren't you?' (the SAC being the Specialist Advisory Committee overseeing surgical training).

'Yes,' I replied.

'Do you think my service in the Gulf will be recognised for accreditation?' he asked. He was at that time a Senior Registrar (a sub-consultant grade) seconded to the Nuffield Orthopaedic Hospital in Oxford as part of his training, and yet in a few days he would be the most senior orthopaedic surgeon in the Gulf. I felt sure his rather special service would be recognised for accreditation. The Welcome Home Parade ended with a buffet lunch for the participants in the Guildhall at which Her Majesty the Queen and other members of the Royal Family were present. The most popular was Princess Diana, who clearly made a special effort to meet and captivate as many servicemen as she could.

Another unique event was the service in St Paul's Cathedral in the presence of Her Royal Highness the Princess of Wales to commemorate the part played by the Fire Services during the Blitz which had begun fifty years before, on 7 September 1940. The bombing of London continued for fifty-seven consecutive nights and thereafter intermittently until May the following year. One of the two lessons was read by Miss Anne Shelton, a popular singer during the War, second only to Vera Lynn in the nation's affections. We remembered the 300 London firemen who died and the 3,000 injured before the War in Europe ended.

The Trustees and Directors of the National Maritime Museum mounted an exhibition 'Henry VIII at Greenwich' illustrating his life and times to mark the 500th anniversary of his birth in Greenwich in 1491. Dr David Starkey, an authority on the Tudors who has subsequently written and presented several popular television programmes on the monarchy, acted as the historical adviser. The Worshipful Company of Barbers possesses more royal gifts than any other livery company, in part at least due to the special relationship between the Sovereign and his surgeon and his barber, both of whom held privileged positions in the Royal Household. Dr Starkey wanted to include in the exhibition the Grace Cup designed by Holbein and made by his goldsmith, John Morrell, in 1543, and the surgical instrument case believed to have been presented by the King to his surgeon, Thomas Vicary, Master of the Company no fewer than five times, in return for which Dr Starkey agreed to deliver the Barbers' most prestigious lecture, the Sir Lionel Denny lecture in 1991. In addition, I, as Master of the Barbers, and Pat were invited to a dinner and a private viewing of the exhibition together with representatives of the other organisations lending their treasures. Her Majesty the Queen was represented by her Chaplain!

The Company as a whole were also invited to a private viewing of the exhibition, on what proved to be a glorious sunny evening, travelling from Tower Pier to Greenwich on one of the many pleasure boats on the Thames with the Master of the Company of Watermen and Lightermen at the wheel. The event proved so popular that we were divided into two groups to view the exhibition and I was fortunate to be in Dr Starkey's group and appreciated for the first time the political significance of many of the artefacts. In particular I remember Dr Starkey explaining the significance of the events depicted in the painting of the Field of the Cloth of Gold when Henry was trying to impress on his formidable French and Spanish counterparts the importance of England and its King by an extravagant show of wealth. On the return journey we had a delicious supper on the boat to complete a most enjoyable evening. Dr Starkey subsequently became a liveryman of the Company and has made several memorable presentations to the livery.

The final social event of the year, the Court Ladies Dinner in July, is attended by the Master of the Worshipful Company of Cutlers of Hallamshire and the Deacon of the Incorporated Society of Barbers of Glasgow among the many guests, and both reciprocate the hospitality by inviting the Master and his wife to Sheffield for the Cutlers Feast and to Glasgow the following year. The Master Cutler reserves a carriage to take his many guests from London to Sheffield by train, providing generous refreshment on the way. Just as the train was about to leave the platform at Euston Station an incoming train broke down and blocked the track. After a short delay the Station Master appeared in a top hat and conducted us to a distant platform to another reserved coach for our party. On the way we lost one of our number but eventually the train left for Doncaster rather than Sheffield. When we arrived, a motor coach was waiting to take us to Sheffield with police motorcycle outriders in front and behind blocking the entrances to the motorway and the roundabouts. The coach sped unhindered to our waiting lunch in Sheffield, an impressive performance illustrating the considerable influence of the Master Cutler! The missing member of our party was the Duke of Norfolk who was discovered travelling on his own in a standard compartment without a ticket!

The Cutlers of Hallamshire, needless to say, have a very grand hall with several beautifully panelled reception rooms and staircases leading to the main hall with its marbled pillars along either side and portraits of past luminaries between them. The hall was lit by three large chandeliers suspended from a very nice ceiling, beneath which the silver sparkled. The 400 or so guests included innumerable members of the aristocracy, including His Royal Highness Prince Philip, as well as church and civic dignitaries and Masters of many London livery companies. An equal number of ladies dined separately but were allowed to sit in the gallery to hear the speeches, which did not go down well with Pat. Prince Philip responded to the toast to the guests and the Right Honourable Lord Wakenham, Secretary of State for the Department of Energy, spoke well when he responded to Her Majesty's Ministers.

At the Trades Hall in Glasgow the dinner was delayed when the principal guest, a lawyer, failed to appear. The chef insisted on serving the meal without him and the Deacon asked me if I would respond to the toast on behalf of the guests. I made a few notes on the back of the menu but in the nick of time the lawyer appeared. I was off the hook, or so I thought, but his speech was disappointing and the Deacon asked me to speak after all.

The Barbers are one of the companies with a history dating back to 'the time when memory runneth not', a wonderfully evocative phrase, and are seventeenth in order of precedence. The order of precedence was very important in medieval times as an indication of status and was sometimes quite literally fought over but more often the squabbles between the companies were resolved by the Lord Mayor. The well-known phrase 'to be at sixes and sevens' (a state of confusion) is the result of a dispute between the Merchant Taylors and the Skinners which the Lord Mayor resolved by ruling that they would each take it in turn to be six or seven, with the result that neither company could remember whose turn it was to take precedence over the other. Precedence not infrequently changed as a result of petitions to the Lord Mayor. The present order was established early in the sixteenth century and subsequently new companies followed in numerical order.

The order of precedence is still quite useful. For example, the Master of the Pewterers at No. 16 would always precede me, the Master Barber, at No. 17 in a procession and I in turn would be followed by the Master of the Cutlers. No. 17 is obviously quite high on the list, which frequently meant a seat at the top table when dining with other companies. I had the good fortune to be sitting opposite his Eminence Cardinal Basil Hume, the Archbishop of Westminster, on the inner side of the top table when he was the principal guest at a dinner, not of a livery company but of the Guild of Freemen of the City of London, held in the magnificent setting of the Guildhall. It was not difficult to appreciate why Cardinal Hume was held in so high regard. It was at a time when unity between the Christian churches was being widely discussed and in the course of conversation I asked the Cardinal what he regarded as the main stumbling block to closer ties between the Catholic and Anglican churches. I might have known the answer: 'the ordination of women.' *Was it something I said?*

Most of the ancient companies possessed their own halls but none survived of those existing before the Great Fire of 1666. The Apothecaries Hall built two years after the fire is the only hall from this period and, although attractive in many ways, its dark panelling makes it rather gloomy. Many companies were unable to afford to rebuild their halls after the fire and if they did several fell into disrepair as the importance of the livery companies declined. With renewed interest in the nineteenth century many were rebuilt, only to be destroyed or damaged in the Blitz. As a consequence most of the halls were rebuilt or restored, like Barber-Surgeons Hall, after the war, nearly all of which I visited during my year in office. It is quite impossible to entertain the Master of every livery company so invitations to dinner are usually extended to companies with similar interests or close ranking in order of precedence. The first twelve in order of precedence (The Great Twelve) tend to entertain each other in their very grand halls which are, however, often used by other companies for special events. The Worshipful Company of Chartered Surveyors invited me together with other Masters to their spring dinner in Merchant Taylors Hall, rebuilt after the war with opulent ante-rooms furnished with antique furniture, leading to the richly panelled dining hall with copious gold-leaf decorations and with a high wood-panelled ceiling. The gallery surrounding the hall led to a massive pipe organ used for the singing of Grace. The Loriners, traditionally the makers of bridles, held their livery dinner at the Mansion House where the Upper Warden, Her Royal Highness the Princess Royal, proposed the toast to the Lord Mayor and Corporation. I found myself sitting next to His Honour Judge Argyle, who responded to the toast to the guests. The Shipwrights held their annual banquet at Whitbread's Brewery in Chiswell Street, sadly no longer used for brewing. Much of the old equipment is on show, particularly the Porter Tun room where, under a huge timber roof, the biggest of its kind in Europe, slate vessels held over one and a half million pints of porter.

Although the Worshipful Company of Constructors are No. 99, the Barbers are on their guest list and the Masters Dinner was held in the crypt of the Guildhall, another marvellous setting, a few yards from the site of the Roman Amphitheatre. The Inn Holders have a lovely old panelled hall with silver candle sconces and wooden chandeliers circa 1670, and a reception room of similar age, which blends well with a new extension. The Company of Watermen and Lightermen have probably the smallest hall, built in 1780, a positive delight with a beautiful Georgian ceiling. The Leatherworkers, in contrast, have a very grand Victorian hall, the dining room being a perfect cube with a domed ceiling shaped like a cushion, with damask wall coverings above the wood panelling. The Armourers and Brasiers have an early Victorian hall, the walls decorated with a representative collection of armour and weapons which survived the Great Fire and the Blitz. The Cutlers, with whom the Barbers have a long-standing association, have a terracotta brick Victorian building with a panelled hall and a hammer beam roof, with carved elephant heads at the end of each 'hammer', from which hang wrought-iron chandeliers. Unsurprisingly they also have a very splendid and enormous carving set.

The Ironmongers, although among the Great Twelve, and the Barbers are near neighbours and their hall, built in the 1920s, was the only steel-frame building in that part of the city, which was completely devastated on 30 December 1940. The photographs of the time show the hall standing in the midst of desolation, which is just as well because some of the Barbers' treasures were stored in its vaults. The remaining halls are mainly modern but tasteful, such as the Founders with the dining hall half above and half below ground with porthole windows overlooking the churchyard of Bart's the Great. The Glaziers and the Scientific Instrument Makers share a converted warehouse on the banks of the Thames, which flows past the windows at eye level, while the Fanmakers converted the Victorian Parish Hall and Schoolroom of St Botoph's, Bishopsgate for their hall. They are one of the many Companies to attract the modern equivalent of their ancient craft, the makers of industrial fans and jet engines. Similarly, the Fletchers (arrow makers) attract their modern equivalent, the Rocket Scientists and Engineers. The Master Mariners, however, stay true to their calling on the *Wellington* moored on the Victoria Embankment, albeit without an engine.

Because it is impossible to entertain representatives of all the livery companies at the court dinners at Barber-Surgeons Hall, a Master and Clerks lunch was introduced in 1991, later to become a dinner. The Cannon Street rail crash occurred on the morning of the first lunch and I had hoped during the course of the morning to find time to make a few notes for the speech I was expected to make, but the casualties clearly took precedence and, instead, my spontaneous speech warned my fellow Masters that unless they brought political pressure to bear by whatever means at their disposal, they and the City would soon be without its only hospital, and without the means of dealing with future disasters. The words were prophetic. *Was it something I said?*

There is a common thread which runs through every livery dinner in the city: the toasts to the Queen and the Royal Family and to the Lord Mayor and Corporation and Sheriffs; the singing of Grace from the *Laudi Spirituali AD 1545*; and the Ceremony of the Loving Cup, a custom that is said to have originated in the precaution to keep the right or dagger hand employed so that the person who drinks may be assured of no treachery such as that practised by Elfreda on the unsuspecting King Edward the Martyr who was slain whilst drinking at Corfe Castle. The cup, filled with 'sack', is passed round the table and as each guest drinks from the cup he is protected by the guest standing on either side of him.

Barber-Surgeons Hall is often used by other livery companies and organisations and the Master, as a matter of courtesy, is invited to attend. In September 1990 shortly after I took office, the Court of Aldermen entertained a large number of dignitaries in the Hall and I found myself sitting alongside Michael Heseltine at one of the tables. The forthcoming General Election and the issues that influenced voters inevitably came up in conversation. He believed that the pound in the pocket was all the voters really cared about. 'What about the Health Service?' I said.

'What's wrong with the Health Service?' he replied. And so I mentioned some of the problems.

'Well, none of my constituents complain to me,' he said.

'Perhaps that's because most of your constituents in Newbury have private health insurance,' I replied. *Was it something I said?*

The Master of a city livery company enjoys many privileges and one of the more surprising is the invitation to lunch with Her Majesty's Judges at the Old Bailey, at the invitation of the Sheriffs who are responsible for providing facilities for them. Perhaps more surprising is the fact that the Judges wore their wigs throughout the meal. The invitation extends to listening to one of the cases after lunch, which unsurprisingly was tedious and did nothing to enhance my opinion of the legal process.

At a glance there seems little to link the City livery companies with the world-renowned Iron Bridge Gorge Museum, but the Industrial Revolution took place in Britain in part because of the pre-existing abundance of skills and the genius and invention nurtured by the guilds and livery companies, and the focal point of national enterprise was the City of London. The livery companies support the museum in many ways and each year their representatives are invited to the Livery Company Day, marking the enterprise and skill of our forbears. I was accompanied by Pat and though it was a very busy weekend for us because of the need to be in Edinburgh for the presentation of the Barbers 'Trophy' at the summer camp of 257 Field Hospital, the Territorial Army Unit attached to the Barbers Company, on the Sunday, and then to be in Liverpool by Sunday evening ready to examine in the Liverpool Qualifying Examination the next morning, it was well worth the rush.

With the changing social and industrial scene in the seventeenth and eighteenth centuries, the livery companies lost their powers and went into decline. Towards the end of the nineteenth century there was a renaissance, with many old companies renewing contact with their former trades and new companies being formed, a process which continues to this day; there are now over one hundred, though only thirty-nine have their own halls.

The Barbers consolidated their association with surgery in 1919 by establishing a joint annual lecture, the Vicary Lecture, with the Royal College of Surgeons. Since 1951 the Court of the Barbers and the Council of the College have dined together after the lecture, an occasion which I particularly enjoy, having a foot in both camps. In 1998, I had the privilege of delivering the Vicary Lecture myself, entitled 'The Court of Examiners', recounting the history of a body of examiners with an unbroken history spanning six centuries. To commemorate the event I presented jointly to the Barbers and Surgeons a silver table decoration to be placed in front of the Master or the President at the dinner each year. The Opinicus, the mythical emblem of the Barbers, and the Eagle, the emblem of the College, between them hold a shield with the arms of the Barbers on one side and of the College on the other, symbolic of their renewed and flourishing collaboration and friendship, both of which I have so much enjoyed.

Table decoration presented jointly to the Barbers and the College on the occasion of my Vicary Lecture, 1997 (Photo Grant Macdonald)

Chapter 11

The British Orthopaedic Association

The British Orthopaedic Association was founded in 1917 with the object of 'the advancement for the public benefit of the science and art and practice of orthopaedic surgery, with the aim of bringing relief to patients of all ages suffering from the effects of injury or disorders of the musculoskeletal system.' The membership embraces almost all practising orthopaedic surgeons in the British Isles including those in training, and is the largest of the many similar surgical specialist associations. It pursues its objectives by organising and conducting regular scientific meetings, sometimes in association with similar organisations abroad, at which members contribute scientific papers, by instructional courses, and by promoting research. It has a symbiotic relationship with the independent *Journal of Bone and Joint Surgery* which publishes original contributions from around the world and is itself unique in its relationship with the American journal of the same name.

I became an associate member of the BOA when I began orthopaedic training as an SHO at the RNOH and like all associates I was encouraged by my teachers to read the *Journal* and to undertake original work with a view to presentation at BOA meetings and to publication in the *Journal*. Over the next thirty years I published more than fifty papers, sometimes by invitation and usually in collaboration with members of the junior staff, mostly in the *Journal of Bone and Joint Surgery*, and I eventually became a member of the Editorial Board. In addition to the published articles on low back pain, joint replacement, fracture repair, arthritis and surgical training, I was invited to contribute chapters on similar topics to fourteen books, over a similar period.

A light-hearted contribution to the Christmas edition of *The Lancet* in 1964 entitled 'Addiction to Plaster?' attracted much unwanted attention from the Press. A slightly built middle-aged woman was admitted to hospital with acute abdominal pain and the general surgeon found it impossible to examine her abdomen because her trunk was encased in a plaster of Paris cast extending from her upper chest to her pelvis. He was more than a little surprised to find that it had been put on in 1939 and had remained unchanged for twenty-five years! She had failed to keep a follow-up appointment and with the administrative confusion at the beginning of the Second World War she had never returned, thinking she would be severely reprimanded for non-attendance. She had managed to keep her trunk clean and free from unpleasant odours by tipping talcum powder down into the cast and then passing a cylindrical garment made from silk over her head and then into the gap between the plaster and the skin and pulling it out at the bottom – rather like cleaning the barrel of a rifle. When the cast was removed her muscles were grossly wasted and she was unable to stand. Before she could leave hospital another cast had to be applied. Sadly I do not know the eventual outcome.

Perhaps the most prestigious of all awards made by the British Orthopaedic Association, second only to the Robert Jones prize and gold medal, is an ABC Travelling Fellowship to North America. Four young British orthopaedic surgeons are selected on alternate years, to be joined by one from Australia, New Zealand or South Africa in rotation, to visit orthopaedic centres in the United States and Canada, from whence a similar group visit the UK in the intervening years. I flew back for the interview from Switzerland, where I, by invitation, was presenting my research on bone healing. As the most junior of those on the short list, I was not unduly surprised when I was not selected, and I was still eligible to apply again in the future. When that time arrived I was a consultant but between the application and the interview Jenny had become ill and I probably should have withdrawn my application. Charles Manning was secretary of the BOA at the time and had probably made the committee aware of the situation. Following the interview, Roland Barnes, the BOA President, took me to one side to tell me, quite rightly, that it would have been inappropriate for me to visit North America at this time, but that I would still be in a position to apply two years later. By then, of course, the Selection Committee had changed and I was not selected, to my great disappointment. John Dickson a member of the Committee wrote:

> My dear Lettin
>
> I had hoped to be able to write to you with congratulations. The majority of votes declared otherwise. It had not occurred to me, even before the privilege of hearing you in person, that this could have come about. I realize that for one of your evident ability and achievement (B.Sc. Hons, MS, Robert Jones Prize & Medal, consultant to Bart's and RNOH) this must seem an incredible decision. It was not one which my vote supported, nor that of a considerable number.
>
> It may be presumptuous for a failed MS from the 'bush' to express opinions, but the fates have placed me on the Executive! I am reminded of the words of my old chief, Professor Kirk – 'It is not given to man to command success, but to deserve it.' Perhaps you have deserved so well that Beelzebub had to step in. There are very many, nevertheless, who see in your career what we should have been proud to have achieved, and who

confidently look forward to success on a wider stage than was presented to you this time.

Yours very sincerely,
John Dickson

Was it something I said?

I played little part in the affairs of the BOA, apart from attending and presenting papers at the meetings until I became a member of the Education Committee on which I served for eight years, five as secretary (1982 to 1987). In that role I was responsible for organising the Annual Instructional Course, which took place over the first weekend in January each year (usually, it seemed, on my birthday) at the City University, and later at Bart's. It soon became apparent that the seniority and experience of those attending was extremely wide and so I introduced almost a double programme to cater for the diversity of the participants' experience. It is noteworthy that all the contributors gave up their weekends without remuneration, accommodated in the vacant student living accommodation! In 1987, I was elected to the Council of BOA, having already been elected to the Council of the Royal College of Surgeons three years earlier. There were obvious tensions between the two organisations and I naively thought that my membership of the governing bodies of both might prove advantageous, but sadly this was not so. The BOA regarded me as a 'College man' and the College as a 'BOA man'. The members of the BOA and its Council were, as the name implies, 'British', including members from Scotland and Ireland, whereas 'the College' was English and the more prominent role of the English college in surgical affairs was often resented by Fellows of the Edinburgh and Glasgow colleges. Furthermore, there was a view among orthopaedic surgeons generally that the Colleges were dominated by general surgeons who had little regard for orthopaedic interests, prompting a move to form a breakaway Orthopaedic College. There was, after all, the Royal College of Obstetricians and Gynaecologists and the number of consultants in that specialty was approximately equal to the number of consultant orthopaedic surgeons, and the ophthalmic surgeons had recently left the College of Surgeons to form their own small College of Ophthalmologists.

The BOA had begun fundraising with a view eventually to purchasing premises during the presidency of Robert Duthie, a Scot! I was firmly opposed to such a course of action, which was attributed to my College loyalties, making the BOA Council meetings a little uncomfortable at times, but in reality I believed that surgical influence in 'the corridors of power' would inevitably be reduced if surgery became fragmented. A common surgical voice was essential and greater orthopaedic influence in the College could be best achieved by increasing orthopaedic representation at the College Council Elections.

The elections were conducted annually to replace retiring members on a first-past-the-post basis. Electioneering was strictly forbidden, although I did achieve a moderate change by persuading the college Council to allow the candidates to submit a short election address of no more than one hundred words with the voting papers. The Fellows usually voted for candidates in their own specialty who worked locally, often from their own medical schools. A large number of general surgeons usually sought election, thus splitting the general surgical vote. By persuading orthopaedic surgeons carefully to assess their prospects before seeking election and thereby limiting the number putting their names forward, there was a greater chance of increasing orthopaedic representation.

Two years after completing my term on the BOA Council I was elected Vice-President Elect, leading automatically to the Vice-Presidency the following year and then the Presidency. My views on a separate college were well known, and my election clearly indicated that the majority of orthopaedic surgeons held a similar view. However, there remained a perception that orthopaedic surgeons elected to the College Council were not representing their orthopaedic colleagues but surgeons in general, in spite of the fact that the vast majority of their votes must have come from their orthopaedic colleagues. The issue was eventually resolved by the College Council inviting each of the Specialist Associations to appoint a representative to sit on the Council as a non-voting Invited Member for a period of two years, and later by the creation of the 'Surgical Senate' with representatives of both the four Colleges and the Specialist Associations, on which I sat first as a BOA and subsequently as a College representative. The enthusiasm for a separate orthopaedic college waned but the fundraising continued through the highly successful Wishbone Trust, which organised the well-known sponsored 'Hip Walks', later to include patients with artificial knees as well as hip replacements. The Trust was recently renamed the British Orthopaedic Foundation, which is entirely devoted to funding orthopaedic research.

The tenure of the BOA Presidency is limited to one year, allowing a larger number of Fellows to achieve high office, but at the same time limiting the President's ability to significantly influence policy in so short a time. The President is therefore effectively elected proleptically two years in advance. Professor George Bentley and Mr Michael Freeman, President and Vice-President respectively, were already concerned when I joined them by the widely held view that there was an overprovision of acute medical services in Inner London. In the course of the next year we analysed the workload and resources available to the orthopaedic teams working in Inner London, using the official data collected by the Department of Health, and compared it with data from a similar number of similarly manned teams, selected at random, from the provinces. We found that although the London teams had fewer beds at their disposal they were used more effectively but even so waiting lists were longer, suggesting that facilities were already inadequate to meet the existing need. This was largely due to the fact that 32 per cent of patients treated in Inner London hospitals and 50 per cent on the waiting lists came from suburban London and even farther afield. The report was sent to the Secretary of State for Health, Mrs Virginia Bottomley, in 1992 but the hospital closures continued, not only in London but elsewhere, with the consequences that are only too apparent today.

The role of chiropodists in the surgical treatment of disorders of the foot had been a recurring issue throughout my membership of the BOA Council and continued to be so subsequently. Chiropodists traditionally limited their operative practice to the skin and nails of the foot but when the restrictions on the administration of local anaesthetic by non-medically qualified practitioners were lifted it opened the way for them to operate on the deeper structures, including the bones and the joints. The prescription of powerful analgesics such as morphine, and of antibiotics, however, remained limited to medical practitioners and the chiropodists (increasingly calling themselves podiatrists) were dependent on the patient's general practitioners to prescribe such drugs when required. This sometimes caused resentment on both sides, particularly when there were complications, such as wound infections.

On the initiative of Robin Ling, the BOA President in 1987, a joint BOA/BMA/College Committee was established on which I represented the College, and at an informal dinner hosted by the BOA it became clear that the podiatrists were seeking the support of the surgeons, in the hope not only of seeking a change in the prescribing regulations but also in persuading the private health care insurers to pay their fees. Nothing came of the meeting but the issue continued to rumble on. At a time when non-medical practitioners generally claimed to take a 'holistic' approach to their patients, in reality their expertise was limited to a small region of the body and only medical practitioners were trained to treat the body as a whole. If the trend continued, manicurists might be doing hand surgery! Another joint committee and its subsequent report in 1995 failed to resolve the issue.

Michael Freeman had done his best to put podiatry to bed during his presidency but he had also taken the initiative in convening a Manpower Committee, which he suggested that I should chair because he appreciated that its deliberations and ultimately its report on consultant staffing requirements for an 'Orthopaedic Service in the NHS' would continue into my presidency. The prediction of future NHS manpower requirements had always proved to be difficult, bearing in mind that fifteen to twenty years elapsed between entry to medical school and assuming independent general or hospital practice. Over the years, attempts to predict future requirements had led to both increases and decreases in medical school entry. At least a quarter of my own medical school entry who qualified are known to have emigrated early in their professional careers for lack of prospects in the United Kingdom. The imbalance between those completing surgical training and the consultant posts available to them was even greater, with many so-called junior doctors, some in their late forties, still seeking permanent consultant appointments.

The belief that patient care should not be left to surgeons in training, the reduction in junior doctors' hours of work and the duration of surgical training with the emphasis on more formal education and training, as well as the increasing demands for orthopaedic treatment, made it imperative that some estimate of future manpower requirements be made in the interests of future patient care. The number of outpatient consultations and the number of surgical operations carried out each year were easily quantifiable using Department of Health statistics, confirmed by the BOA's own figures, leading to the conclusion that every consultant in post would have to work twice the number of contracted sessions if surgeons in training made no contribution to service work. The NHS is virtually a monopoly employer and if higher surgical training were to be reduced to a total of six years and a consultant is in post for thirty years, then in order to achieve a balance between the number of trainees and the number of consultants there needs to be five times as many consultants as there are trainees. This ratio is constant no matter how many trainees or consultants are in post and will only change if the length of training changes or consultants spend more or less time in post. Therefore if trainees carried out the same number of outpatient consultations and operations as consultants, they would still meet only one-fifth of the service demand. If it is assumed that a trainee makes no contribution to service needs at the beginning of training but is capable of taking full consultant responsibility at the end, over the course of training it is reasonable to assume that one trainee is equivalent to half a consultant, but trainees will still fulfil no more than 10 per cent of service needs, and for the purpose of calculating consultant numbers for a consultant-based service then their contribution can be ignored.

This was the essence of the report and doubling the consultant establishment took no account of the current unmet needs or of future developments involving even more time-consuming and complex operative treatment.

10 February 1995
AWFL/BAS
Mrs Virginia Bottomley
Secretary of State for Health
Department of Health
79 Whitehall
London
SW1A 2NS
Dear Mrs Bottomley
I enclose a copy of the report on 'Consultant Staffing for an Orthopaedic Service in the National Health Service' which was published by the BOA a few days ago. It has received a certain amount of publicity on television, radio and in the newspapers of which you may be aware and perhaps it would have been more courteous if I had sent you a copy earlier.

I would like to emphasise that the report is meant to be constructive and is not intended as a criticism of the changes in surgical training or reduction in junior doctors' hours proposed by the Calman Working Party.

The BOA would be very happy to co-operate in facilitating these changes.
Yours sincerely
A W F Lettin MS FRCS
Chairman of Working Party
Past President BOA

Ten years on, shorter training is about to be implemented, not without misgivings among the senior members of the profession, and although there has been a considerable increase in the number of consultant orthopaedic surgeons appointed there is still a need for more, both to achieve a balance and to provide patient care, but the ratio must not be overlooked if the pitfalls of the past are to be avoided in the future.

Injury to the musculoskeletal system is frequently the result of sporting activities. The financial consequences for the NHS, industry and the individual are considerable, and badly treated injuries may lead to irrecoverable loss of athletic performance. The elite athlete, usually, but not always, has access to informed advice but the far more numerous recreational athletes are usually seen over a weekend by a very junior doctor in an overworked A&E Department and then referred to an orthopaedic clinic, with an appointment perhaps several weeks later. The Sports Council, aware of this situation and of the many organisations with an interest in sports injuries whose members varied considerably in their degree of knowledge and expertise, convened in 1990 a meeting in London of all interested parties. The College President, Sir Terence English, asked me to represent the College.

It was a very large gathering at which I recognised several of the participants, particularly Mrs Mary Glen-Haig (later Dame Mary, an international fencer and member of the International Olympic Committee) and, despite their diverse interests, all agreed that there was a need for a co-ordinated approach to the increasing interest in sports medicine and that a Working Party should take the matter forward. Mary Glen-Haig proposed that I should be a member and the proposal was accepted. I had a long-standing interest in sports injuries, having personally suffered a serious knee injury whilst playing soccer as a student. My Monday morning fracture clinic at Bart's became a fracture and injury clinic, attended by among others the students and City workers from the suburbs injured as a result of their weekend pursuits. I also had some experience of treating professional footballers and cricketers as a result of a chance meeting, at a symposium on sports injuries at the Royal Society of Medicine, with Dr Dewi Griffith, a general practitioner and medical officer of Leyton Orient Football Club.

'The Orient' were a lowly professional team in the then third division of the Football League and I mentioned to Dr Griffith that my father had taken me to watch them play when I was seven or eight years old, when they were known as Clapton Orient. My only recollection of the match were cries of 'milk baby' whenever the goalkeeper touched the ball. Apparently he had recently been convicted of stealing a bottle of milk from a doorstep! During the war, some of my school friends and I regularly watched the games from behind the goal on Saturday afternoons, school matches having taken place in the mornings. Most of the professional footballers were in the Services, often as physical training instructors, and the teams were made up from any serviceman who happened to be free and within easy travelling distance of the ground, providing that they returned to their units in time for 8 a.m. parade the following morning.

After the war, the competition for promotion was restored and the Orient were promoted to the second division and, for one season only, to the first division and I remember a visit from Liverpool, the first time I had ever seen fighting at a football match! The maximum wage was only £10 a week but the Orient had to sell their better players to remain financially viable. The FA Cup generated great excitement because there was always hope of defeating one of the more prosperous and glamorous teams from the higher divisions, and many years later when I was the Club's Honorary Surgeon they reached the semi-final, only to lose to Arsenal. The atmosphere in the dressing room after the game was very subdued. My exhortation to 'cheer up, it's only a game, lads' was not well received. *Was it something I said?*

My visits to the Orient as a spectator came to an end when I left school but Dewi Griffith invited me to renew my association and arranged for me to be a guest at the next home match, which I remember was against Reading. It was rather more comfortable watching the game from the

Directors' Box than it had been standing in the rain behind the goal. I was invited to become the Honorary Club Consultant Surgeon and as I was then not unduly busy in my recently appointed consultant post, I could not resist the opportunity of returning to my roots. There was a reserved car parking space for me outside the ground and who should be the police officer in charge of parking but Ron Colman, a useful left back with whom I had played in the school team many years before. More was to come. A season ticket holder in a seat in the stand adjoining the Directors' Box was Jackie Groom, an excellent all-round athlete who had represented Essex schools at football and cricket and, although three or four years my junior, was good enough to play in the first eleven when I was captain. Now a local bank manager, a severe knee injury had brought his playing days to an end. Perhaps even more surprising, the groundsman was Freddie Wellington whom I had not seen since I left Cannhall Road School in 1942!

In those days there were no substitutes so injured players were encouraged to play on if possible. The trainer (usually a former Pro) would run onto the field with a bucket of cold water and a sponge, which usually had a miraculous effect. If players were brought off I would go to see them in the Treatment Room and on a few occasions, when there were serious injuries, I would arrange their admission to Bart's. There was no compulsory private insurance for them in those days and the students enjoyed seeing even minor celebrities in the wards.

The Orient were fortunate in having a qualified physiotherapist, a member of the Chartered Society, which was unusual in those days. Charlie Simpson was very experienced and he and Dr Griffith were a good team. Like many of the club physios he ran a private clinic for all types of sports injuries and suggested the patients consult me, either privately or at the hospital, if the problem required orthopaedic care. In the summer Charlie looked after the Essex County Cricketers, in the days when Essex were becoming a formidable force in the County Championships under the captaincy of 'Tonker' Taylor and subsequently Keith Fletcher, when Graham Gooch (a Leytonstone boy) was a great prospect for the future. I would see them in my Monday morning Fracture and Injury Clinic at Bart's. Charlie moved to Crystal Palace but continued to refer patients to see me and my opinion was sometimes sought from some of the bigger clubs. At around that time I also acted as consultant surgeon to the English netball team.

My sons Nicholas and Jonathan enjoyed accompanying me to the matches on Saturday afternoons and particularly meeting the players after the games, as well as some of the well-known personalities who often accompanied visiting teams as managers or supporters. Alf Ramsey and

Bobby Robson (both later Knighted) and Bill Nicholson come to mind. I particularly remember Bill commenting on a young, athletic very graceful black player whose skills he admired but, in his own words, he wondered about the courage of the increasing number of young coloured players. His concerns never materialized. Laurie Cunningham was, I believe, the first black player to play for England. Jimmy Hill, by then a TV commentator, Eric Morecambe director of Luton Town, and Richard Attenborough, a regular Chelsea supporter, among others, were all entertained in the hospitality suite at one time or another.

In 1991 the Sports Council accepted the Working Group's recommendation that a United Kingdom Sports Medicine Institute should be established to promote sports medicine through education, research and accredited sports medicine and injury clinics, with a committee of management with representatives from the various interested organisations. I was nominated by the Joint Meeting of Surgical Colleges to represent the interests of the Surgical Colleges. It was my good fortune that the Institute would be located in the premises occupied by the London Sports Medicine Institute which it would replace in St Bartholomew's Hospital Medical College, holding its meetings in the evening!

The new organisation became the National Sports Medicine Institute (NSMI) and Ossie Wheatley, a former Cambridge University and Glamorgan Cricket Captain and a member of the Sports Council, was appointed chairman. The prevention of sports-related injuries was regarded as being as important as their treatment. There was a frequent perception that outstanding performance could be achieved by intensive training, but in reality innate ability is a prerequisite, and over-strenuous training often results in injury, particularly repetitive strain injuries (RSI). The education of physiotherapists, trainers, and the athletes themselves would therefore form a large part of the Institute activities, under the direction of one part-time director, with the management of injuries under the direction of another.

There was no recognised sports medicine career structure and although two part-time directors, each retaining a part-time post in the NHS were envisaged, in the event a full-time director, Greg McClatchy, a vascular surgeon and former weightlifter, was appointed. Treatment, and more particularly treatment centres of which several had been established in Scotland, took pride of place. They were usually held in the evenings and staffed by interested GPs and physios and in my view were not the way forward. I believed that treatment should be available in the NHS Clinics and this could be achieved by changing the existing Fracture Clinics, held in every general hospital, to Fracture & Injury Clinics and this I had hoped to promote during my presidency of the BOA, but unfortunately other matters took priority, such as examinations and manpower. However, with Ossie Wheatley and Greg McClatchy, I devised a two-tier examination structure, a basic Diploma in Sports Medicine mainly for GPs, and a second more advanced Diploma as an optional extra for specialists in allied fields. The proposals were put to the newly created Conference of Royal Colleges (now Academy) and were taken forward I believe by the Royal College of Surgeons of Edinburgh.

It was clear that by the time of my presidency of the BOA, orthopaedic surgery was in danger of becoming fragmented into a number of sub-specialties, a development which had already occurred in general surgery. Each sub-specialty had its own association, its own meetings, and sometimes produced its own journal and both the scientific meetings and the journals attracted the best contributions in the field, to the detriment of the BOA meetings and the *Journal of Bone and Joint Surgery*.

The Queen Elizabeth Conference Centre in Westminster had been booked for a combined meeting with the Scandinavian Orthopaedic Association in the spring of 1994. By chance I met the Swedish secretary in San Francisco, at a meeting on orthopaedic education and training, who informed me that the Scandinavians had decided that there was no place for such a meeting since the formation of the European Federation of Orthopaedics and Traumatology (EFORT) would hold its first meeting in Paris in 1993, at which incidentally I was the BOA representative. The numerous conference rooms at the Queen Elizabeth Centre were far in excess of the requirements of the BOA alone and it was too late to cancel the booking and, at the suggestion of David Dandy and with the support of the BOA Council, one day of the meeting was devoted to the specialist societies, who organised their own programmes and permitted non-members to attend their presentations. It was considered a great success, especially by the juniors, and the specialist societies day has been a feature of BOA Conferences since. To consolidate the initiative a secretarial assistant was provided for the societies in the BOA offices and so far the BOA has remained an all-embracing organisation representing the various branches of orthopaedics.

On the flight to San Francisco for that meeting on education and training, the journey all but over, came the announcement that every doctor, or at least most doctors, fear. 'Is there a doctor on board?' I sat tight in the hope that there was an enthusiastic junior somewhere in the economy class. No such luck. After a suitable interval, following the second call, I admitted to the steward that I was medically qualified, at the same time pointing out that I was in fact a surgeon. 'That's better than being a doctor, isn't it?'

'Well, it might be if the passenger's got a broken leg,' I replied.

'Actually, a large German lady has collapsed in the toilets at the rear of the aircraft. We've got her out and she's on the floor.'

I knelt beside her; she was breathing and had a steady pulse. A companion sitting nearby spoke a little English and I asked if she was taking any medication or suffered from any particular disorders. 'I think she has heartache' came the reply. That's not a word we would normally use and I thought her companion had said 'headache'. Not a common reason to lose consciousness. Now, what would a proper doctor do in these circumstances, I asked myself, as all eyes in the seats alongside the gangway focused on me. I asked for the first-aid kit in which there was a booklet intended no doubt to aid both qualified and unqualified practitioners faced with such an emergency. The possible conditions were listed in alphabetical order and on reaching asthma I decided there was no time to go through the whole book. Besides, I detected that the cabin crew and nearby passengers were beginning to lose confidence in me. Ah, I'll take her blood pressure. That's what a proper doctor would do, and proceeded to inflate the cuff and listen for the return of the pulse to the elbow with a stethoscope.

'What is it, doc?' enquired the steward.

'There's too much noise. I can't hear.'

'Do you want me to ask the captain to switch the engines off?'

At that moment I knew that he had completely lost confidence in me. By now the patient had regained consciousness but every time we tried to sit her up she passed out. We were now on our descent into San Francisco and the steward pointed out that international regulations required everyone to be strapped into a seat for landing but our fat lady passed out whenever we tried to sit her up and so I thought it best to keep her flat.

'What about the regulations, doc?'

'I am sure the captain has discretion to overrule them in an emergency,' I said.

Soon the message came back. 'The captain says it is all right for her to stay on the floor providing you stay with her.'

I discovered just how uncomfortable it can be, landing in a Jumbo Jet while sitting on the floor. I was relieved when the paramedics took over immediately we landed and I made my way back to my seat but by then the cabin crew had gathered my belongings together and, with a bottle of champagne, ushered me through the door which had just opened. My celebrity continued through immigration and customs where 'the doctor' was ushered through in record time. A few days later, the meeting over, I checked in at the airport.

'Would you mind stepping aside for a few moments?' enquired the girl at the desk when I handed in my ticket. A rather more senior young lady then appeared and offered me the opportunity to travel home first class, an offer not to be missed. The roast beef carved by the steward, and the Château Lynch Bage to accompany it, seemed more than adequate recompense for my well-intentioned if ineffectual efforts. But that was not all. A week or two later a very nice thank you letter and a travel voucher for £100 arrived through the post from British Airways.

A few weeks later another flight to America was ready to take off and again a request was made for a doctor to come forward. Emboldened by my previous experience I was not quite so reticent and offered my services. A diabetic patient on insulin had forgotten his self-administered supplies and the syringes brought to the aircraft by a nurse from the airport medical centre were different and he was reluctant to use them. Would I be prepared to give him the injection at the appropriate time during the flight? We were in danger of losing our slot and the captain and the passengers were becoming irritated by the delay, so I agreed. When the time came I appreciated the patient's dilemma. His syringes were pre-loaded and although he knew the dose he was reluctant to draw up the insulin from the phial provided. After I had administered the insulin in the galley the steward thanked me but there was no mention of a possible upgrade. 'Is the aircraft full?' I enquired.

'The only empty seats are in economy,' he replied.

The Orthopaedic Associations of the English-speaking world (Australia, New Zealand, Canada, South Africa, United States and Great Britain) are perhaps unique in having a common journal and also an almost identical presidential badge of office. During the year in office the Presidents of the Associations and their partners meet at the annual congresses of each of the constituent associations. A veritable merry-go-round. Besides the strictly educational value of these meetings, the exchange of ideas extends much further. The problems of providing comprehensive health care are not unique to this country and the alternatives can be witnessed first-hand. The privilege of attending and representing one's fellow countrymen at these meetings cannot be overstated. The meeting of the American Academy in the spring of each year attracts so many participants and their partners that there are only three or four cities in North America capable of accommodating it. David Adams, the efficient BOA chief executive, booked accommodation for us at the Holiday Inn but neither he nor I realised that there were several Holiday Inn hotels in New Orleans and we were booked into one about thirty miles from the city centre at what seemed to be the confluence of several motorways and railway lines. Furthermore, our room adjacent to the lift shaft was damp and that characteristic smell associated with long disused buildings filled the air. We informed the receptionist that we would not be staying but she in turn informed us that there were no empty rooms in the whole of New Orleans and so there was no alternative but to spend the night there. The next morning our first stop was the Accommodation Bureau at the conference centre when it transpired that quite incredibly the total number of delegates and accompanying persons was almost thirty thousand and there were indeed no hotel rooms available. Not all delegates register for the whole meeting, however, and we added our names to the waiting list for a room when available.

The health care industry in general and the manufacturers of joint implants in particular mount an enormous trade exhibition at large international meetings and we soon met Jonathan who, after leaving university, worked first for a multi-national drug company and now held quite a senior position with the orthopaedic division of Johnson & Johnson. This company alone had booked 150 rooms for its representatives from around the world. Jonathan suggested that we should have his room; he would share a room with one of his colleagues from the UK, an offer we readily accepted and a small return on our previous investment in his education! Next day a room became available at a beautiful old hotel in the French Quarter, which greatly facilitated our exploration of New Orleans and its many historical and musical attractions, with the memory of its favourite son Louis Armstrong never far away.

At every large conference the scientific presentations are grouped together to accommodate the many and varied interests of the delegates, the different topics presented simultaneously in different lecture theatres. There is obviously a need to select the papers relating to one's own special interests but there is no doubt that the most enjoyable feature of all is meeting old friends. The meeting in New Orleans was a memorable occasion. Besides the official social programme, Pat and I visited Preservation Hall, where jazz musicians join each other every evening for impromptu sessions, something not to be missed. In fact there are small groups of youngsters playing on almost every street corner, with even younger children tap dancing to the sound of authentic New Orleans jazz.

In contrast to the American Academy, the membership of the American Orthopaedic Association is by invitation only and as a consequence the meetings are much smaller. In 1994 it was held in Sun Valley, Idaho, originally built as a ski resort by the American railway magnate and ambassador, Averell Harriman in the 1930s. He was a very keen skier and resented travelling to Europe each year to pursue his hobby and so he had a ski resort built at Sun Valley in the style of an Alpine Village. For good measure he had a branch line constructed to link the resort to the main railway network, and its popularity with the pre-war Hollywood stars was assured. It was the location for a Hollywood musical called *Sun Valley Serenade* featuring Sonja Henie, a pretty blonde Norwegian Olympic Gold Medal ice skater. It was now an all year round conference centre and holiday complex and was instantly recognisable from my memory of the film, particularly the ice rink on which Sonja Henie performed. My recollections of the film seen on one of my many visits to the cinema during my schooldays were confirmed on the evening of our arrival when the film was shown in the resort cinema, with free soda and popcorn to complete the nostalgia for the Americans.

Harlan Amstutz had been President of the AOA the previous year. I have mentioned previously that he and his wife Patti and their young family had spent a year in London when he was working at the RNOH at the time I was a registrar. We became friends and kept in touch, and I had visited him in Los Angeles in the past. He suggested we should fly to Los Angeles and spend a day or two with them and then we would all travel by car to Sun Valley. We certainly did not realise that Sun Valley was 1,500 miles from LA! Our first stop was the Amstutz cabin in the ski resort of Mammoth Lakes. The next day we travelled north passing through Carson City, Reno, Nevada, and Lassen Volcanic National Park, stopping briefly to admire the scenery at Lake Helen, frozen even in June. The second night we spent in a motel in the shadow of Mount Shaster (14,000 feet) before moving on through Oregon to Sun Valley where we shared a log cabin with Harlan and Patti for the duration of the meeting, our journey marred only by the Highway Patrol, which apprehended Harlan for speeding!

The Canadian Orthopaedic Association meeting followed almost immediately in Winnipeg, a modern city where the Hudson Bay Fur Trading Post and an even earlier native Indian settlement had flourished at the centre of the incredibly flat prairie. We were fortunate to be able to return home on board the *Queen Elizabeth II*, which was making a rare transatlantic crossing from New York to Southampton. The view of the city as we made our way along the Hudson River at dusk was breathtaking. At the Captain's Cocktail Party the following evening I was recognised by one of the two medical officers, Mike Beeny, who had been a medical student at Bart's. This fortuitous meeting opened many doors, including visits to the well-equipped operating theatre and the bridge, and not least to the various cocktail parties which added to the pleasure of a memorable voyage.

The South African Orthopaedic Association met in Pretoria in 1994 and we were able to spend a few days exploring Cape Town and the beautiful wine-growing country. By another coincidence our guide happened to be a cousin of Sir Terence English, a former College President. To take the Blue Train from Cape Town to Johannesburg is to make one of the world's finest train journeys. The thousand-mile journey in the well-appointed train with more staff than passengers passes through the beautiful wine-growing valley of the Western Cape, with a spectacular mountain backdrop. The line then enters the Great Karoo Desert with a stop at the attractive little town of Matjiesfontein, which was originally built as a holiday resort 3,000 feet above sea level. The Lord Milner Hotel was the headquarters of the British Army in the Boer War and the little post office next door, from which despatches were telegraphed to the outside world, remains unchanged, like most of the town. The Victorian villas with wrought-iron railings and lampposts would not be out of place in an English spa town.

Sunset over the flat desert landscape is spectacular and as the sun goes down over the never-ending horizon the scrubby vegetation turns blue. The sun rises rapidly next morning when the flat grassland briefly takes on a lilac hue. After a brief stop at Klerksdorp in the dusty mining area of the Transvaal, Johannesburg is not far away. Jos Van Niekirk and his wife Marie-Louise met us at the station and after seeing the highlights of the city we were entertained to dinner at their house, travelling on to Pretoria next day, renewing old friendships and making new ones, particularly when I was made an honorary member of the Rhino Club.

The escalating costs of health care are a worldwide problem but many of South Africa's clinical problems are quite different and this was reflected in the scientific papers. Bone and joint infection and polio, never mind HIV, remain problems, principally in the African communities.

A visit to South Africa is incomplete without a visit to a game park and Jos recommended Sabi-Sabi, a private reserve, rather than the Kruger National Park. Bush Lodge, one of several in the reserve, was a collection of attractive thatched buildings but any resemblance to native dwellings ended with the external appearance for, inside, the facilities and furnishings were anything but primitive. The buildings and the large central compound where we dined around a massive log fire under a starlit sky were surrounded by a stockade through which we were driven each morning into the bush veldt by our ranger and his tracker in a Land-Rover. Zebra, giraffes, wildebeest, water buffalo and warthogs were commonplace but the ranger was intent on making sure that we saw rhino, elephants, lions, cheetahs and leopards in their native habitat. To this end, the rangers in the Land-Rovers communicated to each other by radio when they located the animals and sometimes the ranger and his tracker set off on foot, leaving us and the Land-Rover supposedly to follow the tracks of our quarry, but I suspect that the whole enterprise was rather contrived and the likely whereabouts of these splendid animals was well known to the rangers.

We missed the Australia and New Zealand meeting because it clashed with the inaugural meeting of the Surgical Senate, at which I represented the BOA and which I thought was important to attend, in the knowledge that the combined meeting of the Orthopaedic Association of the English Speaker Associations would next be held in Auckland. The English-speaking Associations hold a combined meeting in turn every six years, providing an opportunity for the whole membership to present their work and exchange ideas. I had been at the meeting held at the Festival Hall in London in 1976 which had ended with a spectacular firework display and the Band of the Royal Marines beating retreat on the riverside. Washington, in 1987, enabled me to visit the last of my father's siblings, then in her 80s, in California before the Congress and to sightsee in the capital city.

The 9th Combined Meeting in Toronto under the chairmanship of the Canadian president, Marvin Tile, whom I had known since his visit to the RNOH many years before, opened with great academic pomp and pageantry, and military and modern music, and the many and varied clinical and research presentations were full of interest. The opportunity to fly over Niagara Falls by helicopter and under the Falls in the *Maid of the Mist* (mackintoshes provided) could not be resisted before travelling west through the Prairies and the Rockies to Vancouver and Vancouver Island. The spectacular scenery is seen at its best reflected in the placid blue waters of Lake Louise and in the view from Château Louise along the lake to the Victoria Glacier. The enormous quantity of delicious seafood at the buffet lunch in the hotel left little room to sample the remaining courses. Throughout the journey we were accompanied by our friends Glyn and Gigi Thomas, members of the Innominate Club, with whom we shared a log cabin when we broke our journey in Banff.

Six years later the New Zealand Association arranged the meeting in Auckland but by then I had retired and, whereas at the previous meetings I had made a presentation or chaired a session, I was now free of any official commitment. The competitors in the Whitbread Round-The-World Race were moored in Auckland Harbour before setting off on the gruelling third leg through the Southern Ocean. Jonathan, now an even more senior executive with Johnson & Johnson's orthopaedic subsidiary, arrived a few hours before the start of the race and joined us on one of the multitude of craft, large and small of all ages brought into service, weaving and bobbing in a sea of foam, a sight as spectacular as the racing yachts themselves as they set off from the starting line.

Waitangi, where the Maori nation voluntarily put itself under the protection of the British in 1840 to avoid exploitation from the French, overlooks the Bay of Islands, one of the most beautiful places on earth. Across the bay lies Russell, and the Marlborough Hotel, the first to be licensed in New Zealand. Rotorua, the spiritual home of the Maoris with its geysers and bubbling mud, is inevitably visited by every tourist. I had not appreciated that New Zealand had experienced its own Gold Rush until we visited Queenstown, the centre of the mining area on the South Island not far from the dramatic Milford Sound with the spectacular

Southern Alps, dominated by Mount Cook, running northwards along the coast.

We spent our last day in New Zealand with Warren Fraser, with whom I had shared general surgical duties at Barnet, and his wife Valerie. After lunch at the Royal New Zealand Yacht Squadron Headquarters we saw the Americas Cup in its protected display cabinet. On our way to New Zealand we had broken the journey in Fiji and on the way back we spent a few days visiting Cairns and the Great Barrier Reef, with a stopover in Singapore.

I was not a particularly active member of the Société Internationale de Chirurgie Orthopaedique et de Traumatologie (SICOT), an international organisation with its origins in the 1930s in France, as the name suggests, but we did attend the meetings in Kyoto, Japan, and in Rio de Janeiro, during both of which I contributed to the scientific programme. Rather surprisingly in Kyoto the slide projectors in all but the main auditorium were manually operated by a projectionist. Before we boarded the Bullet Train en route to Tokyo our guide informed our party that we would have precisely two minutes to board the train with our luggage. It seemed impossible. The doors of the carriages in which our seats were allocated stopped at the precise point marked on the platform and where the group waited. The doors opened and then closed automatically after two minutes and, sure enough, we were all on board and soon speeding past Mount Fuji on our way to the capital. Japan seemed so well ordered at that time and reminded me of England in my childhood, the innumerable crocodiles of sightseeing children of all ages moving in well-disciplined but happy progression from one national monument to the next.

Rio de Janeiro has a reputation for lawlessness and, perhaps rather ill-advisedly, Pat and I walked along the whole length of the famous Copacabana Beach one evening without being molested. From Sao Paulo we flew to La Paz in Bolivia, the highest international airport in the world. As we drove into the city lying in a bowl surrounded by mountains, the lights twinkled and we seemed to be approaching fairyland. I cannot remember if the llama foetuses widely on sale in the town to bring good luck were to be buried under the threshold of a new house or given as wedding presents, perhaps both! We crossed Lake Titicaca, the ancestral home of the Inca Sun and Moon Gods, where people live on floating islands made of reeds, and then we took another of the world's great train journeys, this time the highest, through the Andes to Cusco, the ancient Inca capital. The stone blocks with which the Incas constructed their buildings fitted together perfectly. So accurately were they fashioned there was no need for any form of mortar. A helicopter delivering a white grand piano for a French pop group to make a commercial was a rather incongruous sight in Machu Picchu, the ruined Inca city so long lost in the high Andes.

I was more actively involved with the European Rheumatoid Arthritis Surgical Society (ERASS) but declined the secretaryship in view of my other commitments. Participation in the meetings, sometimes in collaboration with other organisations, led to visits to Russia, Greece, and Hungary. Russia, like Japan, was well ordered but for different reasons. The Communist regime was still in power, with a policeman on every street corner in Moscow. On one occasion I was nearly arrested for stepping into the road to get a better view of Red Square and the Kremlin for a photograph. Naturally all the delegates wanted to visit a hospital, preferably with orthopaedic patients, but it was not until we reached Tblisi in Georgia that this was arranged, and then to a cardio-thoracic hospital. The ubiquitous plain blue and white striped nightshirts and pyjamas were in marked contrast to the colourful carpet of wild flowers in the surrounding fields. Mount Ararat, the mythical resting place of Noah's Ark, was visible from our hotel window. In Yerevan, the capital of Armenia, life seemed to be more relaxed in the Eastern Soviet Republics, but the massive monument to the thousands of Armenians massacred by the Turks during the First World War, in what would now be described as ethnic cleansing, was a reminder of the repeated turmoil in this part of the world. In spite of its enormous size, little of orthopaedic importance has emanated from the USSR, apart perhaps from the Ilyzaroff external fixator, used to stabilise fractures and lengthen limbs. Switzerland on the other hand is a significant source of surgical innovation, not least in the surgical treatment of rheumatoid arthritis and a most enjoyable meeting in Zurich was followed by a visit to Salzburg and then by road to Vienna along the banks of the Danube, where I made more updated presentations on shoulder and elbow replacement.

The opportunity to take our holidays in association with these meetings meant that orthopaedics has been more to us than just bones and joints and although it was my childhood ambition to join the Royal Navy, it is as an orthopaedic surgeon rather than a sailor that I have seen much of the world.

Chapter 12

The Royal College of Surgeons

The company of surgeons established by Act of Parliament in 1745 was short-lived, becoming The Royal College of Surgeons in 1800. The new college was established 'for the promotion and encouragement of the study and practice of the said art and science of surgery' and enjoyed the rights and privileges previously enjoyed by the Barber-Surgeons including the right to 'superintend, rule and govern the Mystery of Surgery'. This it has done ever since by means of its examinations and its educational activities, by regulating the training of surgeons, by promoting research funded by charitable donations, and by fundraising activities. In all of these I was closely involved for more than twenty years.

The most important of the examinations, the surgical component of the Conjoint Diploma (MRCS) and the examination for the Fellowship of the college (FRCS), were conducted by the Court of Examiners but there were several specialist diplomas usually granted in association with other colleges and faculties, one of which, the Diploma in Medical Rehabilitation, was my introduction to the College examinations department.

In 1978 I was invited to join the prestigious Court of Examiners. The Court can trace its origins back to the Middle Ages when the Barbers' Company was granted a charter by Edward IV, which empowered the Master to make ordinances for the governance of surgery, including the power to examine the members of the craft and ensure that they were fit to practise. There has been a body of examiners over the years, in one form or another, continuously to the present day. When I was appointed there were thirty-six examiners, each of whom examined for four days of the week for six weeks each year in all, without financial reward but of course retaining their NHS salaries. A balance was maintained between provincial surgeons and London surgeons, who provided the patients for the clinical examination, and between specialists and generalists. A specialist and a generalist examined as a pair throughout the week, one senior, the other junior, so maintaining a consistent standard. At the end of each day the marks for the different parts of the examination were collated and the candidates either passed, failed or were borderline. The borderline candidates were discussed, each examiner in turn justifying his marks, at the end of which the Court would vote pass or fail. It was indeed a Court.

On one occasion the marks I had awarded to an Indian candidate in the clinical examination were discussed. Among the patients he had been asked

The Court of Examiners at their leaving party at Barber-Surgeons Hall in 1984 in front of the Holbein painting of Henry VIII and the Barber-Surgeons

The author explaining the significance of the cartoon of Holbein's picture of Henry VIII and the Barber-Surgeons to The Queen on her visit to the College in 1989

to examine was one with peripheral vascular disease. He examined the pulses in the feet repeatedly going from one foot to the other. Eventually in exasperation I asked, 'Well, can you feel the pulses or not?'

'Oh yes, sir,' he replied.

'Well, suppose I told you that I can't,' I answered.

'I quite understand, sir. I have very sensitive fingers' was his answer!

I knew if I recounted this conversation the Court would undoubtedly vote as one to pass him but I could not resist the opportunity and my prediction proved correct! *Was it something I said?*

When each group of examiners retired it was customary for them to throw a party for all the examiners with whom they had examined over the previous six years, and in turn they would attend leaving parties for six years to come. I arranged our leaving party at Barber-Surgeons Hall and the Court assembled for a memorable photograph (reproduced on the previous page) beneath Holbein's famous painting of Henry VIII and the Barber Surgeons, who were essentially the examiners of 1540.

The first of many changes which would transform the college examinations resulted from the need to comply with new Health & Safety Regulations. The examinations were held in the Examinations Hall in Queen's Square, jointly owned with the Royal College of Physicians, and as it would have been very expensive to comply with new regulations it was decided to sell the building. This brought the Court into conflict with the Council because no satisfactory alternative accommodation had been agreed. A plan to convert the College basement for the clinical examination was abandoned and temporary accommodation was acquired in the former John Lewis Staff Hostel in Gower Street. Several members of Council, particularly those from the provinces, (especially if spurned by the Court of Examiners in the past) had long held the view that the clinical examinations should be held in hospitals around the country. This provided them with the opportunity to achieve their objective but at the cost of the previously very cohesive Court, and no little expense.

My association with the Court continued after my election to the College Council in July 1984, another entirely voluntary unpaid body. The twenty-four elected members included the president and two vice-presidents, with additional representation from the College Faculties and various co-opted members, and met on the second Thursday of the month for eight months of the year. In addition to attending Council meetings, members served on various college committees and represented the college on outside bodies. Before election to the Council I had represented the college on the British Standards Surgical Implants Committee and the Physiotherapy Board (the regulating body for physiotherapists) and now found myself on its parent body, the Council for the Professions Supplementary to Medicine. Now I was delighted to become a member of the Examining Board in England, the quaint title of the joint committee with the Royal College of Physicians, which oversaw the Conjoint Diploma, becoming chairman from 1988 to 1991.

Maintaining the standard of the various qualifying examinations and entry to the Medical Register is the responsibility of the General Medical Council (GMC), who from time to time closely scrutinise each examination. The 'Conjoint' was reviewed during my chairmanship and the GMC report was particularly critical of the clinical examination in medicine, criticisms which were met before their re-inspection a year or so later. However, the GMC were still not satisfied. The university-based examinations were by now internal examinations, held in the candidates' own medical schools, conducted by their own teachers, with additional external examiners giving a veneer of objectivity. The GMC complained that there were no external examiners, for example, but as I pointed out all the examiners were external examiners recruited from medical schools throughout the country. In reality there were no internal examiners for it was the rule that no candidate should be examined by an examiner from the same medical school. There were no examiners' meetings between physicians and surgeons to discuss borderline candidates (we remedied that), but above all there was no in-course assessment available to the examiners. This was a problem in the obstetric and gynaecological part of the examination because of the not unreasonable reluctance of the volunteer patients to undergo pelvic examinations. This of course applied equally to the university examinations. Candidates in this case were deemed to have demonstrated their prowess during in-course assessment – a dubious assertion! Other non-university licensing bodies (NULB), namely the Scottish Triple Examination and the Society of Apothecaries examination, and, of course, the Conjoint Board, met regularly, and at times with representatives of the GMC, but the Conjoint was eventually abolished and the College lost a major asset, the right to put a name on the medical register. *Was it something I said?*

The Council of the College met in committee on the morning of Council day when important issues were discussed. At the formal Council meeting in the afternoon the gowned members sat in order of seniority on chairs on the back of which they had paid to have their names carved. The chairmen of the various committees rose and presented their reports and proposed they be received, and after a brief discussion proposed that they be accepted. This was very formal and traditional but increasingly time-consuming as the amount of business progressively increased.

In 1988, Roger Duffett succeeded Ronald Johnson-Gilbert as College Secretary, having previously worked in industry with BP. He began to streamline Council meetings, creating a number of boards to which the committees reported, the board chairman then reporting to Council. I remained a member of the Education Committee and the Examinations Board, eventually becoming its chairman in 1991, a time of unprecedented change precipitated by a number of factors coming together fortuitously at a particular time.

The purpose of the 1858 Medical Act was to enable a person requiring medical advice to distinguish qualified from unqualified practitioners, but the medical register a century later did not identify a qualified specialist. Prompted by the Monopolies and Mergers Commission, the GMC decided that they would establish a specialist register recording the names of those who had completed higher specialist training. The criteria for determining the completion of specialist training would remain with the training bodies, the Royal Colleges and their Faculties, who would recommend the award of a Certificate for the Completion of Specialist Training (CCST). The four Royal Surgical Colleges collectively regulated higher surgical training through the Joint Committee of Higher Surgical Training (the JCHST) and its specialist Advisory Committees (SACs) composed of college and specialist association representatives, on both of which I served. An examination at the conclusion of specialist training seemed desirable but there was a widespread view that surgical trainees were over-examined.

The FRCS was no longer regarded as the mark of a fully trained surgeon capable of independent surgical practice, but rather as the gateway to training in one of the surgical specialties, after a basic training in the generality of surgery. It had been a two-part examination for more than a century. The first part, the primary FRCS in the basic sciences, particularly anatomy and physiology, was taken within a year or two of registration and was almost a de facto, if unwritten, entry requirement into basic surgical training. Less than 1 per cent of candidates passed first time and the overall pass rate was between 10 per cent and 15 per cent, candidates frequently sitting the examination repeatedly until eventually passing or giving up the idea of a surgical career. It was a time-consuming measure of determination, as well as knowledge. Success at the first attempt at the final fellowship examination was the exception rather than the rule and, although the overall pass rate among candidates qualified in the British Isles was near 60 per cent, many were perceived to spend too much time preparing for the examination to the detriment of other educational pursuits.

The two-part fellowship examination was amalgamated into a single examination with an applied basic sciences (ABS part) which could be taken separately and which was less demanding than the primary, and the whole examination was renamed the MRCS by the English College, the former MRCS having become the LRCS before the demise of the Conjoint Diploma, but the other colleges retained their individual Fellowships, with their higher pass rates. Understandably many candidates chose to take these examinations, since they provided equal access to higher surgical training and ultimately specialist registration. The proportion of English Fellows was declining, together with their fees and subscriptions.

The disparity in pass rates had been a simmering source of friction for some time and Norman Browse, Avril Mansfield and I had met our opposite numbers in Edinburgh previously to try and establish the reasons for this discrepancy. There were significant differences in the way the examinations were conducted and in the system of marking, but nothing came of this meeting in the short term.

The decision to overhaul the examination system provided the opportunity to reconsider the content and the format and the conduct of the examination. It was thought wise to seek the advice of an educationalist. We had a close marking system which he found difficult to comprehend, even more so when I informed him that often answers were a matter of opinion rather than absolute fact. All the examiners were trying to do was decide if the candidate was 'safe' to proceed to the next stage of training, which he found even more incomprehensible, hence my low opinion of educationalists. He wasn't much help but added a measure of political correctness!

An Intercollegiate examination at the end of Basic Surgical Training had been a long-standing but elusive goal. Quite understandably each college was reluctant to give up its autonomy, yet the Joint Committee for Higher Surgical Training (JCHST) worked well. With this in mind my predecessor as chairman of the Examination Board, Professor John Blandy, was instrumental in establishing the Intercollegiate Basic Surgical Training and Examination Committee in 1993.

When I succeeded him as chairman a year later, the other Colleges would still not agree to give up their individual Fellowships in favour of a common MRCS. It was even rumoured that the Irish College would lose its Royal Charter and it would no longer be the Royal College of Surgeons in Ireland, a title it apparently cherished. It seemed to me that we should concentrate on the things we could agree upon and a common title was not that important. As a result, our three-monthly meetings in the four colleges resulted in the publication of guidelines for basic surgical training in 1994. There would be common entry requirements, a common curriculum, a common format, and common standards for the individual college examinations. It has taken a further ten years finally to establish a common examination!

Meanwhile, the Edinburgh College had introduced specialty examinations in the late 1980s and I had been a member of the Intercollegiate Orthopaedic Examination Board set up in 1988 ultimately to implement an intercollegiate specialty examination, the first of which I organised at the Royal National Orthopaedic Hospital in 1991. The format has remained largely unchanged ever since. Success in the examination is a prerequisite for the award of a CCST and consultant status for British graduates, but alas not for those from other EU member states whose own certificates, which are generally issued after less rigorous training, must be accepted.

I have recounted earlier the haphazard, unplanned nature of surgical training, which prompted me to organise and oversee planned progressive continuous training programmes at Bart's and the RNOH in 1969 to 1970. This type of programme was highly popular and much sought after by the young surgical trainees, usually in their early thirties and often with young families. It was common practice in those days after a tiring outpatient clinic to relax with the junior staff and a cup of tea before undertaking the next commitment. Jonathan Wilkinson, now a successful consultant approaching retirement himself, but then a Registrar, suggested that this type of training programme should be universal and prompted me to seek election to the Council of the Royal College of Surgeons to try to bring this about.

The College supervised basic surgical training at that time by inspecting and approving junior hospital posts at senior house officer (SHO) and registrar level in hospitals around the country. A satisfactory tenure of a series of approved posts over a period of three years was a prerequisite for entry to the FRCS examination. The inspection and approval of the posts was carried out under the auspices of the Hospital Recognition Committee to which I was soon to be appointed. The posts were usually of six months' duration and free-standing, meaning that the trainee was obliged to apply for a new post every six months, often in another hospital in another part of the country, frequently necessitating family moves or long journeys to work. I was not alone in recognising this unsatisfactory state of affairs and eventually, with the support of other members of Council, rotational training programmes, consisting of a series of posts in different specialties in the same or nearby hospitals, was recognised, rather than the individual posts as before. Perhaps this time something I said had influenced events! I was surprised when undertaking my first inspection to find that there were no specific criteria to be met. I mentioned this to my colleague, Terence Kennedy, an experienced and rather self-opinionated general surgeon from Belfast, who told me that I would know as soon as I got through the hospital door whether the posts were suitable for training!

This was quite a contrast to my previous experience as a member of the Physiotherapy Board inspecting physiotherapy training schools for recognition. Their inspections were structured and much more thorough. I suggested to Ronald Johnson-Gilbert, the College Secretary, that a hospital deprived of recognition, which was effectively prevented from recruiting junior staff, might well mount a successful legal challenge overturning the decision. He thought it unlikely but when I became Chairman of the Training Board, guidelines were drawn up but in an ever-changing scene were never implemented. My early misgivings, however, were vindicated quite recently when the Department of Health overruled the College, and responsibility for approving hospitals for training purposes is no longer a College responsibility.

Specialist Advisory Committees (SACs) in the various specialties included representatives of all four colleges and the relevant specialist associations and were responsible for approving posts for Higher Surgical Training. I was delighted to represent the College on the Orthopaedic SAC for eight years and subsequently its parent body, the JCHST. Once again hospital posts were recognised individually. I have already alluded to the fragmented nature of higher surgical training, which led me to devise and implement the planned progressive and continuous programmes at Bart's and the RNOH. After several years of persuasion, comprehensive training programmes became College policy, acknowledged by Bill Steel, of Keele University's School of Postgraduate Medicine and Biological Sciences, in his letter of 11 May 1990.

Dear Alan

You must be very gratified to find that your views on Higher Surgical Training are becoming more widely accepted. I think it would be very timely to have a document for discussion at our next meeting, encompassing your views about the future format of training, its spread between DGHs and academic centres, the place of the intercollegiate exam, thoughts on the appropriate timing of accreditation and the role of advanced training in the sub-specialties. I believe that we should now anticipate future changes and begin planning for the next phase in Higher Surgical Training.

Yours sincerely,
Bill
W.M. Steel, FRCS
Chairman
SAC in Orthopaedic Surgery

The concept of 'seamless' training was finally implemented across all disciplines, following the report by the Chief Medical Officer, Sir Kenneth Calman in 1993. The Registrar and Senior Registrar grades were amalgamated into the new grade of Specialist Registrar. In order to comply with EU directives, Basic Surgical Training was reduced to two years and Higher Surgical Training to six years. It is unfortunate that this so-called Calman Training was introduced at the same time as the European Directive which limited the hours of work for junior staff, for the two became synonymous. The first was long overdue, but the second prejudiced the acquisition of surgical skills.

The College was unique in not only sponsoring medical research but also having research departments within its buildings in Lincoln's Inn Fields and at Down in Kent. Lord Adrian, the neurophysiologist and Sir John Vane, the pharmacologist, had both worked in the College and later both became Nobel Prize Laureates. The departments were also involved in teaching on the various college courses and, as the Institute of Basic Medical Sciences, were partly funded through the University Grants Committee. At a time of financial stringency, university funding was withdrawn but the College Council made a commitment to fund the research departments, which were renamed the Hunterian Institute, for five years. In the meantime there was considerable rationalisation, with research concentrated on a few core areas and a nationwide appeal was contemplated to raise sufficient funds to ensure the survival of the Institute. Many of the departments received considerable support from industry, legacies and endowments, but more money was needed. Although there was a fundraising committee chaired by Lord Leverhulme, whose personal generosity was exceptional, the committee of eminent members, essentially from commerce, was mainly advisory in introducing potential wealthy donors. Redmond Mullen, professional fundraisers, were engaged in 1991 and I was asked to take individual responsibility for fundraising as chairman of a small committee which included Dame Simone Prendergast, a member of the Marks & Spencer dynasty, and John Lumley, both of whose families were exceptionally generous benefactors. I joined Sir Terence English, the president, when the 'great and the good' were entertained to lunch, among whom were Sir Colin Southgate (EMI), Sir Richard Greenbury (M&S), Sir Eric Parker (Trafalgar House), Sir John Blyth (Boots) and Sir Ernest Harrison (Racal). Unfortunately it was a period of industrial recession and furthermore the Hospital for Sick Children, Great Ormond Street, had recently launched a very successful appeal, so little came from these meetings.

To publicise the role of the college, the Cognizance Banquet was organised at the Guildhall jointly with the Barbers to commemorate the award of a cognizance or badge to the Guild of Surgeons in 1493 by Henry VII. The Lord Mayor, Sir Brian Jenkins presided and Robert Hardy, the eminent actor, compèred a pageant illustrating the history of the company and the college. Industry and commerce sponsored the individual tables, but this was not primarily a fundraising exercise but an attempt to recruit support for the college. As an event it was a great success and among the many congratulatory letters the President, by now Sir Norman Browse, wrote on 16 November 1992:

> Dear Alan,
> I am sure that many have already told you that they thought the Cognizance Banquet was a great success. Its conception and development was yours and I am most grateful for all that you have done over the past year in helping and promoting its organisation.
> You can be truly proud of a memorable and extraordinarily enjoyable evening (even for those giving speeches!). Thank you very much.
> Yours sincerely,
> Norman

The academic members of Council particularly believed that research was better undertaken in a university environment. The large animal research at the Buckston-Brown Research Farm at Down in Kent, Charles Darwin's old home, where Sir Roy Calne had carried out his pioneering research on organ transplantation, had already closed, an early casualty of animal rights protesters. The College could not afford to provide security for the staff, many of whom were young girls who looked after the animals. In 1992 the Hunterian Institute was also closed but the College continued to promote research by awarding research Fellowships to surgeons in training.

Our fundraising efforts were not in vain. Ronald Raven, a distinguished cancer surgeon and former member of the College Council and a past Master of the Worshipful Company of Barbers, had been admitted to hospital in July 1991 when I was Master of the Company. I visited him almost weekly until he died three months later, and indeed was present with his sister, Dame Kathleen Raven, when he died. During my visits we discussed College affairs and Ronnie believed that the college needed a Professor of Surgical Education. I persuaded him that before we could appoint a Professor we needed a department of surgical education and unbeknown to me our conversations were passed on to Dame Kathleen.

When Ronnie died Kathleen asked me to write his obituary and to deliver the address at his Memorial Service, which again was well received. I also arranged for the trustees of his estate, of which she was one, to meet College representatives with a view to making the College a beneficiary of his estate. She was rather upset when it was intimated that there was a sort of tariff. So much for an eponymous room, so much for a lecture theatre, and so on. Fortunately I was able to smooth her ruffled feathers, and the Trustees later agreed to provide £1million to establish the Raven Department of Surgical Education, which she opened in September 1993. Among her many personal gifts to me was Ronnie's past Master's badge on which my name has also been engraved, and which I wear at Barbers' functions.

Surgical training is essentially hospital based but surgical education as a means of promoting the 'art and science of surgery' has taken place within the College since its foundation. Until the early years of the twentieth century, pathological museums with preserved specimens illustrating man's afflictions were an important teaching aid. The most famous medical museum of all, the Hunterian Museum, based on John Hunter's collection of human and animal specimens, is housed in the Royal College of Surgeons. Hunter's collection was bought from his executors by the government and placed in the care of the Company of Surgeons in 1799, with funds to 'erect a proper and commodious building for preserving and extending the collection'.

A Board of Trustees was created to oversee the collection, with membership by office of government and academic establishment figures, even including the prime minister, from most of whom there are permanent apologies for absence. The museum and two-thirds of the collection were destroyed in the Blitz and a new museum was opened in 1963, with conventional mahogany and glass cabinets displaying most of the specimens. By the early 1990s the traditional museum format and layout were giving way to more user-friendly displays suitable for public viewing. Plans were drawn up and led to the most acrimonious, time-consuming, and damaging conflict between the Council of the College and the Board of Trustees, or more particularly between Sir Norman Browse, the President, and Sir Reginald Murley, a past President of the College and the chairman of the Trustees. Reggie was a forceful, outspoken and self-opinionated man who undoubtedly had the interests of the College at heart and who regarded any changes to the museum as a matter for the Trustees rather than the Council. Norman Browse took the opposite view and the controversy dominated Council meetings for several months, which many believed was at the expense of more important business. Lawyers were instructed and in their opinion the Trustees were responsible for the collection of specimens and the Council for the building in which they were housed, which solved nothing. Many members of both the Council and the Board of Trustees believed that the proposal should be set aside until funds became available for the scheme, and the more cynical pointed out that Reggie was not in good health. I, and I am sure other senior members of Council, had been approached by some of the trustees to try, in the words of one respected past President, to bring an end to 'all this horrid business' and avoid 'yet another impasse'. As senior Vice-President I felt obliged to acquaint Sir Norman with the views of many Council members, but by now the issue was a matter of principle for the protagonists. Sadly, Norman regarded me as disloyal, believing that I had provided Reggie with confidential information, which was untrue. *Was it something I said?* The Council decided to create a new post, Keeper of the Museum, and an appointments committee was convened and a short list of candidates drawn up. A week before the interviews were due to take place, lawyers instructed by Reggie Murley threatened to serve an injunction to prevent the interviews taking place. The President was abroad and in his absence, and in consultation with Roger Duffett, I met Reggie to try to avoid another impasse. He wanted Professor Bert Cohen, the deputy chairman of the Trustees, to serve on the appointments committee. Reggie accepted that he would be unable to influence the short list but agreed to withdraw the threatened injunction if Bert was put on the committee. Roger Duffett and I could see no harm in this, for the College representatives would still be in the majority, but Norman expressed his displeasure on his return, which did not improve our relationship. The appointment was unanimous and Stella Mason has fulfilled her role with distinction for the past ten years, overseeing the transformation of the Hunterian Museum, recently re-opened by the Princess Royal.

The full-time residential courses in the early post-war years became less relevant, particularly with the decline in overseas participants, and the development of computer-based distance learning programmes. The closure of the Hunterian Institute released space for the Raven Department and the development and the introduction not only of the distance learning courses, but also facilities for the ever-increasing number of practical instructional courses in the various surgical disciplines.

The Courses and Lectureships Committee of which I was chairman from 1986 to 1989 was responsible for awarding the many eponymous prizes and lectures, particularly the Hunterian Professorships. In collaboration with

Professor Miles Irving, by far the most important event during my tenure was the introduction of the Advanced Trauma Life Support Course (ATLS) which is now an obligatory component of every surgeon's training. Developed in the United States this practical course addresses the vital 'golden hour' after serious injury when appropriate management makes the difference between life and death.

The financial consequences of accidental injury are second only to cancer, and rank only behind cancer and cardiovascular disease as a cause of death. Dr Norman Halliday, a Senior Medical Officer at the Department of Health, believed that reports from the Royal College of Physicians had made smoking socially unacceptable and that the Royal College of Surgeons might exert a similar influence by emphasising that accident prevention was a social responsibility. Sir Ian Todd, the President at the time, accepted the challenge and thought me, as an orthopaedic surgeon, the most suitable person to organise a seminar on the subject. Orthopaedic surgeons are skilled at treating the consequences of accidents but have little expertise in their prevention. The symposium took place on 1 February 1989. Mrs Edwina Curry was due to open the meeting but resigned from her Government post the previous day. Her successor, Mr Roger Freeman, the Under Secretary of State for Health, stood in at short notice and although the symposium was well received it was overshadowed by the publication of a White Paper on NHS reforms.

THE MEDICAL COMMISSION ON ACCIDENT PREVENTION

10 March 1989

Dear Mr Lettin

Please forgive this very tardy letter. My colleagues and I very much enjoyed your Seminar last month. It was a splendid and most interesting day and we are just so sorry that you did not receive the publicity you deserved because of the publication of the White Paper on the NHS swamping the media at the same time.

We very much look forward to the publication of the Report. In the meantime, if there is anything we can do to help, please do not hesitate to let us know.

With kind regards,
Yours sincerely,
Andrew Raffle
P. A. B. RAFFLE
CHAIRMAN

In my conclusions at the end of the symposium, I pointed out that speaker after speaker had drawn attention to the serious injuries, mostly to young people, resulting from motorcycle accidents. The most lethal form of transport is in the hands of the most vulnerable and irresponsible age group

The Queen of Thailand talking to Pat after meeting the King at a reception in the Royal Palace in 1989

and more than a quarter of the deaths on the roads in Norfolk, for example, at that time were related to motorcycle accidents. With tongue in cheek I suggested that perhaps motorcycles might be banned from our roads with the exception of the emergency services, or that at least the engine capacity should be limited. The press and the TV commentators picked this up and following an interview on the Jimmy Young Show, hosted in his absence by Glenys Kinnock, the motorcycle lobby directed an avalanche of abusive and vile letters in my direction. An unexpected response to *something I said*! Subsequently I was invited to become a member of the Medical Commission for Accident Prevention and at an early meeting, at which His Royal Highness Prince Michael of Kent presided, I mentioned my somewhat provocative suggestion, without realising that he was a motorcyclist himself! Subsequent legislation raised the age at which a provisional licence was granted and limited the engine capacity of motorcycles for provisional riders. I note fifteen years later that the Essex County Constabulary has launched a campaign to reduce the incidence of accidents (now more than 50 per cent) in which motorcycles are involved.

From time to time the College undertakes combined meetings with surgical institutions abroad and in 1989 met the Royal College of Surgeons of Thailand in Bangkok. The lavish hospitality which accompanied the scientific programme included tea with the King and Queen, to whom we were individually introduced by the President, Sir Terence English, at the Royal Palace. The King, or one of his acquaintances, seemed to have a problem relevant to each one of us for which he sought advice when he was informed of our special interests. We speculated on the discussion that he had with Jack Hardcastle, a rectal surgeon. There followed a magnificent banquet in the evening before we departed for a similar meeting in Malaysia, following which many of us took the opportunity of visiting other parts of the country as part of the usual post congress tours. Together with Pat, I took the opportunity of spending our annual holiday in Rajasthan, visiting Delhi, Agra and the Taj Mahal, Jaipur and the Lake Palace at Udaipur before spending a few days on a houseboat on Lake Dal in Kashmir, probably among the last tourists to visit that beautiful but war-torn country.

The responsibilities of the Examinations, Training and Education Committees, on all of which I had served over the years, frequently became blurred and for a time I acted as chairman of the Education Co-ordinating Committee with the purpose of minimising any conflict. I continued with this role after I was elected one of the two vice-presidents in 1994. John Alexander Williams, my fellow vice-president, was content to allow me to assume responsibility for the boards and committees with which I was familiar, whilst he undertook responsibility for the committees principally involved with the administration of the College. I also represented the president on the Council of the Royal College of Anaesthetists and the Faculty of Dental Surgery, and accompanied him to the regular meetings of the Joint Committee of Higher Surgical Training and the Surgical Senate, and the preparatory meetings with the other presidents which preceded them.

David Blunkett, the Shadow Secretary of State for Health, and other members of the Shadow Health Team visited the College in 1994 to acquaint themselves with its role. After describing the work of the Hospital Recognition Committee I was questioned on the sanctions imposed if recognition was withdrawn. The team was surprised that the only sanction was the withdrawal of recognition which would affect recruitment to junior posts. 'What about sanctions against consultants not fulfilling their teaching and training responsibilities, or even their clinical responsibilities?' they asked. I told them that the college had no disciplinary powers and any such action was a matter for the GMC. 'Would you like such powers?' they asked, a question we were not prepared for, but such powers might have been useful in preventing the problems with paediatric cardiac surgery in Bristol, which subsequently came to light. Informally over lunch we all agreed that the quality of medical care could not be guaranteed by legislation, but only by recruiting to the profession students of the highest intellect and moral calibre.

In 1995, the Crown Prince of Dubai hosted a joint surgical meeting with the United Arab Emirates University in Abu Dhabi. The usual demonstrations and presentations emphasised the opportunities for postgraduate training in the United Kingdom for the first generation of medical students qualifying at the University. The President, the second Vice-President and I had a private audience with the Crown Prince in his palace, primarily to discuss postgraduate training. We waited, in a large, lavishly furnished reception room, to be summoned through doors guarded by armed retainers dressed as in scenes from the Arabian Nights. We sat on cushions on the floor in the Prince's audience room drinking small cups of black coffee which were frequently replenished by more retainers, discussing twentieth century surgical training!

The accompanying lavish hospitality included a trip to the Crown Prince's private island zoo by Hercules transport planes and later a dinner by moonlight on another island, transported this time by lantern-lit sailing ships. We were served the most delicious food as we sat on cushions on rugs overlying the sand, whilst being entertained by belly dancers. Fruit juice accompanied the food but alcohol was available behind the tents! It was an unforgettable evening. From Abu Dhabi we flew to Colombo for a meeting with the Sri Lankan College of Surgeons and after the presentations and workshops again we took the opportunity of spending our annual holiday visiting the ancient religious sites and the Botanical Gardens in Kandi and the famous Elephant Orphanage, before relaxing on the much over-rated Maldive Islands.

Lavish hospitality was not, however, limited to overseas trips and in the past I had been the personal guest of Bill Davis, a wealthy and well-connected former fundraising director at the College, who I think thought that I might be destined for high office. He was a member of the Saints and Sinners Club which included His Royal Highness the Prince of Wales among the many well-known personalities making up its membership. Bill would regularly host a table at their annual dinners and Christmas lunches at the Savoy Hotel and I found myself included among his many influential and wealthy friends from industry, politics and the law.

On the first occasion among the speakers was Dame Vera Lynn, but instead of making a speech she decided to sing. The atmosphere was electrifying, quite unlike anything I had experienced before or since. She held the audience spellbound and elderly guests of wartime vintage, including Lord Porritt, a past College President and Reginald Murley, stood on their chairs wiping away their tears with their table napkins. I can understand why she was remembered so affectionately as the sweetheart of the forces. On another occasion Ronald Reagan was the principal guest, shortly after he had completed his Presidency. After an amusing introduction by the Speaker of the House of Commons he responded in an equally amusing and frequently spontaneous way, which served to belie the view that his mental faculties were already deteriorating. He told the story of the young lady who, as a penance for her sins, had to make her way up a long flight of steps to the church entrance on her knees. She caught the hem of her skirt on the heel of her shoe and asked a following penitent to lift it up.

'Not likely,' he replied. 'That's how I got this penance in the first place.'

The President of the College is elected by the members of Council for one year in the first instance, renewable for a further two. It would be foolish to pretend that I was not disappointed (but not surprised) when I failed to receive that ultimate accolade. The losing Wimbledon finalist must have a similar feeling. David Dandy, one of my registrars but now a world-renowned orthopaedic surgeon wrote:

22 April 1995

Dear Alan,

Thank you for the very generous introduction at the Council Club on Thursday. Thanks to your introduction, my own task was easy and I quite enjoyed it. Nevertheless, I am glad it is over!

I am particularly grateful because I know the disappointment you suffered only hours earlier, yet you remained cheerful and retained your wit and humour.

My 'soundings' before the election made it clear that if the election had been held to select the member held in highest regard, greatest affection, had done work for the College, had the greatest experience or the background most suited to be President, you would have won easily. I only wish I knew why these qualities did not win the day.

The result does not diminish the high regard in which you are held by all those who know you. Perhaps this is worth more than the Presidency.

Yours,
David

But *was it something I said*?

I was also greatly heartened to receive a letter from Sir Geoffrey Slaney, with whom I had a very amiable relationship during his outstanding presidency, when I was first elected to Council, with a quotation from Tennyson – 'Though much is taken much abides' adding that 'your resolution and common sense will be in big demand'.

So I returned to the fray with the same commitments as before, giving the Christmas lectures to the schoolchildren ('So you want to be a surgeon') and the lecture to the new diplomates and their families ('Why surgeons are called Mister'), between the ceremony and the evening banquet as I had done before.

The research facilities at Down, Charles Darwin's home, had long been closed and the upkeep of the house had become a drain on College resources and had been rather neglected. The Natural History Museum was anxious to take on the long-term responsibility for preserving it and the College was willing to sell the property, but not to give it away. As a Charity it was obliged to maximise its assets. The Museum was given the opportunity to raise funds for the purchase, but without success, and in September 1995 gave a dinner in honour of Charles Darwin at the Natural History Museum, hosted by Sir David Attenborough, following a lecture by the American Darwin scholar Stephen J. Gould. This was a belated attempt to raise funds and no doubt embarrass the college. My wife and I deputised for Sir Rodney and Lady Sweetnam but, of course, I had no authority to acquiesce to the Museum's entreaties but merely to report back to the President. It was a wonderful dinner in exceptional surroundings with stimulating company. The Welcome Trust resolved the impasse by purchasing the property and giving it to English Heritage, but the College is given no credit for its role in preserving Down and particularly its contents over the years.

All consultants whatever their specialty receive the same basic salary, but this is augmented by Distinction or Merit Awards, in recognition of service to the NHS over and above the basic call of duty. The lowest or 'C' award was made on the recommendation of Regional Committees, with a representative from every hospital in the Region. I served on the N.E. Thames 'C' Award Committee, both as a member and as chairman, and I remember that year we had to decide who among the 900 eligible consultants from all specialties would receive the thirty awards at our disposal. A formidable task! The Higher Awards Committee, on which I also served, had the easier task of deciding who should be upgraded from C to B and B to A. The Central Committee, chaired at that time most ably and fairly by Sir Gordon Robson, a retired anaesthetist, ratified the recommendation of the Regional Committees, and also awarded the A+ Awards, of which there were at that time 120 for the whole county. I was one of the three College representatives. The system was much criticised, especially by those without awards, and has now been much modified, but I believe overall it was very fair and those involved often agonised over their decisions. If not successful one year, the deserving were usually subsequently rewarded.

It is perhaps surprising that I managed to fulfil my clinical obligations whilst devoting so much time to College affairs, and also to hospital, regional and national committees. I was, of course, not undertaking these various voluntary commitments all at the same time, but spread over a period of twenty years or more. I was fortunate in working in London, within walking distance of Lincoln's Inn Fields, although this meant being asked to undertake more commitments than Council members from the Provinces. Most College Committees began in late morning or late afternoon, giving them time to travel to London, whereas I was able to visit the hospital for at least a few hours every day to supervise the care of the patients. The College administrative staff provided excellent support, particularly Craig Duncan and Martin Coomber, rather like the Civil Service support for a Government Minister. Furthermore, my hospital colleagues John Fixsen and Tom Bucknil very generously allocated the most senior of our junior staff, usually someone ready to take up a consultant post, to deputise for me in my absence.

My twelve years were soon at an end, but not my association with the College for, as a former vice-president, invitations to College banquets continue, as well as the opportunity to dine with the Council Club and the Court of Examiners. Age and infirmity are the only limitations. I appreciated enormously Sir Rodney Sweetnam's gracious letter, thanking me for my 'outstanding contribution to the College, outstanding by any standard', following my final Council meeting.

CHAPTER 13

The National Health Service

IT IS DIFFICULT TO BELIEVE THAT THE NHS was conceived in 1942, during the dark days of the Second World War, and became a major plank in the vast programme of social legislation intended to ameliorate the vicissitudes of life of all the citizens of the United Kingdom from the cradle to the grave, and ultimately enacted by the newly elected post-war Labour Government. The needs of war had spawned the Emergency Medical Service, which provided co-ordinated comprehensive hospital care for all, replacing the rather haphazard arrangements previously provided by the voluntary and local authority hospitals. On this foundation the NHS was built to provide a complete package of health care funded by general taxation but free at the point of delivery, which was soon proclaimed 'the envy of the world'. Why is it now described, however unjustly, as no better than a Third World service?

The NHS was born on 5 July 1948, just over a year before I began my medical studies at University College London, and so I was not present at its birth and perhaps I missed its neonatal development, for it was not until I began the clinical part of the course at University College Hospital in 1952 that I became involved in patient care, albeit as little more than an onlooker initially, but I witnessed its infancy. As a junior doctor I took part in its childhood and adolescence, and as a consultant and a committed member of the workforce, I played an increasing role in its adult life and sadly witnessed its decline until my retirement in 1995, three years before the fiftieth anniversary of its birth, and by then no longer the envy of the world. Why does it no longer meet the expectations of those in need of medical treatment and those who provide it?

Sir William Beveridge and the founding fathers were incredibly naive in thinking that the cost of the NHS would fall as the health of the nation improved as a consequence of the new welfare state. As the health of the nation improved so life expectancy increased and the demand for health care increased with it, for it is the elderly who make the greatest demands on the medical services. Furthermore, conditions previously untreatable become treatable, but at a cost. For example the introduction of total hip replacement in the 1950s and the development of artificial replacements for other joints damaged by injury or disease are undoubtedly beneficial, but at a cost which increases year by year. Organ transplantation allows many patients, who would previously have died, to lead nearly normal lives but the costs are not limited to the initial surgical procedure and the lifelong drug treatment which follows, for after several years the transplant frequently fails and further transplantation is necessary. The compulsory wearing of crash helmets has saved the lives of innumerable young motor cyclists who would previously have died from their head injuries, but now their associated injuries must be treated, initially in expensive intensive care units, and even after months of treatment and rehabilitation the unfortunate victims are often left with permanent disability. At the seminar on accident prevention in 1989 it was reported that every year more than a thousand young people survived accidents which resulted in permanent paralysis due to damage to the spinal cord. It was estimated that each victim will cost the community, though not specifically the NHS budget itself, approximately £1.5m over a thirty-year lifespan. Low birthweight babies now survive with expensive neonatal care, but sadly many subsequently have learning difficulties and remain a lifelong burden on the State. The great advances in resuscitation and in intensive care enable patients of all ages to survive who would previously have died. There is a general expectation that life must be preserved, whatever the cost. High Court Judges are now called upon to decide, at great cost, what is best for a patient, rather than doctors trained to make such decisions, just to satisfy the usually unrealistic expectations of relatives and pro-life campaigners. Increasingly sophisticated methods of investigation such as computerised tomography (CT) and magnetic resonance imaging (MRI) are not only expensive to install but expensive to operate, and are soon superseded by even more expensive equipment. Investigations are often undertaken unnecessarily in response to patient pressure and expectation, and the fear of litigation.

At the inception of the NHS the hospitals were funded on the basis of their previous historic costs with increments each year to match increasing expenditure. It was appreciated in the 1950s that the system was unsustainable and successive Governments believed that the costs could be contained by administrative changes. The teaching hospitals had occupied a privileged position outside the mainstream of district general hospitals, separately funded and administered by an independent Board of Governors with their individual administrative structures, picking and choosing the patients they would admit on the basis of their value for teaching and research but, that apart, admission was open to all from anywhere in the United Kingdom, and it was a truly National Health Service.

The first major reorganisation took place in 1974. The Boards of Governors were abolished, and all hospitals were managed and financed by District and Area Health Authorities, and ultimately Regional Boards. This arrangement at least meant that services could be rationalised and unnecessary reduplication of the more esoteric and expensive services could be avoided. Inevitably it led to a decline in the importance of Centres of Excellence and to the gradual fall in standards of care. Moreover the re-organisation failed to achieve its objectives and added to the echelons of administration. In 1976 the Resource Allocation Working Party (RAWP) was created to direct resources from what were perceived to be over-resourced to under-resourced areas of the country. It was as though the housing shortage in one part of the country could be solved by knocking down houses in another part with adequate housing to equalise availability. Robbing Peter to pay Paul satisfied no one.

The Districts were funded on the basis of their resident population which was satisfactory in well-defined rural areas where one or two hospitals served the residents of circumscribed populations. In the large cities, with their inner city hospitals and small resident populations, but still serving a large non-resident commuter population from the suburbs, the difficulties in providing a satisfactory service were exacerbated.

Surprisingly, in view of the financial constraints, the hospital service had become more and more efficient in terms of the number of patients treated, but, unlike the manufacturing industries, where increased productivity leads to lower unit costs and more profit, there is no profit to be made by treating more patients, only more costs. Although the cost of treating each individual patient may fall, the total cost increases.

Mrs Thatcher appreciated the simple economics: if increasing throughput increases costs, then reducing the number of patients treated will reduce total costs, even though unit costs will arise. It is the total cost which is of course the concern of politicians. For example at St Bartholomew's Hospital, the most cost-efficient of the London teaching hospitals, two beds were removed from each of the surgical wards to reduce the number of operations. When this failed to produce significant savings each of the operating theatres was closed for a week in rotation, and finally each surgeon's operating sessions were reduced. Instead of spending two half-days a week in the operating theatre I was now allowed only one. A limit was placed on the number of patients seen in each outpatient clinic, an easy way to reduce waiting lists for in-patient treatment. Elsewhere, whole wards and even hospitals were closed, not to increase efficiency but to contain cost.

Mrs Thatcher believed that competition was the answer to almost every problem and the most effective way of controlling the NHS budget was to create a market for health care. To quote from the White Paper, *Working for Patients, Caring for the 1990s*:

> An NHS Hospital Trust will earn its revenue from the service it provides. The main source of revenue will be from contracts with health authorities for the provision of services to their residents. Other contracts and revenue will

> come from GP practices with their own NHS budgets, private patients, or their insurance companies, hospital employers, and perhaps other NHS Hospital Trusts. This form of funding will be a stimulus to better performance. There will be an opportunity to finance improved and expanded services because the money will flow to where patients are going. Hospitals which prove more popular with GPs and patients will attract a larger share of NHS and other resources available to hospital services. A successful hospital will then be able to invest in providing still more and better services.
>
> Health Authority funding will continue to be cash limited and this will place authorities under a strong incentive to secure value for money through their contracts. Performance-related contracts of employment will similarly provide strong incentives for hospital managers to improve the quantity and quality of the services on offer. Competition with other hospitals, where it is effective, should also constrain costs.

The immediate effect of the internal market, of course, was to increase the number of administrative staff, but sadly with no improvement in patient services or care. Now both the purchasers and the providers of health care needed accountants to calculate costs and staff to shop around for the cheapest option and to administer the complex system of cross-border flows and immediate admissions from A&E departments where admission was guaranteed irrespective of contracts and budgets. The administrators were at a loss to understand why the number of emergency admissions increased towards the end of a financial year. The answer was only too obvious. The fund holders had exhausted their budgets or exhausted their contracts and so referred patients to Accident & Emergency departments, knowing that they would not be responsible for the cost. Was any thought given to the fate of the hospitals which would prove less popular with GPs and patients, and so attract a smaller share of NHS and other resources? Presumably the demoralised staff were expected to try harder but in the meantime the waiting list of popular hospitals would presumably increase and the less popular ones, by now more expensive, would decrease.

In 1990, the most far-reaching re-organisation of all brought about the fragmentation of health care, the consequences of which could have been foreseen. Patients and referring doctors no longer had the freedom to choose the hospital or consultant of their choice as the following letter illustrates:

> Dear Mr Lettin
>
> Re: Patient Number . . . . . .
>
> The above patient was referred to you by Dr . . . . . Unfortunately, we do not have a contract for your specialty with Barking, Havering & Brentwood Health Authority, which is where the patient resides.
>
> Although we have contacted the purchasing authority to request authorisation for treatment, they have refused this. The patient and her GP have been

informed and details have also been sent to your business manager so that he can monitor this information.

We hope that the Health Authority will change their decision very soon and allow us to proceed.

Yours sincerely
Dominic Conlin
Assistant Patients' Services Manager

I didn't know I had a business manager!

Contracts had to be fulfilled and the freedom for one consultant to refer a patient to a more competent colleague was curtailed, perhaps a contributory factor to the unacceptably higher mortality in some units. Fund holders were not prepared to pay for future follow-up consultations, vital for orthopaedic surgeons to assess the long-term results of joint replacements for example, and essential for the training of junior staff.

Teaching takes time and the reciprocal arrangements by which the universities paid academic staff treating NHS patients and the NHS paid consultants teaching medical students came to an end. Although the costs were ultimately borne by the taxpayer they now came from different pockets. More bureaucracy! Many consultants served on local regional and national committees and clearly could not be treating patients at the same time, adding to the cost of their units and reducing the capacity of the unit to compete for contracts. When the Chief Executive of the NHS addressed a meeting at the College of Surgeons to explain the new arrangements, I asked him at the end of his presentation if hospitals would now be reimbursed for the time I and other members of the College Council, for example, spent on College affairs. (*Was it something I said?*) He replied that he hoped that the free and easy arrangements that existed in the past would continue in the future. This was not the view of some of the now all-powerful hospital managers, who attempted to prevent such absences but were eventually overruled by the Chief Medical Officer. Their units, however, were further disadvantaged by the fact that some individuals were in receipt of Distinction Awards, further adding to the cost of running that unit. Fortunately the highest of these awards were soon paid centrally, but the problem should have been anticipated.

Patients were no longer selected for admission from the waiting lists for in-patient treatment by doctors on the basis of producing a balanced operating list which could be completed in the available time, taking into account the needs of postgraduate and undergraduate training. A surgeon in training spends only a limited time on a particular unit and in that time needs to take part in as wide a variety of procedures as possible, not the same operation week after week. Patients were now admitted by administrative staff in chronological order irrespective of the time it might take to carry out a particular operation or, indeed, of clinical need. For example three total hip replacements could not be completed in a half-day operating list, the duration of which was by now being rigidly enforced. Operations would be cancelled and patients sent home. The uninformed might think that the operation could be carried out the next day, but the theatre would almost always be occupied by another surgeon who already had a full list of patients to operate on, and the first surgeon would inevitably have other commitments already booked. Patients sometimes had their operations cancelled two or three times. At the other extreme, two or three patients might be booked who required relatively simple operations which might be completed in half the time available, so wasting valuable theatre time. The problems seemed to be endless, which only increased resources and administrative changes might resolve.

Although the salaries of the medical staff account for only a very small portion of the NHS budget, the number of consultants and junior staff were very strictly controlled by the Department of Health in the early days of the Health Service. Increases were only grudgingly approved if a need could be established. I have already alluded to the lack of regular time off and paid holidays for housemen in the 1950s and 60s and, even when I had joined the staff at Bart's, housemen were expected to find their own locums (usually senior students) when they took a holiday. The long hours and emergency commitments of the higher training grades were not much better but they were accepted in the expectation of good times to come. Unfortunately the imbalance between the number of junior posts and the anticipated consultant vacancies meant that the good times never materialised for many, who emigrated, often after many years in the training grades. The NHS was the envy of the world, at least in part, because of the exploitation of the workforce and the goodwill not only of the doctors but also of the nursing and ancillary staff. Extra beds were willingly put up when the wards were full, to accommodate emergency admissions, usually without extra staff, although sometimes nurses were moved from other less busy wards to help out. Theatre staff remained on duty until the operating list ended, and operations were never cancelled, whatever the time of the day or night. I remember mentioning to a Minister of Health some years later at an informal lunch that the Health Service had been and still was very good value for money, and he agreed. A week or two later he was replaced. Was the room bugged? *Was it something I said?*

It took some time for the goodwill and the ethos of the old voluntary hospitals to evaporate. First the ancillary staff and then the nurses demanded better pay and conditions. As a reward for their labours nurses command a special place in the nation's affections but soon the plight of the underpaid and overworked junior doctors gained considerable media support. It must be remembered that 'junior' in this context included men and women in their late thirties and early forties, often with families to support, earning far less than their contemporaries of a similar age in other professions, usually with less-demanding training. In practical terms it was difficult for them to obtain a mortgage in a buoyant property market and in 1976 they went on strike.

Sir Keith Joseph, the Secretary of State for Health, responded, not by increasing their basic salary, which is what they wanted, but by paying them overtime, a costly mistake for both the profession and the Exchequer even though the rate of overtime pay was less than for daytime work. Medicine ceased to be a profession in which doctors were paid to do a job. It was now a trade paid by the hour. An all-embracing definition of a profession is elusive, especially when applied to such diverse occupations as the oldest profession, prostitution, and professional football, which has spawned the professional foul, although I suggest that both professions are committed to the entertainment of their respective clients. Membership of a profession does, however, imply certain obligations and for doctors the obligation is to put the welfare of patients above all else, to put their interests above one's own. Doctors should not be bound by the clock, and should not be exploited, but at the same time they should ensure that the job they are paid to do is done. The essence of a true profession to manage its affairs in the best interests of those it serves was now replaced by a more rigid system of control.

For the Exchequer the cost was far more than they had anticipated, for in the smaller specialties such as neuro-surgery and thoracic surgery a unit might have only a single Registrar or Senior Registrar, who was on call in case of emergency twenty-four hours a day seven days a week, even though he might be at home. Income soared although the overtime was paid at a lower rate than normal time. Even juniors in the bigger specialties with less onerous duty rosters were now paid more than their consultants, whose salaries had also fallen behind compared with those with similar responsibilities in comparable professions.

It is easy to blame politicians for such errors but they can only act on the information and advice provided by their civil servants, who presumably include the many doctors employed by the Department of Health, and ultimately the Chief Medical Officer. Most of them will inevitably be out of touch with grass roots, for much will have changed since they abandoned clinical medicine for the ivory towers. There can be few idealistic young people contemplating a career in medicine, with the ultimate ambition of becoming a civil servant in the Department of Health!

The dilemma for the Exchequer was ameliorated by limiting junior doctors hours to seventy-two a week ostensibly to improve their conditions of employment, although the juniors themselves regarded it as a cynical way of reducing their income, and they were also concerned by the effect this would have on patient care as well as on their own training. Such misgivings are still pertinent, as the European Directives limiting doctor's hours to fifty-two per week is now being implemented and they are forbidden, for example, even to spend their own time watching rare and unusual operations, which they may never see again during their training.

Out-of-hours surgery, which consultants were expected to cover as part of their contracts, some of which, but not all, provided for a notional paid session for emergency work, was further limited by postponing all but life-threatening emergency treatment to the next day. This inevitably limited the number of elective operations that could be performed, leading to frequent postponement and cancellations and increasing waiting lists for admission. The problem was partly resolved by setting aside operating theatres for daytime treatment of emergency admissions such as broken bones, but sometimes elderly patients, particularly with hip fractures, could wait several days for definitive treatment. The quality of care was perhaps approaching what might be expected in the Third World and was not to be envied.

The introduction of the internal market loosened the control on manpower just at the time when the Royal Colleges and the Department of Health had reached an agreement on 'achieving a balance' between the number of potential consultants in training and the number of anticipated consultant vacancies. The newly created Trusts were by and large allowed to spend their budgets as they saw fit and often increasing the number of orthopaedic surgeons was a priority. As the backlog of fully trained juniors competent to assume independent practice as consultants was exhausted, increasing reliance was placed on recruiting staff from overseas, particularly from the member countries of the European Union.

Basic medical education and specialist training, and indeed medical practice, in the English-speaking world are very different from Continental Europe. Since the creation of the European Union it has been an unrealised ideal to harmonise training in the Member States. Committees with representatives from the member states have wrestled with the problem without success and it is incumbent on each of the members to recognise the qualifications of all the others, not only in medicine but also in all professions. The Certificate of Completion of Specialist training is valid throughout the European Union, but whereas in the past there were insufficient consultant posts to satisfy the number of fully trained UK specialists, now there were insufficient candidates trained in the United Kingdom with a UK CCST to fill the increased number of vacant consultant posts, which are consequently frequently filled by those with less exacting training. Teams of non-UK-trained specialists are being recruited on a short-term basis to reduce waiting lists, often with disastrous results, leaving their complications behind them. The DOH attempts to reassure the public that they are all registered with the GMC, like all doctors working in the NHS, but fails to mention that the GMC cannot refuse registration if they have a CCST awarded anywhere in the EU.

The NHS has always been dependent on overseas-trained staff, except perhaps in its infancy when a large number of doctors who had served in the Armed Forces became available to fill the posts relinquished by consultants who had stayed on beyond retiring age to keep the Emergency Medical Service and later the NHS working. The junior grades particularly at Registrar level were always dependent on overseas doctors, mostly from the old Commonwealth, whose undergraduate and postgraduate training was comparable to our own. They came over as ship's surgeons to gain experience and 'to cut the poms', as the Aussies put it and to take the British Fellowship Examinations. Lord Nuffield funded Nuffield House adjoining the College in Lincoln's Inn Fields as a place for them to live whilst on full-time College courses. During my training in general surgery at the Barnet General Hospital I worked with two of them on a one-in-three rotation. They were ideal members of the NHS workforce, competent, hardworking, and after two or three years went home, rarely staying to compete for consultant posts, thus to some extent redressing the imbalance between the number of trainees and the number of consultant vacancies. Once their own Colleges established comparable Fellowships and training programmes, the need to travel to Britain for training receded, except for highly specialised training, and the junior posts were then filled from the Middle and Far East and increasingly by women, who generally opted for a less demanding career than hospital medicine. Like the overseas trainees, they occupied junior posts without competing for consultant vacancies, often working part-time, an unpalatable truth for the politically correct, as I found to my cost in the circumstances I have already recounted. Today when 60 per cent of medical students are women, only 3 per cent occupy consultant posts, certainly not as a result of discrimination but perhaps because of the arduous and exacting training until now demanded by the profession. The women themselves to their great credit have never sought or expected concessions, but part-time working inevitably increases the duration of training; working half-time will make training twice as long.

The College under the Presidency of Sir Terence English set up a committee, Women in Surgical Training (WIST), chaired by the highly respected vascular surgeon Professor Avril Mansfield. I asked in a loud aside if this meant the College would be running Whist Drives and was admonished for being flippant (*was it something I said?*) and I recalled the words of the famous lawyer F. E. Smith (later Lord Birkenhead) 'Just because you are grave, it doesn't mean you're wise and just because I'm flippant, it doesn't mean I'm foolish' or words to that effect, but for once I kept quiet; even so I found myself the only male on the committee!

Although the GMC may recognise an overseas qualification as equivalent to a UK qualification, which would allow the holder to practise in the United Kingdom, communication between patient and doctor could be dangerously impaired when English is not the doctor's first language and so the PLAB Test (Professional Linguistic Assessment Board) was introduced. It became essential to pass a language test administered by the British Council in one's country of origin before travelling to Britain where a written test of basic scientific and medical knowledge preceded a further test of clinical skills.

Passing the PLAB Test did not guarantee a job of one's choice and an aspiring orthopaedic surgeon might find that the only post available was in psychiatry, for example. Sir Ian Todd, with some financial support from the Department of Health, introduced the Overseas Doctors Training Scheme (ODTS) in an attempt to overcome the disappointment of many young predominantly Asian trainees. They were sponsored by a senior person in their own country before setting out to fill a specific training post at SHO level in the United Kingdom, with the prospect of promotion to a reserved registrar post, subject to satisfactory progress, before returning home. Many preferred to remain in the UK and the scheme proved to be disappointing. Citizens of the European Union, however, are not obliged to take the PLAB Test and their primary qualification and their Certificate of the Completion of Specialist Training must be accepted, making them eligible for appointment to consultant posts, even if their knowledge of English is poor.

An editorial in the *British Medical Journal* in October 2004 pointed out that 'Germany, for example, has an intense hierarchy where the chief specialist is one notch below God – or one notch above, with junior staff promoted on a whim or shunted to a dead-end post in a flash of irritation' or, one might add, banished to the UK providing he or she has the CCST! The new members of the European Union present an even greater challenge.

Nursing is even more dependent on overseas-trained staff, mainly from countries in the Third World, who may also have language and cultural problems although compassionate and kind. By far the biggest reason for the shortage of nurses, 'Project 2000', is rarely mentioned. Traditionally a ward was staffed by a sister and one or two staff nurses who were fully trained State Registered Nurses (SRN) and the remaining workforce was made up of nurses in training, described as student nurses, pupil nurses, or learners of varying seniority, some in the first year and others in the second or third years of training. They were the nursing workforce and were taught on the wards by their sisters and sister tutors and from time to time would spend several weeks relieved of their ward duties, receiving theoretical instruction in the nursing schools. Project 2000, though I am sure welcomed by patient groups, ultimately decimated the workforce because henceforth all the nurses on a ward would be fully trained. Nursing is not a job for life for the majority of nurses, who leave nursing a year or two after State Registration to bring up a family. Although they may return in later life, it is often on a part-time basis. I recall a presentation made by a member of the Department of Demography at Sheffield University who had calculated that every 16-year-old girl leaving school would need to become a nurse to compensate for the loss of student nurses on the wards. Furthermore the teaching and training no longer took place in the nursing schools attached to the hospitals but in local colleges of further education or the newly created universities. Any placement on the wards during training is supernumerary to staffing requirements. The nurses, now truly students, although perhaps sound in theoretical knowledge, have little experience of patient care when they eventually work on the wards and often relate to patients with difficulty. They, like their predecessors, leave after perhaps a year or two of clinical nursing, after three years in a College of Further Education.

The role of the ward sister has long been downgraded and she or her male equivalent, the charge nurse (why not ward brother?), are no longer responsible for the cleanliness of the ward, which is in the hands of the Domestic Superintendent and a contracted-out service. Antibiotic-resistant bacteria and wound infections are a source of concern. Similarly the ward sisters are no longer responsible for distributing the patient's meals, which frequently remain untouched, unless relatives take it upon themselves to visit at mealtimes. 'Bring back Matron' is a frequent cry, but the old-style matron would need old-style sisters. Dame Kathleen Raven, the longest serving former Chief Nursing Officer, and responsible herself for many much needed changes during her fourteen years in post, was prevailed upon by a group of senior nurses (not members of the nursing establishment!) to chair a committee of senior nurses and doctors in an endeavour to remedy what they perceived to be an unsatisfactory situation, but sadly she died soon after and nothing came of this initiative.

Research shows that reorganisation seldom delivers the promised benefits and this has certainly been my own experience. John Major adopted a different approach, believing that League Tables and Citizens Charters would bring about that elusive improvement, not only in the NHS but also in almost any other Public Service. His officials must have realised that hospitals with high death rates were not necessarily worse than those with low death rates. Survival after surgery does not solely depend on the skill of the surgical team. There are surgeons renowned for their expertise in treating particularly complex or rare conditions with a high mortality or morbidity. The hospitals in which they work and they themselves will inevitably be at the bottom of the league if mortality is the criterion. Surgeons who refer all the difficult problems to their colleagues, conversely, will be league leaders and consequently patients can be easily misled. The best surgeons cannot treat everybody. It also does little for a patient's confidence to find that they are admitted to a hospital with a low rating, and it does little for the morale of the staff.

'Audit and Appraisal' is now a mandatory part of clinical practice. There is clearly merit in all doctors formally analysing and assessing the consequences of their interventions. This invariably takes time, time previously devoted to clinical care. In the past, audit was part and parcel of that care on ward rounds and in outpatient clinics, not in time set aside at the expense of clinical commitments.

No patient should wait longer than fifteen minutes before being seen in an Accident & Emergency Department, according to the Citizens Charter, the implication being that the overworked staff are deliberately keeping patients waiting. If you are kept waiting then complain, advises the Charter; in fact, if you are not satisfied, complain about your treatment or about anything that takes your fancy, and so take up more staff time. Complaints have burgeoned and there are now departments in hospitals that do nothing else but deal with complaints, whereas in the early years they would be dealt with expediently by the matron and the consultant concerned. Inevitably time has passed by the time the complaint is made. The notes must be scrutinised and reports compiled, which from my own experience can take the best part of a weekend of one's own time unless operating lists or out-patient clinics are encroached upon. Fortunately for the first twenty years as a consultant I cannot remember a single complaint, and subsequently only one led to Counsel being instructed, but the complaint, after being soundly refuted, was withdrawn before Court proceedings, but at the cost of a great deal of time and legal fees. The lawyers always win!

In the meantime the annual subscription to the Medical Defence Societies had risen exponentially. I recollect the subscription was five guineas a year when I qualified and was £5,000 a year when I retired. The Department of Health decided to assume responsibility for litigation and compensation for NHS patients, and so my subscription to the Medical Defence Union provided cover only for private practice and would have become exorbitant if the state had not taken over responsibility for NHS litigation. Many of the complaints are frivolous and are withdrawn or resolved without legal proceedings, but almost all cases that reach the courts are legally aided. Effectively claimants and their lawyers have everything to gain and nothing to lose, for, unlike a self-financing litigant, who will perhaps be deterred by the thought of meeting the defendant's costs if the case is lost, the legally-aided loser is not liable for the costs of a successful defendant.

Most cases never come to court and in order to minimise costs the NHS will often accept liability when a claim for damages is small, which encourages future disgruntled patients and their lawyers to make unjustified claims which are ultimately dependent on the opinion of so-called medical experts. These are chosen because the lawyers believe they will be sympathetic to their cause, rather than impartial servants of the legal process. Although they may be selected from a register of experts, such a register signifies nothing other than the ability to pay an annual subscription to have one's name included. They are more likely to be seen in the courts than in the hospitals from which, presumably, they derive their expertise. Such experts are frequently criticised for their evidence, but surely it is the duty of the lawyers in cross-examination to question its worth. In 1996 I represented the College at Lord Woolf's enquiry into 'Medical Negligence and the role of the Expert Witness' and pointed out that the lawyers regard as experts all witnesses giving a professional opinion rather than witnesses of fact, whereas the medical profession regard as experts people respected for their knowledge by their colleagues in their field of expertise.

Much is made of the possible advantages of 'no fault compensation' but the issue is not necessarily a matter of apportioning blame, but of deciding whether the claimant has any significant disability. It is extremely difficult to prove a negative. Who can say whether or not the patient is suffering nightmares or flashbacks or sexual dysfunction, other than perhaps the patient's partner who cannot be regarded as an impartial witness. Even so mundane a complaint as backache is impossible to disprove. Unfortunately, human nature is such that, if there is a chance of financial gain, that chance will be taken by the majority at a cost to the NHS of billions of pounds which could be better used treating patients. The claimants ritually recite: 'It is not the money that matters; we just want to ensure that no one else suffers as we have done.' Yet how many claimants refuse to accept their compensation or hand it to a charity?

Lord Taverne, QC, a Liberal Democrat Peer and former Labour Minister, writing in the *BMJ* recently, questions what rational grounds there can be for awarding damages to the parents of children whose organs were retained at the Alder Hay Children's Hospital. To dare to question the outcry about the 'body part scandal' is almost to commit sacrilege. Failure to meet a patient's unjustified expectations and the compensation culture were not features of the early years of the NHS when patients were grateful for any help they received and accepted that the results of treatment were not always what they had hoped for. Now, if their expectations are not met, someone must be at fault and compensation due.

Patients' expectations are not limited to the indigenous population. Tuberculosis was almost eradicated from the United Kingdom twenty years ago, but in recent years the disease has been reintroduced by the immigrant population. 60 per cent of new sufferers from Aids are recent immigrants, each of whom costs £10,000 a year to treat and it is hardly surprising that residents of poor countries of the world seek admission to the United Kingdom by any possible means when they know that their expectations of free treatment will be met. Their expectations are clearly not unrealistic but can the NHS accept the burden of treating the Third World sick, anymore than it can afford to spend £100,000 per annum to treat a single patient with a very rare disease?

A change of Government brought a change of emphasis – quantity rather than quality of health care. Dr James Le Fanu, a GP and regular contributor to the *Daily* and *Sunday Telegraph* newspapers, writing in May 2004 believes that money is the best medicine for the NHS. Expenditure doubled in seven years from 35 billion to 67 billion pounds a year and it is predicted to increase to 90 billion pounds a year in the near future. More doctors, more nurses, more equipment, more patients, but inevitably ever more new initiatives, committees and administrators. Hospital admissions, however, are still postponed or cancelled and clinicians see little improvement in patient care.

Staff morale remains low and consultants retire early and devote their time to private practice or medical-legal work. White male school leavers are no longer attracted to medicine as a career, despite reports that universities are receiving extra funding to take pupils with lower examination grades. 60 per cent of medical school entry is female and with a disproportionate percentage from ethnic minorities (30 per cent compared with 8 per cent of the general population). Alarmingly 65 per cent of junior doctors who qualified in 1999 did not definitely intend to practise medicine in this country, according to a recent survey reported in the *BMJ*. Working conditions and quality of life were blamed yet both have undoubtedly improved in the lifetime of the NHS. Perhaps it is because the doctor is no longer the final arbiter of the patient's best interests and is subservient to the managerial hierarchy.

The Right Honourable Michael Portillo delivered the Kathleen Raven lecture in 1998, which he entitled 'The Bevan Legacy', the legacy of a health service funded by the taxpayer and free at the point of delivery, which has become so much a part of society that no political party dare challenge the concept. The Private Funding Initiative (PFI) is an attempt to introduce capital from private sources but short-term expediency can only lead to greater long-term costs. Private capital borrows at higher rates of interest than the Government and the countless consultancies, contracts and monitoring agencies add to the burden. The early reputation for cost-effectiveness depended on minimal management costs and trust in the workforce, without the need for constant monitoring and supervision, and by and large that trust was not misplaced.

It is easier to identify the reasons why the NHS in its adult years is no longer the cost-effective envy of the world than it is to find solutions. Changes in working practice and the consequent increase in the workforce have inevitably led to increased costs, but sufficient numbers of doctors must be trained in the UK to restore and maintain standards. More expensive, complex methods of investigation can be justified and more expensive methods of treatment may prove cost-effective but there is little justification for preserving life at all costs. Patient expectations cannot necessarily always be fulfilled and the National Health Service must not pretend that they can. Litigation and compensation surely must be controlled.

Repeated administrative reorganisation, market forces, and Citizens Charters have, if anything, exacerbated the relentless increase in costly bureaucratic administration and reduced the morale and efficiency of its most valuable asset – the workforce. In its vigorous infancy and childhood, and perhaps adolescence, the managers endeavoured to serve the patients' interests by accepting the recommendations and advice of the doctors, but in the decline of the adult years the doctors must accept the dictates of the managers to meet the targets set by the politicians, who are at a loss to find solutions. Perhaps the time has come to reverse the roles once more, before the NHS drifts into senility, but above all patients must appreciate that medical care comes at a cost, which they must meet one way or another.

Chapter 14

Retirement

By the time I retired from the NHS I had made up my mind that I would leave the Health Service and all its problems behind, and make no attempt to keep up-to-date with clinical practice and the changes in the provision of health care. The NHS that I have described is as I saw it through my own eyes and as I experienced it before I retired. There is little doubt that much has changed since, particularly in relation to surgical education and training, administration of the NHS and the governance of the profession, to which I have alluded without first-hand experience. Change is inevitable but it is not synonymous with progress and most of the changes I have witnessed seem to be for the worse rather than the better. Now I tend to avoid the ever-increasing television programmes, newspaper and magazine articles dealing with health care, because they leave me despondent and depressed. My contemporaries and I are relieved that we have retired, grateful that we worked in the NHS in its heyday. We feel sorry for our successors. Unlike most of my contemporaries I decided that I would neither undertake private practice (which in any event had always been limited by my other commitments) nor medico-legal work because it is rather artificial, adversarial, time-consuming, and inefficient.

Shortly before I completed my twelve years' service on the Council of the Royal College of Surgeons, I was invited by the recently established Academy of Royal Colleges to represent the medical profession on the soon to be created General Osteopathic Council and I was duly appointed by the Privy Council as the sole medical representative to the Council designate in 1996.

I had long had an interest in manipulation and soon after appointment to the staff at Bart's I joined the British Association of Manipulative Medicine (BAMM), a group of medically qualified 'manipulators' to increase my knowledge of manipulation, and even acquire some practical expertise. It soon became apparent, however, that it was too time-consuming for inclusion into the practice of an orthopaedic surgeon in NHS clinics, with the frequent need for repeated treatment, often in a matter of days, impossible with clinics booked so far ahead. I did, however, contribute regularly to their Instructional Courses, usually lecturing on the surgical treatment of back pain and came to know Dr James Cyriax, an extremely well-known medical manipulator and a consultant physician at St Thomas's

Hospital. This proved to be a very profitable association insofar as he regularly referred patients to me for operative treatment when manipulation had failed.

One of my contemporaries in the Sixth Form at the LCHS had been Colin Dove, with whom I had completely lost touch but, quite by chance, I regained contact through a mutual patient. He was now the Dean of the British School of Osteopathy and a much-respected leader of the profession. I look back with amazement to the occasion, when it was a disciplinary offence for a medically qualified doctor to associate professionally with non-medically qualified practitioners, when I was invited by Colin Dove to lecture to the osteopaths and felt obliged to consult the BMA, to be sure that I would not fall foul of the GMC! How times change. Later, Colin accepted my invitation to take part in a symposium on the treatment of low back pain with, among others, James Cyriax, which I organised for the British Orthopaedic Association. Now, Governments encourage patients to make use of complementary medical practitioners, no doubt to ease the burden on the NHS.

The osteopaths had never been represented on the Council for the Professions Supplementary to Medicine on which I had served in the past, regarding themselves as complementary rather than supplementary, a significant distinction, making osteopathy an alternative – in some eyes – to orthodox medicine, a view which no doubt resulted in the antagonism that undoubtedly existed between the respective professions in the past. It was not uncommon then (and perhaps even today) for patients to say, 'I don't know whether I should tell you, doctor, that I have been to see an osteopath', to which I would reply, 'Did he do you any good?'

'Well, he did at first, doctor, but then the improvement got less and less and that's why I've come to see you.'

In all fairness only the patients who ceased to be helped by osteopathic treatment and not the successes returned to orthodox medicine. I think that perhaps the antagonism declined after the creation of the NHS because doctors no longer competed with osteopaths for patients, or more particularly for their fees!

The osteopaths had been seeking statutory recognition since the 1930s but they were a disparate group, with several schools of osteopathy running their own courses, some by correspondence, granting their own qualifications and generally run as profit-making businesses, who were reluctant to relinquish their autonomy. As the result of political lobbying and the recommendations of King's Fund Working Party report on osteopathy, their aspirations were now realised with the passing of the Osteopaths Act in 1993, which established the General Osteopathic Council with power to regulate the education and conduct of osteopaths and maintain a register of qualified osteopaths. Ultimately anyone not on the register but calling themselves an osteopath would be committing a criminal offence. 'Osteopath' had become a protected title, something not available to a surgeon and something I remember the physiotherapists sought when I served on the Physiotherapy Board, but which they failed to achieve.

There were fifteen osteopaths on the Council, initially appointed, I believe, to represent the various factions but ultimately (on completing five years' service) to be replaced by members elected by Registered Osteopaths. The nine lay members (non-osteopaths) of which I was one were presumably nominated by organisations with a public interest in osteopathy. I was a little apprehensive about the reception I might receive from the osteopaths but that apprehension proved to be misplaced and my reception was very cordial. The Act stipulated that there should be four statutory committees. I was asked to chair the Health Committee and I was delighted to be made a member of the Education Committee, expecting my previous experience of medical education, training, and examinations would prove to be valuable.

The Council and its committees initially spent most of their time devising a Business Plan and securing an overdraft of £1.4m to be repaid by the osteopaths themselves in the future by registration, a source of very troublesome dissent when the Register ultimately opened. The Council was entirely self-funding and the money was needed to pay for accommodation and staff, and some of the osteopathic members expected to be remunerated, which was quite understandable as they depended on their practices for their livelihood. I had never faced this situation in the past and certainly not now that I had retired. I undoubtedly had suffered from lost earnings from private practice whilst serving the College and the BOA, but this I am sure had been taken into consideration when the Distinction Awards were made. Codes and standards of practice needed to be created before the Register could be opened and a draft Code of Practice was published in October 1997 and presented to His Royal Highness the Prince of Wales at a reception at St James's Palace when he became Patron of the GOsC. The Code of Practice was rather anodyne and applicable to almost any organisation including the Cubs and Brownies!

The full implementation of the act took place over a two-year transition period ending in May 2000 with the opening of the Register, but meantime scores of osteopaths were qualifying from the unregulated schools, who would subsequently need to demonstrate their proficiency. Rather than accredit the schools first, the Education Working Group (later Committee) decided to concentrate on the registration of existing osteopaths. The Council decided against retrospective recognition of qualifications, quite reasonably in view of the wide variation in standards, but at the same time thought it unfair to expect osteopaths who had been practising safely for several years to take examinations.

The Working Group was chaired by Dr Brian Jolly, a psychology graduate whom I had first known in the 1980s when he was a member of the Medical Illustration Department at Bart's, producing two excellent reports on undergraduate teaching, with the Orthopaedic Department easily topping the league. He had subsequently acquired a reputation as a medical educationalist, fully embracing the ethos and vocabulary, and he persuaded the Committee to use Personal and Professional Profile Portfolios (PPP) as the route to registration. A forty-seven page document (including fourteen pages of guidelines) was developed which could be completed in the applicant's own home, which elicited details of the applicant's professional work and practice and self-assessment of osteopathic competence, managements and skills. A sixty-eight page document of subjective and objective criteria was devised for use by the evaluation teams! It proved to be a very time-consuming and unpopular means of assessment, open to widespread abuse, the only checks being the threat of random visits to the applicants' practices. Needless to say I had misgivings.

My misgivings were even greater when the Council turned its attention to the accreditation of teaching institutions, which were invited to submit details of their courses for evaluation. The Council steadfastly refused to accept that there should at least be a core curriculum, common to every institution because it might prove undesirably rigid. John Armistead, a medically qualified osteopath, produced one at the request of the Education Committee but it was never discussed. I came to the conclusion that my views could not be reconciled with the decisions being taken and I resigned, only to be persuaded to withdraw my resignation by Simon Fielding, the GOsC Chairman and Brian Jolly, and several individual Osteopaths. I decided that perhaps it was I who was out of step and I decided to seek reassurance from Lord Walton who had introduced the Osteopaths Bill to the House of Lords in 1992 and subsequently retained a keen interest in the Council.

I had first met John Walton when, as Professor of Neurology at Newcastle Medical School, he came to lecture at the RNOH and I had subsequently met him on social occasions at the College when he was President of the GMC. In April 1999 we met at his suggestion at the House of Lords when I expressed my misgivings, which I subsequently set out in a letter to the Chairman of the Academy of Medical Royal Colleges in December 1999, part of which I quote:

> In May 2000 a Register of Osteopaths will formally open and it will be an offence for anyone to practise osteopathy or to use the title 'Osteopath' if they

> are not registered. . . . Already osteopaths are treating many patients within and outside the NHS on the recommendation of medical practitioners and the integration of this and other forms of complementary medicine with orthodox medicine is likely to increase in the not too distant future. I believe it is important for the profession to appreciate that once a patient is referred to an osteopath the medical practitioner has no further control over that patient's treatment . . .
>
> Most members of the profession, and indeed the public, would, I think, accept the BMA's (1993) definition of osteopathy as 'a system of diagnosis and treatment whose emphasis is on conditions affecting the muscolo-skeletal system using predominantly gentle manual manipulative methods of treatment to restore proper bio medical function.' This definition is too limiting for the generality of osteopaths to accept and they are more likely to believe that osteopathic health care is essentially an 'ecological perspective of health, illness, and disease'. (Corr, 1995 Editorial *Osteopathy Today*, December 1999). Many osteopaths do not limit their activities to manipulative methods of treatment and practice, including among other things acupuncture, aromatherapy and herbal medicine, and within the field of manipulative practice, cranial and visceral manipulation and veterinary osteopathy! Registration may be seen to confer on such methods of treatment recognition which was probably not intended when the Osteopaths Act was passed.
>
> I believe that it is important that medical practitioners should realise when referring a patient to an osteopath, that forms of treatment may be employed that they did not envisage. These treatments are unlikely to be harmful in themselves (except to the pocket) but if provided by the NHS may well divert funds from orthodox treatments of proven effectiveness. . . . As your nominated representative, if that is the right description of my position, it seemed an appropriate moment to bring these matters to your attention and, perhaps through the representatives of the Royal Colleges, wider dissemination.

Unfortunately the Act made no attempt to define osteopathy or the scope of osteopathic practice, which in reality made it impossible to devise an examination which covered and included the variety of treatments that patients might receive. The osteopaths on the GOsC would not accept the BMA definition which most members of the public, and many osteopaths themselves, would accept as a reasonable description of their work.

Lord Walton asked me to keep him informed of developments, which I did in a series of letters and I was reassured that he shared my concerns:

> I must say that I share your reservations about cranial and visceral osteopathy and the like and I have expressed my views on this topic in the past. (31 January 2000)

> I am sure you are right to continue to press the Council to be much more active and prescriptive in this connection, not least in the relation to the Core curriculum. (3 April 2000)

> It is at least good to know that the schools have been approached with respect to the possibility of accepting a Core curriculum. (18 September 2000)
>
> It is good to have been in touch with you about these matters over the last few years and I am sure that everyone in the medical profession is grateful for your efforts. (17 November 2000)
>
> Like you, I was surprised to learn that for osteopaths in training pelvic examination and other relevant details are included as part of the course. This would seem to me to lie far outside the boundaries of the proper practice of osteopathy. (14 May 2001)

I completed my term on reaching the statutory retirement age of 70, in January 2001. I had anticipated that my previous experience might be of benefit to the new Council but on the whole they preferred to reinvent the wheel and learn by their own experience. In spite of these misgivings I believe my membership of the General Osteopathic Council was not without its benefits. Andrew Gilmour, a fellow member of the Council, is a practising osteopath in Ipswich with whom I travelled back from meetings on several occasions and to whom I have turned for treatment, to good effect, on more than one occasion since.

We moved to Suffolk in 1996, to the small village of Cretingham, in the valley of the River Deben, some fifteen miles from Ipswich from which there is an excellent train service to London. This enabled me to arrive in time for the 11 o'clock start of the GOsC meetings, within a couple of hours of leaving home. A return service runs late into the evening conveniently for Court meetings and dinners at the Barbers and social events at the College.

When I began to use this service, I was rather surprised that some of the late trains stopping at the intermediate stations were still using the old type of rolling stock, with individual compartments across the width of the carriage with bench seats and manually operated doors at both ends. On one occasion, just as the train was pulling out of Liverpool Street Station, the door was flung open by a panting City gent in striped trousers, black jacket and waistcoat. He climbed in, placed his bowler hat and briefcase and rolled umbrella on the luggage rack, made himself comfortable in the corner of the compartment and immediately fell asleep. An hour or so later the train stopped rather suddenly. He leapt up, grabbed his belongings, opened the door and promptly disappeared into the night. Realising that he was now on the railway track and not on the platform, he scrambled back into the compartment, turned to me and in a very upper-class voice said, 'Oh, I say, I am a fool.' He then promptly opened the door on the other side, with exactly the same result! This was an unscheduled stop in the depths of rural Essex on a very dark night.

Moat Farm. The moat is largely obscured by the trees

We had previously lived for seventeen years in a nice old farmhouse with a couple of acres of land in Chigwell Row in Essex, just in the Green Belt and adjacent to Hainault Forest with Epping Forest close at hand. We had never really been part of the local community, our social lives revolving around the hospitals where I worked, the Barbers Company, and the College and the British Orthopaedic Association. Our local friends were more acquaintances whom we met through the children's schools. It was very convenient to travel to work on the Underground Central Line, but I never thought that I would spend the rest of my life there, although Pat would have been quite prepared to do so, particularly as her elderly parents lived in a cottage in the same village.

I had known Michael Youngman, who was my anaesthetist at the RNOH and who worked with me in private practice, since 1960 when we were both Registrars at UCH and by coincidence we had the same duty days. He was born and brought up in Suffolk and with his wife, Ann Price (then Fashion Editor of *Country Life*), had a weekend cottage in the village of Sweffling where we stayed quite frequently. We would often scan the property pages of the local papers and sometimes visit properties in the very attractive local villages. Once we were on an estate agents' books their brochures arrived at regular intervals and shortly after I retired we received the details of an Elizabethan farmhouse in an acre of rather non-descript garden but completely surrounded by a moat situated in the middle of 112 acres of farmland, bounded on one side by a tributary of the River Deben.

It was a very attractive spot about a mile from the small village of Cretingham with its own post office and shop, pub and church.

The house was a classic Suffolk timber-frame farmhouse with a massive central chimney stack and a room on either side, which would have originally been called the parlour and the hall (now the sitting room and dining room), each with a large open fireplace. Leading from the hall were the two service rooms, which originally would have been known as the pantry and the buttery where the barrels or butts of food and drink were kept but which would, for us, become the kitchen and the laundry. This basic design had been obscured by various alterations over the years but was retrievable and during restoration the original high-quality oak studding and ceiling beams were revealed, without a trace of woodworm. The timbers in the three rooms on the first floor were of similar high quality, complemented by wide oak floorboards. The very large attic above reached by a stepladder (later replaced by a staircase) running the length of the house included a further bedroom beyond the chimney stack.

The quality and abundance of the timbers was hardly surprising, for the house had been built in 1602 by Richard Cornwallis, a member of the very influential family, with estates scattered over East Anglia, whose ancestors and descendants were prominent in the history of England. There is evidence that the house is on the site of a previous house built by Richard de Kettlebars who, according to the historians, 'Gave his name to the Manor and built a Manor House encompassing it with a moat in the reign of Henry II (1154–1189).' I have been unable to trace the current Lord of the Manor of Kettlebars – perhaps it might be me!

It seems likely that the timbers from the old house were reused to build a lower wing at one end of the main house, and this would have provided self-contained accommodation for Pat's elderly parents whom she was reluctant to leave behind in Chigwell. Sadly her father died a few weeks before the move but her mother remained largely independent in this accommodation until she died at the age of 96 following a fall, as so often happens.

I had always been quite a keen gardener and with help the garden was completely re-made. I had also enjoyed building things, particularly using recycled materials and thanks to my father I had acquired the necessary skills at an early age. The bricks and timbers removed during the renovation of the main house provided materials for a summer house; only the thatch was new and the thatcher the only professional help. Other recycled materials were also used to build a workshop, a field shelter and for alterations to the farm buildings. It is as well that these major tasks were undertaken in the early years after the move because inevitably, with the passage of time, I am now no longer able to undertake such major projects and even routine maintenance is becoming a problem. However, I don't think we could contemplate another move! There are still unpacked boxes in a barn from the last one.

The land in East Anglia is particularly suited to growing cereals and is probably the most productive acre for acre of any in the world. A hundred of our acres are contract farmed, that is, we pay for a neighbouring farmer to do the work as required and after the crop is sold we share the profits. After all expenses have been met, even with subsidies there is very little profit to share and even if, as owner/occupiers, we were using our own labour and not paying for the work to be done, it would not be enough to live on.

The ill-informed cry out for the abolition of subsidies, which in itself is laudable, but without them agriculture in this country would become unviable. The pretty green fields turning gold at harvest time will disappear. Who will care for the trees, the hedges and the ditches? This green and pleasant land will revert to scrub. It sometimes seems there is a wish that England should become a huge theme park, but even a theme park must be maintained. The link between subsidy and farm produce has now been broken (de-coupling) and will in future be based on the area of the farm. 56 per cent of farms changing hands at present are being bought by people such as ourselves with alternative sources of income, according to the Royal Institution of Chartered Surveyors. We are effectively subsidising the countryside. No wonder farmers are being encouraged to diversify!

'Oh, Granddad, where are the animals? We thought you'd bought a farm' was the chorus of disappointment from our young granddaughters on their first visit to the farm. A day or two before the next visit I bought half a dozen newly hatched chicks but this provided only temporary respite for, after all, chickens are not really animals, particularly in the eyes of young children. Their next visit coincided with a smallholders' show at the local agricultural college and they were enchanted by the Southdown sheep and their lambs, which bore a passing resemblance to teddy bears, with wool on their faces and legs, unlike most breeds.

'Oh, you must buy some of those, Granddad.' And so I did, at the smallholders' show the following year – a ewe and her twin ewe lambs – in the meantime having attended a course for smallholders at the agricultural college.

The Southdown is a small well-proportioned sheep with short dense wool covering the entire body and most of the face, except around the large bright eyes and over the bridge of the nose but including the small ears. They are thrifty and hardy and easy to manage. Ideal for retirement! Although now classified as a rare breed it was one of the first breeds to be selectively refined in the eighteenth century Agricultural Revolution and has been used in the breeding of many other breeds of sheep scattered around the world. From our original ewe and her two lambs we have bred a small flock of Pedigree Southdowns which graze on part of the twelve acres of land unsuitable for arable use. Although we sell our surplus lambs to our local butcher and we have received a small subsidy for each ewe (now gone) there is no profit in the enterprise, bearing in mind, for example, that it costs three times as much to shear a sheep as the value of the wool. We and the family do, however, enjoy the home-grown lamb and it is perhaps noteworthy that Southdown lamb was chosen by the Prince of Wales for the main course for the celebratory dinner for Her Majesty the Queen and the Duke of Edinburgh marking the fiftieth anniversary of her Coronation.

At The Chase in Chigwell Row the grandchildren spent many happy hours in the swimming pool and all became excellent swimmers, no doubt due in part to the time they spent in Australia. In the absence of a pool at Moat Farm we thought that a pony might perhaps be an attractive alternative. We had a stable and plenty of grazing and we happened to see an advertisement on the notice board in the Co-op Store in Framlingham for a home for a middle-aged white Connemara pony. The owner turned out to be a former Middlesex Hospital RNOH-trained nurse who now ran a local nursing home and, after inspecting us, decided that we would provide a suitable home for its remaining years. The grandchildren's initial interest waned whilst they lived in Australia and was never really rekindled on their return but I became quite fond of the pony and was very sad when it had to be put down because it had developed laminitis, a rather curious condition which no one really seems to understand.

Not all the non-arable land is suitable for grazing and there are a couple of acres of rather marshy land and a large pond with a small island which forms a haven for wildlife. A pair of Canada geese nest on the island every year and in the spring bring the goslings up to the garden before they eventually depart. The ubiquitous mallard share the pond and the moat with ducks of mixed parentage. A kingfisher flashing over the water is a joy to see and butterflies of varying hue and dragonflies and damselflies abound. The occasional grass snake slithers away and, though there is ample evidence of muntjac deer, they are rarely seen. Rabbits, of course, are everywhere but we see hares less often. Among the wild birds a barn owl regularly quartered the wild areas but sadly the tree in which it roosted was blown down in a gale and it has made its home elsewhere, but the presence of a kestrel or two is some compensation.

Sadly, Pat is unable to enjoy the wildlife or garden except from the house, for longstanding back problems make standing and walking painful, in spite of two surgical operations in the past. Late onset diabetes, with numbness and pain in the legs, as well as deteriorating vision, add to her

The author and his wife on the occasion of their Golden Wedding

problems. Many pursuits that we had hoped to enjoy during retirement and which were put off as a result of my busy working life are, unfortunately, not possible. However, we make the most of the many activities which take place in our small village.

Within a week or two of our arrival we were invited to the annual village barbecue, one of several events organised by the Village Committee. I suppose we must have looked a little lost until Michael Pinner, a longstanding village resident, introduced himself and made us welcome. He and his wife Pamela have been kind friends ever since and a valuable source of information about the village and its inhabitants. Beetle Drives and quizzes provide opportunities to meet other residents besides raising funds for other events such as the Village Lunch provided without charge by many willing helpers.

The Parochial Church Council (PCC) organises the Summer Fête on our village green, which is dominated by one of the most splendid oak trees one is ever likely to see. A variety of games, stalls, food and drink raise funds, this time for the Church to fulfil its commitments. Although a non-believer and in spite of a very non-conformist background, I enjoy taking part in the church services which mark the main religious festivals. Our small, simple, unspoiled church with its box pews and double-decker pulpit provides a tranquil place for contemplation and a link with those who have lived in the village over the centuries.

Stuart Barber, a barrister dividing his time between the village and his London home and a church warden at the time of our arrival in the village, recognised that there were many residents who were not churchgoers but nevertheless appreciated the presence of the church and the need to preserve it as part of our heritage. Largely through his initiative a third village group, Friends of St Peter's Church, was formed, and at the inaugural meeting I found myself on its committee. *Was it something I said?*

The first chairman was George Ralli, a distinguished figure who had given up the City to become a farmer. If the village possessed a squire it would be George. Stuart became the first secretary and inevitably drew up the Constitution and sorted out the charitable status, as well as managing the finances before Chris Barker agreed to take on the role of treasurer. The rules ensured a turnover of officers and committee members and in due course I became chairman. Fortunately Stuart, initially, remained secretary and there seemed to be very good reasons why we should frequently meet on a Saturday evening with a glass or two of wine and often a meal to discuss Friends' business. Happily the meetings have continued, although neither Stuart nor I now hold any official office. The law and medicine are after all two of the three oldest professions and we have much in common. Stuart is a superb craftsman, painstakingly creating wonderful furniture in his well-equipped workshop. He is a cabinet-maker and I am a mere carpenter! We both have an interest in conservation, particularly of ancient buildings and the village church, and medico-legal matters generate lively debate.

The committee has been blessed with excellent officers, Pamela Pinner succeeding Stuart and Robert Hadley following Chris Barker as treasurer. Weekenders are often criticised for adding little to village life but my successor, Tony Whitmarsh, is the exception that proves the rule, if indeed there is such a rule. The committee has raised over £50,000 since its formation eight years ago. A few generous covenants have been supplemented by the proceeds from the recycling bins, open garden events, car boot sales, and lectures during the winter months for which a charge is made. Fund-raising is never easy.

We have been fortunate to find ourselves in such a friendly village served so well by Margaret in the village shop and the proprietors of The Bell and, of course, the priest in charge, the Reverend Clare Saunders. The medical services are excellent and the senior partner in our local general practice, Dr Paddy Fielder, just happens to be a Bart's man. We could not survive without Susan's help indoors, and Colin's help outside. Melvyn, the postman, cannot be faulted and we were fortunate in securing the services of Bruce Hinton and his farm manager Philip, who run the arable side of the farm. We have never had better meat than that bought from John Hutton, the butcher in the neighbouring village of Earl Soham.

There is no doubt that the pace of rural life is more relaxed. Drivers, on the whole, are more considerate, and most assiduously observe the speed limits. I was, therefore more than a little surprised, when shortly after we moved here, as I approached a sharp right-hand bend in the road, I was forced onto the grass verge, by an elderly open-top Morris Minor, driven by an equally elderly lady, taking the bend very widely. As she passed she shouted 'Pig,' as though I was to blame for this near accident, but on resuming my journey and turning the corner, to my surprise, there was a large pig strolling along in the middle of the road!

Our new friends have not supplanted the old and, particularly, the members of the Innominate Club, who have been meeting regularly twice a year since 1965. It is difficult to believe that the formation of an orthopaedic club in the UK came about as a result of the granting of independence to Nigeria, but for several years a registrar from the RNOH had been seconded for a year to the orthopaedic hospital in Kano in Northern Nigeria. With independence the Colonial Medical Officer in charge, Frank Bryson, returned to the UK leaving the registrar (Malcolm Swann) unsupervised and so Sir Herbert Seddon persuaded the members of the Arbuthnot Lane Orthopaedic Club to go to Kano for three months at a time, to provide consultant cover.

Geoffrey Walker, who had previously worked in Kano, was invited to a meeting of the Lane Club to explain to the members, who were all consultant orthopaedic surgeons, what to expect, and he so enjoyed the experience that he suggested to one or two of his senior registrar colleagues at the RNOH that it was time to form a new comparable single generation orthopaedic club. In March 1965, Geoffrey, Ernest Kirwan and I met at the Karachi Restaurant close to the RNOH and made a list of senior registrars and newly appointed consultants whom we thought might be interested. The members were to be drawn from a wide geographical area but not from the same training programme, although, as it happened, all but one of the subsequent members had spent part of their training at the RNOH.

The first formal meeting of the ten original members was held at Stanmore in May of the same year. A clinical meeting with the presentation of interesting patients was followed by a business meeting, where it was decided that the aims of the new club would be to debate medical politics,

Members of the Innominate Club on their visit to Spain. The author is on the extreme left of the picture, with Glyn Thomas, Philip Yeoman, Ernest Kirwan, Kim Poul-Manresa, Geoffrey Walker, Brian Andrews, John Chalmers and John Gibson

particularly the design and construction of new hospitals, and the training of orthopaedic surgeons, as well as other orthopaedic topics. Members then retired to The Vine to continue the search for an appropriate name for the club but as no startling suggestions were made it was decided to call it The Innominate Club. Our current members are Brian Andrews, John Chalmers, John Gibson, John Goodfellow, Michael Heywood-Waddington, Leslie Klenerman, Robin Ling, Ernest Kirwan, Glyn Thomas, Geoffrey Walker and myself. With the passage of time we have lost Patrick Chesterman, Norman Shaw, Philip Yeoman and Kim Poul-Manresa. We have been very lucky that everyone has got on extremely well together and after nearly forty years we continue to have a very good attendance, although the meetings are now entirely social and we have ventured abroad from time to time.

Four of our members have served as presidents and one as vice-president of the BOA. Three have been BOA secretaries, two have been members of the Council of the Royal College of Surgeons (one a vice-president), two have become professors, one president of World Orthopaedic Concern and one editor of the journal *Bone and Joint Surgery*. Four have served as Presidents of the Orthopaedic Section of the Royal Society of Medicine. It is somewhat surprising that a self-selected group of surgeons coming together at the beginning of their consultant careers forty years ago should have assumed such important roles in their specialties.

There was sufficient expertise among the members of the club to present by invitation a Scientific Programme in Barcelona and then in Madrid on one of our early trips abroad. At the dinner in Barcelona one of our Spanish hosts complimented me on my excellent pronunciation, much to the amusement of my English colleagues, adding that he had no need of the simultaneous translation. I mentioned that I had received similar, if unexpected, compliments after presentations at various European meetings. Someone, presumably English rather than Spanish, suggested that this was because I kept my vowels open, a remark that caused great hilarity among my friends, who for several years afterwards taunted me by asking if I was still keeping my vowels open. *Was it something I said?*

The Percivall Pott Club is a rather different organisation, increasing its membership year by year. Mention has already been made of the establishment of the formal rotational orthopaedic training programme at Bart's in 1969. As the trainees left the programme on completion of their training to take up consultant appointments, such was the camaraderie that had developed between them that they decided that they would like to maintain the friendships in the future. Louis Deliss, now retired from the Orthopaedic Department of Ipswich Hospital, and a near neighbour and firm friend, was the prime mover and the inaugural meeting and dinner was held at Bart's on the 3rd November 1973. Percivall Pott was an eminent eighteenth century Bart's surgeon who made many original contributions to surgical practice including disorders of the bones and joints, perhaps the most well-known of which is Pott's Fracture. It seemed appropriate to commemorate this connection with Bart's and the speciality of orthopaedic surgery.

The Club meets twice a year, once at Bart's continuing the tradition with a dinner in the magnificent Great Hall in November, and once elsewhere in the summer. The membership increases each year as the members become consultants and in spite of their new responsibilities and appointments throughout the United Kingdom, it is gratifying that many continue to attend the meetings from time to time. Many have taken on important and responsible roles within the College and the BOA. David Dandy, Hugh Phillips, and David Jones have already been presidents of the BOA and John Getty will follow in the near future. Three are serving as members of the Council of the Royal College of Surgeons at present, Hugh Philips occupying the most prestigious position of all as president, only the third orthopaedic surgeon to have done so in the history of the College.

I suppose my formal retirement began following my last working day at Bart's which in contrast to the first almost thirty years before passed

An early photograph of the Percivall Pott Club. Charles Manning is seated in the middle of the front row (photo Norfolk and Norwich Hospital)

unnoticed. The orthopaedic wards had already closed, and the junior staff transferred to the Royal London Hospital. My last outpatient clinic, for reasons I can no longer recall, took place on a Wednesday morning rather than the usual Wednesday afternoon. The clinic nursing staff had also departed. A single nurse, a stranger to the clinic, ushered in the few patients with follow-up appointments. It was all over by mid-day and, feeling rather miserable and depressed, I left for home. It had been customary for retiring members of the consultant staff at Bart's to have the opportunity of bidding a formal farewell to their consultant colleagues and the senior nurses at an informal cocktail party in the Great Hall. They were thanked for their services and a presentation was usually made, and subsequently they were invited to become honorary or emeritus consultants, but my departure seemed to have been overlooked. Nonetheless, it had been a privilege to have worked at Bart's and follow, unworthily perhaps, in the footsteps of so many illustrious members of the medical profession.

However, in due course I was more than amply rewarded by the members of the Percivall Pott Club and their partners at a splendid banquet held in the Great Hall where Percivall Pott himself had stood almost two hundred years before at the banquet given by the Board of Governors on his retirement. It is said that he was so overcome by emotion that he was unable to speak. It was not until later that I was overcome by similar emotions when I read the reminiscences of the fifty-seven members of the Club to whose training I had contributed. Mrs Trish Phillips had collected them together with a photograph of each of them in a beautiful leather-bound volume. In addition to this wonderful and treasured memento of my years at Bart's they presented me with a silver goblet, a replica of the goblets used by the Master of Wardens of the Worshipful Company of Barbers which were presented to the Company by Edward Arris who was Master in 1651. I would like to end this book by quoting from two of these reminiscences.

> AWFL was appointed consultant at Bart's in 1967. In those days a non-Bart's-trained consultant was rare but perhaps, surprisingly, given Bart's notorious reputation for snootiness and insularity, they adapted to and accepted him quite rapidly. At that time, Alan, 'the East End barrow boy' as he was sometimes unkindly referred to but not at Bart's, and Mike Freeman, from the affluent cigar family and recently appointed to the London Hospital, were seen as the two bright young boys of the London orthopaedic scene. His first major contribution to Bart's was to revolutionise the undergraduate teaching of orthopaedics. Until then students only attended to observe a couple of clinics a week with no ward or theatre experience. It was Alan, I am pretty sure, who persuaded the Dean to give the students six weeks full-time orthopaedics, considered rather revolutionary at the time. When I

returned to the Department in 1969 (on appointment to the Percivall Pott rotation) this was just starting and AWFL got me and the other SRs considerably involved in developing the syllabus and course of lectures and devising structured student assessments, including compiling a multiple choice exam, which they took at the end of their six weeks. For a long time after this, orthopaedics was frequently voted 'best course' by the students.

But as all who have trained on the Bart's rotation know full well, it was Alan's vision and drive which first set up our training scheme and made it into still arguably the best in the country, which is his main contribution. Professor J. I. P. James in Edinburgh and Professor Frank Holdsworth in Sheffield were I think the most influential orthopods to persuade the Royal Colleges that four or more years as an SR, staying throughout in one post, was too narrow a training and a more structured training was needed with rotations to include experience in the major elective sub-specialties as well as trauma, the latter often at a good district general hospital. While Charles Manning contributed the political clout, I think much of the vision, scheming and certainly all the hard work was Alan's. Alan's ideas on how orthopaedic surgeons should be trained were tested on our rotation and are only next year to be introduced for all specialties, which says much for his foresight over twenty-five years ago and we have much to be thankful for.

Paul Moynagh (Consultant Orthopaedic Surgeon – Bart's undergraduate and orthopaedic trainee).

Alan, there can be few people who have given as much to surgery as yourself. Your registrars have good reason to know this better than anybody. The most loyal of supporters, a rock in times of trouble, a wise adviser, and (in case we have all forgotten) the author of magnificent references. You have never grudged the time and effort spent fighting on our behalf. Your contribution to surgical training was enormous. The Bart's Programme ran for twenty-five years before the continuum was reinvented. At the College you reorganised the Training Board, made possible the success of the Education Department, brought agreement between the four surgical colleges, and much more. As always you gave your time and energy and ideas far beyond the call of duty.

It is a source of sadness to many that you seldom received the official recognition you deserved but at least there is one group, your registrars, who are not afraid to acknowledge your contribution to surgery as a whole and the help you gave each of us as individuals. You can retire secure in the knowledge that the members of the Percivall Pott Club and their wives and families know exactly how much you have given to surgery and how much you have shaped our careers. Thank you.

David Dandy (Consultant Orthopaedic Surgeon, Past President BOA; member of Council and Vice-President of RCS).

Was it something I said?

P.S. ESSEX BOY ASPIRES TO DO WELL LIKE NOTORIOUS LEYTON BONE SURGEON WHO DONE GOOD. BEST WISHES. ANIL CHAKRABARTI (Consultant orthopaedic surgeon and former trainee)

Select Bibliography

Burns, Ian (ed.), *The Company of Barbers and Surgeons*, 2000

Cholmeley, J. A., *History of the Royal National Orthopaedic Hospital*, 1985

Cope, Zachary, *The History of the Royal College of Surgeons of England*, 1959

Couch, L., *Leyton County High School for Boys – A Sketch of the First Fifty Years 1898–1948*

Dobson, Jessie & Milnes Walker, R., *Barbers and Barber-Surgeons of London*, 1979

Estcourt, Paul, *Leyton County High School for Boys – At its Peak*

Hollingshead, John, *Ragged London*

Medvei & Thornton (ed.) *Royal Hospital of St Bartholomew 1123–1973* (1974)

Waddington, Keir, *Medical Education at St Bartholomew's Hospital 1123–1995*

Williams, Francis, *Fifty Years March – The Rise of the Labour Party*

British Medical Journal

Leyton County High School Magazine

Pass the Port, published for Oxfam by Christian Brann Ltd, 1976

Index